Documentary Dilemmas
Frederick Wiseman's *Titicut Follies*

CAROLYN ANDERSON
AND
THOMAS W. BENSON

SOUTHERN ILLINOIS UNIVERSITY PRESS
CARBONDALE AND EDWARDSVILLE

94 93 92 91   4 3 2 1

Library of Congress Cataloging-in-Publication Data

Anderson, Carolyn, 1939–
  Documentary Dilemmas.
  Bibliography: p.
  1. Titicut Follies (motion picture) I. Benson, Thomas
W. II. Title.
PN1997.T553A54 1991   791.43'72   88-29834
ISBN 0-8093-1518-1 (pbk.)

The paper used in this publication meets the minimum requirements of
American National Standard for Information Sciences — Permanence
of Paper for Printed Library Materials, ANSI Z39.48–1984. ⊗

For our daughters

Kimi and Kisa Takesue
Sarah and Daisy Benson

Contents

Preface

Frederick Wiseman has been making documentary films for more than twenty years. For nearly that long, we have been watching the films as they were released, usually on public television, teaching them in our classes, and occasionally writing about them. Finally, we saw that our work was leading us to attempt a full-length study of the films, which was published by Southern Illinois University Press in 1989 as *Reality Fictions: The Films of Frederick Wiseman.* In that larger work, we have attempted to give words to the interpretations that the films seem to invite, and the rhetorical structures by which those interpretations are induced; and we have gone behind the rhetorical structure of the films to offer a glimpse of the people and processes behind the films. Since Wiseman's films speak to his audiences so deeply of their own experiences of American institutional life, it seemed important to examine in context the issues of ethics and epistemology, and the elements of convention, craft, collaboration, finance, distribution, and legal restraint that constrain the production and reception of the films.

Documentary Dilemmas, the present work, is a revision and expansion of the first two chapters of *Reality Fictions,* making available in a relatively inexpensive paperback edition the story of Wiseman's first and most controversial film, *Titicut Follies,* a documentary filmed at the Massachusetts Correctional Institution at Bridgewater. When the film was completed in 1967 its release was challenged by the Commonwealth of Massachusetts, setting in motion a series of litigations and restrictions that continue twenty years later and that are unique in American film history. For over twenty years, exhibition of *Titicut Follies* has been restricted by order of the Massachusetts courts. In *Reality Fictions,* we traced the story of *Titicut Follies* to April 1988. The present book carries that story forward to September 1990, through a complicated and mostly unsuccessful attempt by Wiseman to open the film to unrestricted exhibition. In addition to adding the story of the most recent legal developments in the case, we have included an extensive chronology of *Titicut Follies,* which appears as an appendix. We offer this analysis of the film's history as a case study in independent documentary film making, and in the legal, ethical, aesthetic, and rhetorical issues that the case has raised.

In the years during which we have developed the various parts of this book, many colleagues and students have offered encouragement and advice. Fern Johnson, Jack Shadoian, Hermann Stelzner, and Richard Stromgren of the University of Massachusetts at Amherst commented on early drafts. Other colleagues and students, a group too large to identify individually, have encouraged us with questions and suggestions, and we deeply appreciate their support. This project was partially funded by grants from the Institute for the Arts and Humanistic Studies, the College of Liberal Arts, and the Department of Speech Communication at The Pennsylvania State University and by a faculty research grant from the University of Massachusetts. Our department chairs and deans—first Robert Brubaker and Stanley Paulson and then Dennis Gouran and Hart Nelsen from Penn State, and Barnett Pearce and Glen Gordon from U-Mass—provided additional support. The manuscript for this book was edited on the mainframe computer system at Penn State and relied during its preparation on Bitnet, an interuniversity electronic mail system. For computer assistance at our universities, we thank Glen Kreider, Donald Laird, William McCane, Tom Minsker, Gerald Santoro, William Verity (Penn State), and Pat Driscoll Kochin, Kevin Jordan, Serafin Mendez, Michael Morgan, and Judy Smith (U-Mass). The text was entered on the Penn State mainframe computer in the Waterloo SCRIPT formatting language, which produced a manuscript for revisions and copy editing. Then SCRIPT was used to produce a PostScript file that was sent to an Apple NTX LaserWriter, to create page proofs. Once the page proofs were approved, a PostScript file was used to run camera ready pages at a resolution of 1240 dpi on Penn State's Linotronic 300 Typesetter. We are grateful to Tom Minsker, who devoted many days of computer consulting to the job of setting the text of this book on the mainframe computer at Penn State. Wayne McMullen and Joe Gow each spent a summer as our research assistants at Penn State. We also thank Catherine Egan, Larry Fay, Phil Green, Richard Halgin, James Hallowell, Ronald P. Johnson, Jeff Kaplan, P. J. O'Connell, Anne O'Toole, David Robinson, Jay Ruby, Len Siebert, Sylvia Snape, John Stacey, Barbara Sweeney, and Judy Trochi.

Dozens of people kindly shared information, opinions, and memories regarding *Titicut Follies*. They include June S. Binney, Kent Carroll, Ken Colpan, Kevin Crain, Ellen Feingold, Oliver Fowlkes, Charles Gaughan, Phil Glassanos, Stephen A. Jonas, Katherine Kane, Thomas Kurcharski, Michael Leja, Lorna Marshall, John Morrison, Francis X. Orfanello, Michael Perlman, Blair Perry, Wesley Profit, Jerry Rappaport, John Roberts, Deac Rossell, Mitchell J. Sikora, Jr., and Harvey A. Silvergate. We are grateful to the staff of the Southern Illinois University Press for their help and support on this large and complicated project, and especially to James Simmons, Kenney Withers, Susan Wilson, Yvonne Mattson, and Natalia Nadraga. Special thanks go to cinematographers John Marshall, Richard Leiterman, William Brayne, and John Davey for their candid interviews and to Karen Konicek of Zipporah Films.

We must say a word about our relationship to Fred Wiseman. This book is not an authorized study of Wiseman's association with *Titicut Follies*. Over the course of several years, in person, by telephone, and in writing, he has answered many of our questions. But Wiseman is in no way responsible for any of our interpretations, either in the analysis of the film, or in the account we give of its production and distribution. Wiseman has been in a particularly difficult position, because the *Titicut Follies* case involves so many disputed recollections, so many charges and countercharges of bad faith, and ongoing litigation concerning the film. For the most part, Wiseman preferred not to discuss the *Titicut Follies* case with us. To do so, he told us, might have seemed to place him in the position of collaborating with our version of the story, or in the equally difficult position of being quoted as disputing our version. In the summer of 1987, Wiseman read a nearly final version of the first two chapters of our manuscript for *Reality Fictions* and offered some corrections dealing with factual matters in a memorandum to the authors, with the understanding that this did not commit him to a view as to our interpretation of the case. He declined our requests for an extensive interview on his work and declined to provide photographic reproductions from his films. We have tried to respect Wiseman's privacy, and we think it is clear how much we respect his work. On the other hand, he has often said that his films are about public issues and exist in the public sphere and that where the public's right to know conflicts with other interests, the public's right to know should prevail. Wiseman's actions and assertions, and the litigation concerning *Titicut Follies*, have made his films and his working methods into public issues, the legitimate subjects of critical analysis and searching inquiry.

Wiseman, and others, as participants in the *Titicut Follies* case, will no doubt disagree not only with some of our interpretations, but with some of our allegations as to the facts. We have relied, in our account, on the published record, on trial transcripts, and on interviews and correspondence with participants. Even a trial transcript, although it is taken under oath, is not a transparent record of the events it describes, since it occurs in an adversarial setting—it is making history, not just reporting history. Whatever the limits of various documents and the unreliability of human memory, the story is important and needs to be told. Our version is offered in good faith as one supported by the record. We make it public here in the spirit of scholarly inquiry, in the hope that where it is wrong it will be refuted.

As a critical reconstruction of the history of *Titicut Follies* and the issues it raises, our work is necessarily concerned with motive. We have tried to avoid attributing motives to any of the men and women involved in the story. And yet it is clear that each of those men and women acted as they did partly on the basis of their understandings of the motives of the other participants in the story and that, when things began to go wrong, each side began to attribute—in public—motivations to their opponents. The Commonwealth, when it brought suit against Wiseman, both declared and implied that Wiseman was acting in bad faith to further his own artistic and financial ambitions, and when he began to seek the widest possible distribution for *Titicut Follies* they interpreted his actions as confirmation of their suspicions. According to such an interpretation, Wiseman had obtained the footage out of which he made *Titicut Follies* under false representations, by hook or by crook, and once he had the film finished appealed for protection to the First Amendment. According to those sympathetic to Wiseman, the officials of the Commonwealth, who claimed to be protecting the rights of the inmates, were instead acting as classic bureaucrats and protecting themselves from exposure and censure, since all of them were arguably, in some measure, responsible for conditions at Bridgewater.

Hence, it is impossible to make sense out of the story of *Titicut Follies* without understanding the ways in which these people were depicting to the court and the public, and perhaps to themselves, each others' behaviors and motives. Still, though the record shows how important the matter of motivation is to understanding how the story unfolded, and how helpful it would be to understand what the actual motives of each person were, the actual motives are not and cannot be part of our story. We can describe, from the record and from interviews, what people did, and what they said about themselves and each other; we can indicate the points at which someone (who, it may never be known) must have been mistaken or telling a lie, but we cannot see into the hearts and minds of Fred Wiseman, John Marshall, Charles Gaughan, Elliot Richardson, and the others who acted out the story of *Titicut Follies.*

Readers, of course, will themselves be tempted to reconstruct the motives of Fred Wiseman, his friends, and his detractors. While such an impulse is understandable, and perhaps inevitable, we urge caution, skepticism, and sympathy. We cannot know wholly what happened or what was thought or felt more than twenty years ago. The history of *Titicut Follies* is partly the story of how a documentary film came to be made and restricted. But the story of both Bridgewater and *Titicut Follies* continues. To what extent, if at all, should *Titicut Follies* and the story of its production inform the debate about the care of men such as those at Bridgewater? To what extent should a judgment about whether Fred Wiseman broke or finessed an oral contract to allow the state final approval of his film govern a judgment about whether exhibition of *Titicut Follies* should be restricted? Should prior consent (tacit or explicit) be subject to reconsideration, legally or ethically, when it leads to a documentary as aesthetically and rhetorically provocative as *Titicut Follies?* What *were* the circumstances and understandings under which Wiseman obtained consent to film *Titicut Follies?* Whatever those circumstances, should claims of invasion of privacy, in 1967 or now, prevent the general exhibition of *Titicut Follies?*

We are grateful to the institutions, associations, and journals that have allowed us to present our work to audiences who contributed to shaping what is presented here. Parts of this book were presented in early versions at meetings of the Speech Communication Association, the Society for the Study of Social Problems, and the Image Ethics Conference at the Annenberg School of Communications, University of Pennsylvania. For permission to reprint our work, we thank *The Journal of the University Film Association* and *Current Research in Film.*

We especially thank our families—Andy Anderson, Kisa and Kimi Takesue, and Margaret, Daisy, and Sarah Benson—for their encouragement and support.

Documentary Dilemmas

Chapter 1

The Trials of *Titicut Follies*

Frederick Wiseman is the most successful independent documentary filmmaker currently working in the United States.[1] His work rivals that of the most distinguished originators and practitioners of the genre. And yet Wiseman stands apart from the documentary film movement as such; he has not started a movement or even a group of filmmakers of his own, has no followers, and may be impossible to imitate. He has stretched the limits of what counts as documentary film to the point where it has challenged what at one time appeared to be fairly settled matters of style, practice, and politics, of the relations of documentary to its subjects, its audiences, its means of knowing, and its claims as art.

Wiseman has sometimes referred to his films as *reality fictions.* The term was used by Wiseman as early as 1974 and at one level is a way of referring to the same problem John Grierson pointed to when he said that documentary film was about "the creative treatment of actuality."[2] One works from social actuality but necessarily imposes form upon that actuality, turning it into what may be implied by the terms *art* or *fiction.*

Wiseman has sometimes used the term *reality fiction* to disclaim a responsibility to represent social actuality "objectively." At other times, he seems to use the term to advance his claim to be making "art," with all that term implies about artistic freedom, complexity, and worth in a romantic and modernist frame. At still other times, Wiseman has turned the phrase against its apparent roots in other attempts to name a hybrid form that emerged in the 1960s in film, journalism, and fiction: an inventory of such terms would include the cinema verite of French documentarians Jean Rouch and Edgar Morin; the direct cinema associated with Americans Robert Drew,

Richard Leacock, Albert and David Maysles, and Donn Pennebaker, and with the Canadians grouped around Allan King (who once referred to his work as "actuality drama"); the nonfiction novel of Truman Capote; and the novel-as-history, history-as-novel of Norman Mailer. Wiseman at one time referred to his work as "reality dream," and only later as "reality fictions"; later, he commented that he had used the term *reality fictions* as a parody of attempts to label what he and other documentary filmmakers were doing.[3]

Wiseman's use of the term *reality fictions* is characteristic of his relations to the press and public. At times, he has used the term as an apparently serious attempt to point to the inevitably constructive nature of documentary film. At other times, he has used the term in a more combative way, either to disclaim any responsibility to maintain a literal accuracy to the "reality" he records on camera and tape or to assert the claims of his films to be regarded as art and to be read with the same level of interpretive complexity as serious fiction. He has also used the term as an apparent thrust at the implied claims to truth of cinema verite and direct cinema. Coming full circle to pull the rug out from under those of his own admirers who were willing to take up the banner of "reality fiction" on his behalf, Wiseman has also said that "partially in reaction to the concept of cinema verite, I came up with my own parody-pomposity term called reality fiction."[4] Wiseman's use of the term *reality fiction* seems less like a claim upon film theory than a way of pointing at the inevitable tension between social actuality and film form.

Our approach to Wiseman's work is drawn, broadly speaking, from a rhetorical perspective. A rhetorical approach is nowadays widely understood as being interested in the way meanings are constructed and communicated through a variety of symbolic actions and processes. In ancient Athens and Rome, rhetoric had to do with the theory and practice of public, spoken argument. As the rhetorical tradition has evolved through the nearly two thousand years since the theories of Plato, Aristotle, and Cicero, it has come to be used as a way of referring to what Kenneth Burke has called "symbolic inducement," that is, to the ways in which humans make meanings out of the forms they construct and perceive in the world.[5]

A rhetorical perspective points the critic-historian at the whole enterprise of communication. Essential to a rhetorical inquiry is the notion that it is justified by an interest in actual human practices. At one end of the process, people sit before their television screens, or in auditoriums, watching Wiseman's documentaries, making sense out of them, experiencing the thoughts and feelings that the films somehow arouse.

Frederick Wiseman's documentaries are both artistic experiences and social documents. The films speak to us about the politics of American institutions, and about difficult legal, social, educational, scientific, and other public matters. After their first showings on public television, they are widely seen in secondary distribution in classrooms. Because they speak so profoundly and with such a liberating freshness of the experience of institutional politics and the petty oppressions of everyday life, it seems especially important to understand not only what they say and by what cinematic/rhetorical means they construct their meanings, but also how they come to be made, through the whole process of identifying subjects, locating willing institutions, securing consent to film, collaboratively recording the sound and images that will make up the film, gaining access to funding and audiences, maintaining an independent distribution company, and coping with the legal and other challenges that sometimes arise in dealing with controversial material. These matters are of considerable historical interest to those who make or study documentary films, but they must also be a concern to anyone who would make use of documentary films as a way of knowing something about the issues and institutions they depict.

At every step in the process of production and distribution, the filmmaker, no matter how independent, is making choices that constrain the form of the work and its reception and interpretation by the public. Frederick Wiseman has been notably successful as an independent producer of documentaries. As is clear from his films, and from his many interviews, he regards independence as a central issue in human experience. When we mentioned to him, for example, that we were interested in his films, in how he maintains the freedom and independence to make them, and in the constraints within or against which he finds himself working, he replied, "What constraints? There are no constraints. I get the money and I make the films. There are no constraints." Such a reply is valuable as evidence of Frederick Wiseman's view of the world and of his work, but it cannot brush aside the question of how his films come to be as they are. Clearly at the center of the whole enterprise are Wiseman's intelligence, sensibility, and willpower. But readers who are interested in Wiseman's films not only as expressions of his character, chapters in his autobiography, but also as social documents, may wish to consider the whole series of shaping forces that intervene in various ways between the institutions Wiseman observes and the films we see on the screen.

This book offers a historical account of *Titicut Follies,* Wiseman's first documentary, and of the largely successful attempts of the Commonwealth of Massachusetts to restrict its exhibition. The trials of *Titicut Follies* raise crucial and ongoing issues about the relation of social documentary to its subjects and audiences and provide a rare opportunity to see the issues of documentary ethics, consent, filmmakers' intentions and methods, and exhibition argued in an adversarial setting, and under oath. Our account of the *Titicut Follies* case, relying on interviews, journalistic accounts, and especially on the legal record, including the *Commonwealth v. Wiseman* transcript, provides a special opportunity to consider the issues and forces that independent documentarians must contend with in shaping their work.

Titicut Follies occupies a unique position in American film history: it is the only American film whose use has court-imposed restrictions for reasons other than obscenity or national security.[6] As this book goes to the printer, Wiseman continues his campaign in the courts to remove these restrictions. Whatever the courts' eventual decision, the case of *Titicut Follies* provides a clear and compelling means to consider the tension in a democracy between the public's right to know and the individual's right of privacy.

Titicut Follies is a bitterly critical documentary account of the prison hospital for the mentally ill at the Massachusetts Correctional Institution at Bridgewater.[7] After allowing Wiseman access to the institution to shoot the film, the Commonwealth of Massachusetts took him to court to prevent the film from being shown on the grounds that Wiseman had violated an oral contract to allow the state editorial control over the film and that he had invaded the privacy of an inmate at Bridgewater.

Wiseman's documentaries are built upon a method of film making that deliberately courts questions of invasion of privacy. To watch the films is often to feel that we are seeing deeply into other people's private experiences. In the *Titicut Follies* case, the issue of invasion of privacy became a legal issue; in all direct cinema it is an ethical and aesthetic issue.

Because the struggle for control of *Titicut Follies* entered the courts, a debate regarding the intentions, procedures, and effects of this film was made public. By examining that debate and constructing from it a history of *Titicut Follies,* told primarily from the public record, we hope to offer a sense of the complex interaction that takes place among filmmakers, subjects, and audiences in the negotiation for the meaning and use of documentary films. The legal battles over *Titicut Follies* prompted Wiseman and his supporters to articulate the case for documentary access in a way that has not been repeated. So, too, has the case for restricted access and exhibition been made by Wiseman's opponents in litigation that has raised questions not only about Wiseman himself but also more general questions about privacy, the rights of institutional inmates, and the procedures for securing informed consent.

No later Wiseman film has met with the organized resistance leveled at *Titicut Follies,* but many of the questions raised about the Bridgewater documentary continue to be asked about documentary in general—especially when it addresses difficult public questions.

We present the history of *Titicut Follies* as a narrative in generally chronological order, with each chapter organized around a dilemma central to the case of *Titicut Follies* and endemic to the documentary enterprise—especially to the form known as direct cinema, which Wiseman has so greatly influenced.

Chapter 2

The Politics of Asking and the Myth of Informed Consent

Speaking before a university audience a decade after the 1967 release of *Titicut Follies,* Fred Wiseman was questioned about the controversial documentary. He quipped, "Bridgewater, like any maximum security prison, is not the kind of place you parachute into and hide in the hills and make forays into the cell blocks when nobody's looking. [Hesitation] It took a year for me to get permission to make *The Follies.*"[1] The filmmaker's sarcasm anticipates and mocks any suggestion of clandestine film making in the *Titicut Follies* project. The film's history begins not with claims of journalistic rights, although such rights later became the filmmaker's primary legal defense, but with what Wiseman has called the "politics of asking."[2] Whether one sees the litigious and often acrimonious history of *Titicut Follies* as a demonstration of an unfortunate, avoidable breakdown in communication, an exercise in cross purposes and sensibilities, or an example of personal betrayal, consent—as bureaucratic procedure, ethical imperative, and oral contract—is the key concept of the first stage in the film's history.

There is wide consensus that consent is not valid unless it was given under conditions free of coercion and deception, with full knowledge of the procedures and anticipated effects, and by someone competent to consent.[3] A documentary filmed at a state institution with characteristics of both a maximum security prison and a mental hospital strained each condition of validity. Still, the incarcerated subjects stood a chance of gaining if the film led to improved conditions at Bridgewater. In documentaries dedicated to social reform, consent negotiations with persons in power are particularly problematic, since full disclosure of intent could easily result in withdrawal of support. The balance of risk and benefit thus presented a dilemma of procedural ethics for the Bridgewater documentarians.

Wiseman began his pursuit for permission to film a documentary at Massachusetts Correctional Institution-Bridgewater, a permission required by state law,[4] by the most direct and standard of procedures: he personally contacted the superintendent of the facility. Identifying himself as a member of the instructional staff in sociology at Brandeis University, Wiseman telephoned Superintendent Charles Gaughan in the spring of 1965. Their conversation concerned Wiseman's instructional work in the area of legal medicine. That May, Wiseman met with Gaughan to discuss a potential documentary film. In his capacity as a Boston University law instructor, Wiseman had first visited Bridgewater in the spring of 1959, shortly after Gaughan's appointment. Later Wiseman recalled, "Ever since I began to take law classes to Bridgewater, I'd wanted to do a film there."[5]

Although Wiseman was a novice filmmaker in 1965, he held impressive personal and professional credentials upon which to draw in presenting himself to state officials. Fred Wiseman's parents, Jacob Leo Wiseman and Gertrude Kotzen Wiseman, were respected professionals in the areas of law and mental health care in Boston.[6] Jacob Wiseman was born in 1884 near Kiev, Russia, and immigrated to the United States as a child. He attended Boston English High School and Hildrith's Classical School, then worked as a cigar clerk and a railroader while he studied at Boston University Law School. Jacob Wiseman was admitted to the Massachusetts bar in 1907 and began a long and distinguished law career: he was an assistant attorney general in the 1920s, served as an auditor for the Massachusetts Superior Court system, and practiced law for sixty years. He was a staunch and active Republican and a leader in Boston's Jewish community. He was a founder of the Young Men's Hebrew Association, a trustee of Beth Israel Hospital, and president of the Combined Jewish Appeal, the Associated Jewish Philanthropies, and the Jewish Community Council. Gertrude Kotzen was born in Chelsea, was educated in Chelsea schools, and lived in the Boston area for seventy-eight years. Like her husband, she was active in community and philanthropic work, serving on the board of directors of Hecht House and as head of the women's division of the Combined Jewish Appeal. She was administrator for the James Jackson Putnam Children's Center in the Roxbury area of Boston from its founding in 1941 until the early fifties; she continued her career in child health care as an administrator of the psychiatry department at Children's Hospital Medical Center in Boston from 1954 until her retirement in 1971. Jacob and Gertrude Wiseman's only child, Frederick, was born in 1930. Fred Wiseman received a classic New England education: Boston Latin, Rivers Country Day School, Williams College, Yale Law School. After Fred Wiseman graduated from Yale, he worked briefly in the Massachusetts attorney general's office and then was drafted. While in the army, he served as a court reporter for the judge advocate general's office in Fort Benning, Georgia, and Philadelphia. In May 1955, while on a three-day pass from the army, he married Zipporah Batshaw, a Canadian who had been in his law class at Yale.[7] After his military discharge in 1956, Wiseman spent two years in Paris, where he first studied at the Sorbonne on the G.I. Bill and then worked for an American attorney. While in France, Wiseman bought a movie camera and shot eight-millimeter film of life in the Parisian streets.[8] Returning to Boston in 1958, Wiseman was a research associate at Boston University's Law-Medicine Institute and, later, a lecturer at Boston University's Law School; he received a Russell Sage grant in 1961 to study in the Department of Social Relations at Harvard; in 1963, Wiseman was awarded a National Institute of Mental Health grant, which coincided with his appointment as a research associate in the Sociology Department at Brandeis University.

Wiseman's experience as a film producer began in 1960 when he purchased the film rights to Warren Miller's novel *The Cool World* for five hundred dollars. An adaptation of Miller's grim story of Harlem street youth was produced by Wiseman, directed by Shirley Clarke, and released in 1964. Wiseman's experience with *The Cool World* convinced him that he wanted to direct and that "there was no mystery in the process."[9]

Holding an undergraduate degree from Harvard and graduate degrees in English and psychiatric sociology, Charles Gaughan had worked as a social worker, a community organizer, and an administrator for the State Commission on Alcoholism and the State Department of Public Health before going to Bridgewater in 1959. During his superintendency, he had been conducting an active and largely unsupported campaign to improve the antiquated, understaffed facilities at Bridgewater.

A large, complex facility with 139 buildings spread over 1,500 acres, MCI-Bridgewater was divided into four divisions with four distinct populations: a state hospital for the criminally insane (with approximately 600 men), a prison department for alcoholics sentenced by the courts and voluntarily committed for drug addiction and inebriety (with 600 to 1,000 men), a facility for defective delinquents suffering from gross retardation (with around 150 men), and a treatment center for the sexually dangerous (with around 150 men).[10] Although only approximately 15 percent of the total population had ever been convicted of a crime—many were sent there for a twenty- to thirty-day observation period—the institution was administered by the Department of Correction, rather than the Department of Mental Health. These two state units, often representing quite different and even contradictory goals, participated in a precarious alliance at Bridgewater. Correction officers were accustomed to taking medical instructions from doctors and security commands from supervisors.[11] In 1965, the oldest of Massachusetts' twelve mental hospitals and the most confining, Bridgewater served as a threatened destination to patients or inmates in order "to allay difficulties in other mental health or correctional facilities."[12] Institutions like Bridgewater became "Siberias"[13] for correctional and medical staffs, who were frequently undertrained, underpaid, and overworked. Doctors who were marginal within their own profession often provided the treatment in such institutions.[14] In the mid-sixties, Bridgewater used the services of foreign physicians practicing on partial licenses. At the time *Titicut Follies* was filmed, two psychiatrists and one "junior physician" cared for 600 men in the hospital section of MCI-Bridgewater.[15] Gross shortages existed in all personnel areas: security, medical, nursing, and social work. It was not uncommon during the early 1960s for a state official to visit MCI-Bridgewater, publicly express outrage at the miserable conditions, demand reform, promise support, and then go on to other projects.

Encouraged by Gaughan's expressed interest in a Bridgewater film project, Wiseman, accompanied by *Boston Herald Traveler* journalist George Forsythe, returned to the institution in early June. Forsythe had previously visited Bridgewater with a district court judge and at the time had indicated a special interest in the prison department and its treatment of alcoholics. Wiseman and Forsythe spoke to Gaughan of grant funding, broadcast on National Educational Television (NET), use of the film by institutions and organizations, and the possibility of tracing an alcoholic inmate from the initial court disposition to confinement at Bridgewater. Other subthemes were discussed. Superintendent Gaughan was particularly eager to educate the citizenry about the variety of services at Bridgewater and the difficulties the staff encountered in providing those services adequately. At that time, both Wiseman and Gaughan assumed that heightened public awareness would improve conditions; both subscribed to the Griersonian notion that a documentary film could be a direct agent of change. Both saw opportunities in the documentary tradition of social indignation.

Seeing Wiseman's documentary proposal as an extension of his courageous informational campaign, Gaughan became Wiseman's "internal advocate."[16] Gaughan introduced Wiseman to James Canavan, the public relations director for the Department of Correction, at a meeting in mid-June, at which Canavan screened a documentary made at MCI-Walpole and Wiseman showed *The Cool World.* Gaughan later recalled describing the Walpole film as "didactic" and expressing the hope that a Bridgewater film would "not follow that general outline" (Tr. 4:19). Wiseman's recollection of Gaughan's reaction to the screening session suggests a sensibility and an optimism rare, if not misplaced, in a prison administrator.

> After viewing both films, Mr. Gaughan . . . said . . . he did not want a film made like the one that had been made at Walpole because . . . it was a phony film, that it only expressed one point of view, that it had no depth and that it didn't accurately portray, as far as he knew, the conditions at Walpole and . . . it was more a public relations job. He said the kind of film he wanted made at Bridgewater was a film that would be beautiful and poetic and true, and . . . that *The Cool World* was such a film. . . . He also said . . . that there was no film that I could make at Bridgewater that could hurt Bridgewater. (Tr. 13:20)

Wiseman had Gaughan's firm support by midsummer, but that was not enough; the project required the approval of the department head. Therefore, Gaughan talked to his immediate supervisor, John A. Gavin, on Wiseman's behalf. Gavin's recent appointment as Commissioner of Correction by Governor John Volpe had followed the controversial dismissal of a well-respected, reform-minded penologist. After meeting with Gavin and two of his deputies in August, Wiseman sent a letter of request to film, accompanied by a five-page proposal to Gavin.

Dated August 19, 1965, and written under the letterhead "Wiseman Film Productions" (with Wiseman's home address in Cambridge), the letter announced that the proposed film on Bridgewater "would be made for showing on NET," would also be available "for teaching and training purposes," and was under negotiation for NET or foundation funding.[17] Although the letter implied that releases would be obtained, it did not mention who would collect the releases or who would be released from liability. Judgments as to competency were delegated, however. Wiseman wrote, "No people will be photographed who do not have the competency to give a release. The question of competency would in all cases be determined by the Superintendent and his staff and we would completely defer to their judgment."[18]

The letter included an offer of additional information beyond the enclosed proposal and closed with self-references of respect, gratitude, and hope: "appreciative of a chance to talk with you . . . very grateful for the courtesies extended . . . by you, Superintendent Gaughan, and Mr. Canavan . . . I look forward to hearing from you."

The attached proposal, although certainly not belligerent, displayed the confidence that flows from elaboration and enthusiasm. It fluctuated between specificity and vagueness, between predictions of a rather routinely scripted documentary and plans for an ambitious and determinedly innovative work. Counsel for the state would later seize upon details of the proposal as promises unkept.[19] Superior Court Judge Harry Kalus, in his summary of facts found by the court, included three of the ten paragraphs of the proposal as "pertinent excerpts."

> This will be a film about the Massachusetts Correctional Institution at Bridgewater. Bridgewater is a prison for (1) the criminally insane, (2) defective delinquents, (3) alcoholics, (4) narcotics addicts, (5) sexual deviates, (6) juvenile offenders. The prison therefore has a cross-section of the problems confronting the state in dealing with a wide range of behavior of individuals whom the state must (1) Punish, (2) Rehabilitate, (3) Treat, (4) Segregate. The purpose of this film is to give people an understanding of these problems and the alternatives available to the state and its citizens.
>
> The story of the film would be that of *three people*—an inmate most of whose adult life had been spent at Bridgewater; a youthful offender committed from the Roxbury District Court for a 35 day observation period (Judge McKenney, Chief Judge of the Roxbury, Massachusetts, District Court, has granted us permission to photograph the sentencing); and a Correctional Officer intimately concerned with the day to day functioning of the institution. In showing the day to day activities of these *three people* it will be possible to illustrate the various services performed—custodial,

punitive, rehabilitative and medical as well as the conflicting and complementary points of view of prisoner, patient, guard, family, legislature, etc.

This will be a film about a prison and the people who are in it and those that administer it, as well as their families, friends, and the institutions, groups, agencies and forces within the community that either aid or hinder the custody, rehabilitation, punishment and return to community life of those who have been sentenced by the courts to prison. [emphasis added by Kalus][20]

Kalus did not mention Wiseman's unrealized prediction that the documentary would be "written by George Forsythe," but he did note Wiseman's listing of consultants: Superintendent Charles Gaughan and Brandeis sociology professors Morris Schwartz, John Seely, and Maurice Stein. The proposal also mentioned employing two more staples of the traditional educational film, neither of which was used: interviews and professional actors—"if it becomes apparent that a significant segment of the reality of prison life is impossible to obtain from a participant." Yet running throughout the outline was the promise (or threat) of a self-consciously poetic work that would tap the metaphoric potential of Bridgewater and attempt innovation in both content and form. Thus, two voices emerged: one a cautious traditionalist, the other a restless experimenter. Wiseman straightforwardly stated:

Bridgewater will be shown as an institution where conflicting and complementary forces within the larger community . . . meet.

Implicit in all our experience is an awareness of how similar problems have been dealt with in other countries, therefore . . . the prison itself becomes a metaphor for some important aspects of American life.

The technique of the film . . . will give an audience factual material about a state prison but will also give an imaginative and poetic quality that will set it apart from the cliche documentary about crime and mental illness.

The bringing together of seemingly disparate material [audio and film footage from two different sources] will be used to provide a kind of condensation and counterpoint necessary to make the film dramatic.

Wiseman's summary of his intentions—in their radical willingness to challenge conventional notions of confinement and in a simultaneous effort to praise the status quo—exhibited the complex, even contradictory, impulses that characterize the entire proposal. "Therefore, the content and structure of the film will [among other goals] dramatize the sometimes great, and often slight, differences that exist between those inside and outside of prisons and mental hospitals and to portray that we are all more simply human than otherwise . . . [and will] develop an awareness of . . . the dedicated and skillful work involved in the attempt to provide rehabilitation and dure [*sic*]."

It was the proposal of an intelligent, imaginative, eager producer-director; it was a declaration of possibilities too numerous to find their way into a single film. Therefore, it is easy to imagine how a dedicated, optimistic administrator, weary of the didacticism of state-sponsored projects, might read his own dreams into this proposal *and* how anyone committed to the smooth running of a frequently criticized and routinely underfunded state department might see the documentary as one more risk easily avoided. Whatever their reasons, Gaughan continued to support the project and Gavin, after first notifying Wiseman that he would "explore aspects of doing the film with his staff," wrote a letter of denial to film (Ex. 3).

Gavin's letter to Wiseman stated that he had made a careful judgment, after "considerable discussion with [his] staff and others regarding the total implications of such a film . . . and with full awareness of several complications which may arise." Although Gavin's reasons were vague, his answer was clearly no. "I am sorry to inform you that I cannot permit the filming of this story."

Gavin's letter emphasized his "careful review of [the Wiseman] proposal," but at the subsequent legislative hearing regarding the film he testified that there was no enclosure with the Wiseman letter of request (which began, "I am enclosing a statement of the proposed film on Bridgewater"). At the trial, Gavin said that his earlier testimony had been in error. He had received the proposal, but only "scanned" the memo of request and referred the Wiseman correspondence to Deputy Commissioner Falls, supposedly accompanied by an interoffice memo written by Gavin which stated that "it is also understood that nothing will be filmed or included that is not approved by the Department of Correction" (Tr. 3:82).

Certainly many requests pass through the office of a state department head. It is possible that the initial decision to deny was made not by Gavin, but by a staff member. Saying no is a routine duty for many assistants, and no documentary film had ever been made at

Bridgewater, so it was a request with no precedent of approval; however, the letter does bear Gavin's signature. Gaughan did not receive a copy of the denial and later testified that he did not realize that Gavin had reached a decision that summer (Tr. 4:147).

For a less determined filmmaker, a denial from the Commissioner of Correction's office would have meant the end to the project, but Wiseman did not accept no as his answer. At Gaughan's suggestion, Wiseman made arrangements to contact Lieutenant Governor Elliot Richardson. Widely regarded as a shrewd politician and a gentleman, Richardson was an important bridge figure in Massachusetts politics in the 1960s. A Brahmin by education, social background, and personal style, Richardson nevertheless sided with the liberal Democrats on many civil rights issues that were dividing the nation and the Commonwealth. In the 1964 campaign, John Volpe had promised Massachusetts voters that if the Republican "team" were elected, Elliot Richardson, as lieutenant governor, would have heavy responsiblities in the areas of health, education, and welfare.[21] Volpe did narrowly achieve the reelection he had been denied in 1962, and Richardson also was elected by a slight margin in what was "increasingly a one-party Democratic state."[22] As lieutenant governor, Richardson had visited Bridgewater twice in 1965. Appalled by conditions at the prison hospital and the lack of public interest in improving them, he pledged his support for their reform.

In the fall of 1965, Katherine Kane, a young liberal Democrat who held a seat in the Massachusetts General Court (the state legislature) from the influential Beacon Hill district of Boston, arranged for Richardson and Wiseman to meet. Kane and her husband had invested in *The Cool World* and strongly supported Wiseman's creative aspirations and his expressed goals of institutional reform. Describing Wiseman as an accomplished documentary filmmaker, Representative Kane asked Richardson to see Wiseman, which he did, in early October. On meeting Wiseman and reading his written proposal, Richardson telephoned Gavin, said he knew Wiseman personally, and asked the commissioner to reconsider his earlier decision about the Bridgewater documentary. Several months later, in January of 1966, Kane, a member of the Committee on Public Welfare and of the Special Commission on Sentencing and Release, telephoned Gavin to indicate her support of the Wiseman project. Later, under oath, both Gavin and Richardson strongly denied that any political pressure had been exerted on Gavin.

Gavin did reconsider his decision. In late January, the commissioner met with Wiseman and Gaughan and gave his verbal go-ahead for the film, pending advice from the state attorney general regarding whether he had the *right* to approve such a project. There is no written record of this meeting; the reconstructions of the three participants are in disagreement regarding crucial facts. According to Gavin, Wiseman agreed that any release of the film would be contingent on the final approval of the Correction Department (Tr. 3:89–90, 119). Wiseman has consistently denied such contingencies, claiming that the only conditions agreed upon were that the film crew would be accompanied by a Bridgewater staff member at all times during filming; that only competent inmates and patients would be photographed, with competency determined by the prison staff; and that several individuals (notably Albert De Salvo, the self-proclaimed "Boston Strangler") would not be photographed (Tr. 14:63). There was no written contract. Within the week, Gavin wrote Attorney General Edward Brooke for a legal opinion. Although the letter was written under the MCI-Bridgewater/Gaughan letterhead and cosigned by Superintendent Gaughan, Gavin never referred to the Bridgewater official in the text of the letter; all five first-person references were singular (Ex. 4). Once again, Gavin exhibited an unusual style of indicating, while somehow simultaneously rejecting, joint decision making with Gaughan. A combination of assertiveness and caution is a bureaucratic phenomenon; certainly the tendency to court and abdicate responsibility was pronounced in Gavin's consent style. Subsequent trial testimony revealed that Gaughan had written "almost all" of the text (Gaughan, Tr. 4:159). Gavin had made a few changes, which Gaughan adopted, then the superintendent drafted the letter, signed it, and served it to Gavin for his signature.

Earlier Gavin had asserted his power to say no to Wiseman, but he later doubted his right to say yes. Gavin signaled his awareness of potential legal complexities when he wrote Brooke: "I have told [Wiseman] that I would give him permission to make the film. Provided, however, that the rights of the inmates and patients at Bridgewater are fully protected. . . . I would very much appreciate your views on the question of whether or not I can give permission to do this" (Ex. 4). In describing the precautions Wiseman would take, Gavin mentioned the photographing of only those who were competent to sign releases, which Wiseman had promised in his letter of request. The commissioner did not mention Wiseman's stated expectations that the Bridgewater staff would determine competence. Gavin also claimed that Wiseman had assured him that he would "obtain a written release from each inmate and patient whose photograph is used in the film," an assurance that Wiseman never made in writing and consistently denied (Tr. 4:103–4).

There is no indication by joint address or carbon copy notation that Wiseman was sent a copy of Gavin's letter to Brooke, but Wiseman was aware of the request. The lawyer-filmmaker actively sought a favorable legal opinion when he visited Brooke personally at the attorney general's office in late February or early March. There he was informed that an opinion was being prepared.

Brooke's advisory opinion, dated March 21, 1966, quoted a Massachusetts General Law that designated the superintendent as the party responsible for prisoners.[23] Brooke then stated: "Unless your rules or regulations provide otherwise, the granting of the requested permission would be within the discretion of the Superintendent of the Institution at Bridgewater, who is co-signer of your request. There does not appear to be any provision, whether statutory, constitutional or common law, to the effect that a *consenting* inmate at the Institution may not be photographed (assuming that such an inmate is mentally competent to give his consent)" (Ex. 5).

Brooke cited legal decisions that supported both the jailer's duty to exclude intruders and his large discretionary powers "in determining at what time, under what circumstances, and what persons not having legal authority may be permitted to enter the jail or to have access to prisoners." Brooke thus informed Gavin that it was not the commissioner's decision, but Gaughan's. Again, oddly, copies were not noted.

The same day—March 21—Gavin sent a copy of the Brooke letter and a cover letter to Gaughan. The commissioner's letter of transmittal indicated that he still perceived himself as a vital link in the Commonwealth's decision chain. "On the basis of the attached, you have my permission to proceed to make appropriate arrangements with Mr. Wiseman and get started with the usual precautions" (Ex. 5a).

Here Gavin doubly qualified his responsibility by noting that his approval was based on Brooke's opinion and contingent on Gaughan's following "the usual precautions." These precautions, left unspecific then, became rigorous indeed in Gavin's later testimony before the legislature: "The usual precautions are that no faces are shown in any of our institutions in filming, that no man's picture is shown under any conditions unless he signs a legal release, that he has to be competent to sign such a legal release and that the filming of such inside an institution would be supervised."[24]

A week after the release of Brooke's opinion, Wiseman went to Gaughan's office, where he obtained the (oral) consent that was now Gaughan's to give. It had taken a year to get, but Fred Wiseman finally had his permission to make a documentary film at MCI-Bridgewater. Although not an attorney, Gaughan later claimed he explained the conditions of Brooke's advisory opinion when he gave a copy of it to Wiseman and that the lawyer-filmmaker said, in substance, "I can live with that." Gaughan later insisted that these conditions included a final right of approval by the state; Wiseman has been equally insistent in denying any censorship agreement. Such conditions are not stipulated in the advisory opinion. The opinion does quote Gavin's assumption that Wiseman would be responsible for obtaining releases from all photographed persons. Wiseman never made objection to that expectation in the meeting with Gaughan or in writing later. Charlie and Fred, as they addressed each other by then, seem to have assumed an equal familiarity with and acceptance of each other's intentions regarding the Bridgewater film. It was an assumption that would prove unfounded for both of them.

The same day that Brooke and Gavin issued their approval of the film project, NET wrote Wiseman to offer advice and the possibility of broadcasting a completed film, but denied funding. Wiseman's request for foundation support was also rejected, so he turned to the most common financing method known to the independent filmmaker: a combination of personal investment by crew and friends and lab credit. By this time, George Forsythe had been more or less replaced by David Eames, another journalist and a Cambridge neighbor of Wiseman's. The two men had met earlier in the year and Wiseman had interested Eames, then a free-lance journalist with some peripheral movie experience, in the Bridgewater project, yet Eames never saw the formal proposal Wiseman had sent Gavin until litigation against the film began; neither did John Marshall, the film's cinematographer and codirector, see it.[25] Since there was neither scripted dialogue nor narration in the film, Eames's contribution as a writer per se was limited to composing letters to potential investors in the spring of 1966. As associate producer, Eames joined Wiseman in the difficult task of being frank, yet encouraging, with potential investors. Eames claimed, "We told the investors that there was little likelihood of it being a commercial success" (Tr. 7:34), yet they also indicated that they hoped to return initial investments.

Although not officially incorporated until the following November, the Bridgewater Film Company (BFC) was formed to handle all business transactions connected with the film project. A letter to a potential—and subsequent—investor assured him that "all the proceeds from the sale of the stock are to be used for the sole purpose of producing, distributing, and otherwise turning to account the documentary film tentatively entitled Bridgewater" (Tr. 7:36). Five personal friends of the director—Carl Binger, Henry Kloss, Stephen Paine, Douglas Schwalbe, and Warren Bennis—invested a total of ten thousand dollars. Wiseman, Eames, and John Marshall, who joined the crew that spring, each contributed to the financing of the film and received no compensation for labor. Following an independent tradition, the production budget was sparse. Cinematographer John Marshall had two sixteen-millimeter cameras; Wiseman, doing sound for the first time, used Marshall's Nagra recorder; Eames assisted by changing magazines and tapes, keeping records, and providing a VW van for transportation between Bridgewater and Cambridge.

Of the three-person crew, cinematographer and codirector Marshall was certainly the most technically experienced filmmaker and even his experience was limited. He had worked briefly as a cameraman for NBC in Cyprus and made ethnographic films in Africa. Marshall was best known and respected for *The Hunters* (1958), part of a family research project among the San (Bushmen) begun in 1951 when Marshall was still a student.[26] In 1966, Marshall—then in his mid-thirties, as were Wiseman and Eames—was a Harvard graduate student in anthropology.

When questioned about his motives in making *Titicut Follies,* David Eames testified that he wanted "to gain a great deal of experience in filmmaking, particularly in the documentary field. . . . Another motive was, by making the film, to try to let the public at large understand some of the conditions and problems and situations at Bridgewater which we had observed while filming there" (Tr. 7:146). Certainly when Wiseman and Eames were formally presented to the Bridgewater staff at a special meeting called April 6, 1966, for the expressed purpose of introducing the film project, it was not as men looking for some documentary film training. Their stated goal was to "educate" the public about the institution. The superintendent asked the staff members present to cooperate fully with the film

crew and, according to the testimony of Gaughan and correction officers, assured them that the state had been guaranteed final approval
rights (Tr. 4:40). Wiseman has contested both the guarantee and its
announcement at the meeting of prison personnel. After an introduction by Gaughan, Wiseman screened *The Cool World* for the staff,
answered several questions from the audience, described the noninterventionist methods of film making that would be employed and the
technical innovations that made them possible, thanked the staff in
advance for their cooperation, and told them that he hoped the group
assembled in the prison auditorium would be among the first to see
the completed Bridgewater film. Neither the filmmakers nor the
superintendent gave any instructions for determining competency or
for release procedures. It was made clear that anyone who objected
would not be filmed, yet it was also made clear that the superintendent wanted all personnel to support the film project.

In late April, the crew began shooting footage at a rehearsal of
"The Titicut Follies." An annual inmate-patient-staff variety show,
"The Titicut Follies" was "a kind of religious event at Bridgewater in
the sense that it was something that the inmates and the staff looked
forward to six months before it happened and talked about after-
wards."[27] ("Titicut" is the Indian name for the area in which the institution is located.) According to his own testimony, the superintendent had been eager to have scenes from "The Follies" included in
the film; he was especially pleased that approval had come in time for
the spring event to be filmed, since he felt it would provide some
lightness (Tr. 4:168–69). Before any footage was shot, David Eames
told the performers in the review about the documentary project in
general, indicating that the film crew would try not to interfere with
any activity while they filmed at Bridgewater. He explained the technical procedures of the filming and said that anyone who did not want
to be photographed should so indicate (Tr. 13:64–65). It was an introduction that the filmmakers repeated again and again over the next
few months.

Portions of each of the four performances of "The Titicut Follies"
were filmed. During some performances, a friend of John Marshall's
and a fellow anthropologist, Timothy Asch, operated a second camera.
Edward Pacheco, a senior correction guard who was the producer,
director, and a featured performer in "The Follies," expressed an
interest in escorting the filmmakers. Wiseman spoke to the superintendent on Pacheco's behalf. The director later recalled telling

Gaughan, "I thought it possible that Mr. Pacheco would be an important person in the film because I felt that he had a great deal of
charm and personality and was photogenic and I very much admired
his manner with the inmates because he seemed to treat them so cor-
dially, so affably, and so individually" (Tr. 13:67). Pacheco received
the guide assignment and became so devoted to it that he sometimes
accompanied the film crew on his days off.[28] Soon on a first-name
basis with the filmmakers, Pacheco often jokingly addressed Wiseman as "landsman."[29] Eddie Pacheco became another internal advocate for Wiseman.

The three filmmakers were issued passes to the institution signed
by the superintendent; their presence became routine, expected.
With the exception of several minor restrictions (for example, no filming of Albert De Salvo), Gaughan permitted the crew to film anyone,
anywhere in the institution. This freedom was curtailed when Dr.
Harry Kozol, the director of the Treatment Center for the Sexually
Dangerous, made strong objections in writing to any filming there
without compliance with explicit written conditions.[30] Neither
Gaughan nor Wiseman challenged Kozol's right to make these restrictions; no footage was shot at the center. (In the completed film, several patients from the center appeared in a chorus number in "The
Follies," which was noticed and criticized by Kozol.) Kozol's demands
that filming privileges—and he definitely saw them as just that—be
subject to explicit, written conditions contrasted sharply with the
implicit, oral nature of many other supposed agreements between the
Bridgewater administration and the film crew.

Known as "the movie men," "the boys from Channel 2" (the Boston
NET channel), "the candid camera crew," "the TV guys,"[31] Wiseman,
Marshall, and Eames found the correction officers, inmates, and
patients generally cooperative and extremely curious about the filmmaking equipment and the process of movie making. No hidden cameras or microphones were ever used, but the use of relatively new
high-speed film (which enabled shooting in entirely natural light) and
telephoto lenses made it possible for the filmmakers, at times, to go
unnoticed without being surreptitious. The directional microphone
that Wiseman operated could, on occasion, pick up sounds the ear
could not.[32] Yet most of the time it was perfectly clear what Marshall
was filming and Wiseman was recording. Rarely did anyone object.
The people of Bridgewater permitted the filmmakers to record their
lives. They filmed Commissioner Gavin delivering a lecture at the

training school for correction officers at Bridgewater; they filmed Superintendent Gaughan conducting an interview with an inmate and being interviewed by Wiseman (off-camera). Soon after their arrival, the crew began to receive suggestions from guards of situations or persons that would be "interesting" to include in the Bridgewater movie. Following such leads, the crew photographed a skin search on Ward H, a high school tour of the institution, a physician interviewing a recent arrival, the same physician force feeding an inmate, a man who sang standing on his head, a burial.

There were rare objections to filming particular activities; most of these were raised by staff members on behalf of inmates or patients. Father Mulligan's request that an inmate's confession not be recorded was followed; Officer Moran's objection to the photographing of his interview of a boy under age was honored.[33] Officer Lepine later claimed he objected to the filming of nude men and was supposedly told that they would be shown only from the waist up—Wiseman denied the promise and Marshall said the agreement was misunderstood.[34] In each of these cases, prison personnel acted in their role of *parens patriae*, making consent decisions for the confined men.

In all of the consent negotiations, staff consent was assumed. Correction officers had been told by their superiors to cooperate with the photographers. One staff member, preparing a corpse for burial, objected to being filmed. Wiseman later claimed the man was reluctant because he was an unlicensed mortician, who feared the disapproval of local undertakers (Tr. 13:104–5). Wiseman testified that no inmate ever *said* he did not want to be photographed, and any inmate who expressed an unwillingness to be photographed by a gesture such as "waving away the camera, putting a hand over the face, turning around, turning a coat collar up" was not photographed (Tr. 13:132).

Marshall has described his camera work at Bridgewater, not as an activity "directed" by Wiseman, but as an emotional, personal contact he had with the people photographed.[35] He has claimed he was always sensitive to the desires of his potential subjects, yet also remembers that once he began shooting, it would have taken "a hand in front of the lens" to stop him.[36] Yet the competency of these men to consent remained highly problematic. No objections to filming were made based on determinations of incompetence to consent by the professional staff or by the correction officers who accompanied the filmmakers, which leads one to speculate that the guards had never been given the charge of determining competency, which Wiseman said he assumed. It was, not incidentally, a charge for which prison guards were unqualified.

It is not difficult to believe Gaughan's claim that he assumed the guards were with the filmmakers for security purposes only, although Gaughan was never able to clarify exactly when or by whom competency was to have been determined in his scheme of things. Nor is it difficult to believe Wiseman's claim that he was willing to invest considerable amounts of his time, money, and energy only because he assumed that anything the crew was allowed to shoot and record he would be allowed to use in the Bridgewater film. In at least one instance—a filmed incident in which guards taunted a distraught man in a sequence which became central to the case against the filmmaker—Wiseman claimed he asked the accompanying correction officers if it would be all right to film and he was told that it was.

Added to the vagueness of the consent procedures during filming were the related, and equally vague, conditions involving releases. There was never any written agreement specifically determining who would be expected to sign a release, to whom the releases would run, what form they would take, or who would expedite this process. In Wiseman's letter of August 19, 1965, he intimated that releases would be taken, but did not promise responsibility for collecting them when he wrote, "No people will be photographed who do not have the competency to give a release." Gavin's letter to Brooke, included as an interior quote in the Brooke decision, stated that "Mr. Wiseman has assured me that . . . he will obtain a written release from each inmate and patient whose photograph is used in the film." Yet the attorney general did not explicitly state that his opinion rested on the necessity of obtaining releases.

A release is a precautionary measure; it is a protection from liability and, therefore, assumes a position potentially antagonistic to that of the releasor. Although the state's later position would be that its officers assumed that releases running to the Commonwealth had been obtained, at no time during their period at Bridgewater did the film crew receive a release form, directions for formulating one, or inquiries about such collection. When filmed, neither Commissioner Gavin nor Superintendent Gaughan asked to sign a release or questioned why releases were not being presented for signatures. Gaughan later testified that he did not know what a release was when the matter was first discussed in January 1966.

In the spring of 1966, Wiseman, a member of the Massachusetts bar, drafted the following:

> That in consideration of the sum of $1, lawful money of these United States, to me in hand paid by the Bridgewater Film Company, with offices at 1694 Massachusetts Avenue, Cambridge, Massachusetts, and for other good and valuable considerations [sic], receipt of which is hereby acknowledged, I hereby grant to the aforesaid, the Bridgewater Film Company, its successors and assigns, the right to use my name and likeness and to portray, impersonate or simulate me and to make use of any episode of my life, factually or fictionally, in a motion picture tentatively entitled Bridgewater. This grant shall extend to remakes and reissues of the aforesaid picture, to television rights and to all phases of the exploitation of the aforesaid picture, including publicity, advertising, promotion and the like. (Ex. 19)

A form similar to the one Wiseman used during the filming of *The Cool World,* this release provided wide artistic latitude for the filmmaker and legal protection for BFC investors. Eames and Wiseman obtained signed releases from some 106 individuals, most of them staff members (Tr. 7:127). No one was ever paid the one-dollar release consideration (Tr. 7:39).

Despite a filmmaker's intentions, the procedures of direct cinema filming, whereby a small crew becomes as inconspicuous as possible, often mitigate against efficient release operations. This efficiency is further curtailed when an incident of heightened emotional import has been filmed. Of course, just such incidents are most in need of the protection to subject and filmmaker afforded by a signed release. At the trial David Eames answered a question about "missing" releases. "At the time of filming these individuals there was either too much commotion or confusion or too much activity involved in the filming to make it appropriate or, indeed, possible at that time to approach them" (Tr. 6:144). And, when asked about another instance, he stated that "the obtaining of a release from this inmate was at the time, in my mind, secondary to other duties that I had to perform at the time, such as mechanical or technical duties" (Tr. 6:148).

The direct cinema adage of "shoot and record now—decide later" worked against a systematic cataloging of persons photographed and releases obtained; however, there were "scenes" that Wiseman felt fairly sure would be in the final edit, even as filming ended in late June. Eames volunteered to return to Bridgewater to obtain a release from an individual who had previously refused to sign one, but had been the focus of several provocative filmed incidents. Eames and Wiseman agreed that Eames would get a release from anyone else that he happened to see that he "recalled not having gotten a release from during the filming" (Tr. 6:173). During that haphazardly organized trip, Eames obtained three or four releases from patients at the Treatment Center for the Sexually Dangerous who had been filmed during a performance of "The Follies."

Eames did not get a signed release from the inmate identified as No. 54 in the trial proceedings, but referred to in the film by name—Vladimir. This young inmate took advantage of the filming to state his case, frequently saying, "I want to say this to the camera" (Tr. 13:116). In at least three situations, two of which were included in *Titicut Follies*, Vladimir was filmed complaining to the staff about his treatment. Yet, when first asked to sign a release, he told Eames "he would sign it on the condition that [the filmmakers] arrange to get him out of Bridgewater and not until then" (Tr. 6:170). Eames recalled that in August Vladimir "said he would not sign a release until I showed portions of the film to members of the federal government and until I arranged to have him deported out of America and back to another country" (Tr. 6:174). Vladimir's demands, despite, and even because of, their outrageousness, showed a rare lucidity. This subject realized his reproduction on celluloid was something valuable to a filmmaker; it was a commodity to be negotiated. He did not sign a release; yet his frustrated attempts for a transfer from Bridgewater did become a central part of *Titicut Follies*.[37] Vladimir's story is a capsule version of the complexity of the consent dilemma.

Throughout the spring and summer of 1966, Wiseman and Marshall received dailies from their New York developer, Du-Art Film Labs. Neither Gaughan nor Gavin ever asked to see any of the rushes, and the filmmakers did not volunteer to show any footage to them. So unfamiliar was Gaughan with the process of film making that he later claimed he assumed no film was developed until the filming was entirely completed. Whether because he trusted the filmmakers' judgment and good will or believed in the state's right of final censorship, the superintendent did not interfere in any way with the filming itself. Although Gaughan testified that he reminded Wiseman of his agreements with the state on a number of occasions during the filming period, the filmmakers' freedom while shooting is apparent from the footage they took with them when they left MCI-Bridgewater.

Chapter 3

The Paradox of Reality Fiction and the Aesthetics of Uncertainty

Eleven months elapsed between the time the film crew finished shooting and recording sound at MCI-Bridgewater (June 29, 1966) and the completed editing of the film, which Wiseman would call *Titicut Follies*. While the images and voices that John Marshall and Fred Wiseman had captured on celluloid and tape remained frozen in time—raw material from which Wiseman was constructing a film—the country, the state of Massachusetts, the Boston-Cambridge area, and MCI-Bridgewater reeled in a period of flux and conflict.

The political tensions of 1966–67 created a context of discord that the Bridgewater documentary entered and extended. A national trend to reject the programs and supporters of the Great Society in the elections of 1966 spread into Massachusetts. Republicans won four top state offices: John Volpe was reelected governor by a huge plurality; Elliot Richardson narrowly won the attorney general position vacated by Edward Brooke, who was elected to the U.S. Senate; Francis Sargent replaced Richardson as lieutenant governor. Democrats retained their control of the state legislature; Representative Katherine Kane was reelected to the Massachusetts General Court. State political feuds took on an edge of particular seriousness, even bitterness, as politicians and their constituencies became polarized over national issues such as civil rights and military involvement in Vietnam. The busing of school children to integrate Boston schools continued to divide the city.[1]

Not surprisingly, given its large student population, Cambridge became a center of antiwar activity—the Berkeley of the East Coast. In April of 1967, Martin Luther King, Jr., and Benjamin Spock, accompanied by reporters, visited sympathetic Cambridge residents in a search for volunteers in the antiwar campaign. Among homes visited were those of the Wiseman and Eames families. Attorney Zipporah Wiseman, wife of the producer-director of the Bridgewater film, pledged her support to these two national leaders emblematic of civil disobedience. Here is an account of that visit, as published in a Boston paper:

> The Marty and Benny show begins at the Wiseman's place, the first act in a season-long extravaganza that is to be known as the Vietnam Summer Happening. It is an anti-war production which could put the stars on a Presidential ticket in 1968. . . .
>
> Of course when Mrs. Wiseman opens the door she doesn't get just Marty and Benny. She also gets about 40 newspaper and television reporters in her living room. Plus several hecklers in the front yard who call themselves the Sons of Liberty and sing an old hit, "The Star Spangled Banner," to try to upstage Marty and Benny. . . . The first doorbell ringers [out of thousands of volunteers] are Marty and Benny on Martin Street in Cambridge, and it is disappointing because it is a setup. The Wisemans have been informed that they are to be visited, and they are known sympathizers. . . . Mrs. Wiseman says, "We're honored by your visit. . . ." And the Marty and Benny Show moves on, driven by honest concern and despair through a bewildered country that respects their accomplishments but doesn't know what to think of them now.[2]

Against this general background of political volatility in 1966–67 came the sudden explosiveness of several incidents at Bridgewater. After the film crew left the institution, Superintendent Gaughan continued his personal campaign for attention and increased funding for the forgotten men at Bridgewater. The legislature was appropriating ninety million dollars for statewide mental care already; Volpe had promised to introduce measures to establish one hundred mental health centers in the state, which would divert funds from Bridgewater. Then Dominic Rosati, a suspected murderer, was found naked and dead in his cell at Bridgewater. An examination revealed that he had died of rat poison. The reaction to his cause of death and the revelation that some men at Bridgewater were kept naked because they were possibly suicidal provoked a cycle of wide media coverage, a public outcry about the conditions and the need for reform, and a legislative investigation that resulted in minor changes in some procedures at the prison hospital. During the January 1967 investigation prompted by the scandal, a state legislative committee heard Superintendent Gaughan, medical and legal experts, and social workers describe Bridgewater as "a 'dungeon' throwback to the Dark Ages."[3] Attorney F. Lee Bailey, whose client Albert De Salvo, the self-proclaimed Boston Strangler, was sent to Bridgewater the same month, declared, "The entire institution should be leveled and I'd be happy to do it with my own plane."[4] Once again, criticism of conditions at Bridgewater filled the Boston newspapers. By the end of January, the legislature had responded by appropriating $3.5 million for a new building at Bridgewater.

Still another weakness in the antiquated institution became obvious when De Salvo and two other inmates escaped from Bridgewater in February 1967. Superintendent Gaughan appraised the security situation. "We're holding murderers in what amounts to a hen coop."[5] A Boston journalist described public reaction to the escape: "Bay State citizens were laughing the laugh of sarcasm, of dismay, of complete disgust with responsible officialdom."[6] Still another special legislative commission was formed to investigate the conditions at Bridgewater, and once again, the pattern of reaction to particular events, rather than a general concern for treatment, prevailed.

During the many months that Wiseman was editing the film—a period of intense criticism of the conditions at Bridgewater and a time of personal vulnerability for the superintendent—Gaughan called the filmmaker at least half a dozen times to check on the documentary. Each time Wiseman told the concerned administrator that the work was going very slowly (which it was) or that he had just returned from or was going out of town (which was common for him during that period). Wiseman made no offer to show Gaughan any of the footage, nor did the superintendent demand to see it.[7] Commissioner Gavin had no contact whatsoever with Wiseman during the editing period. In the spring of 1967, at Gaughan's suggestion, senior correction officers Edward Pacheco and Joseph Moran visited Wiseman at his office in Cambridge. There Wiseman introduced them to his associate editor, Alyne Model, showed them a sequence of the film in which Pacheco appeared, and took them to lunch at a Cambridge restaurant. Their meeting was cordial, but Pacheco and Moran returned to Bridgewater with little new information regarding the final film, other than an assurance that there was indeed some developed film that had been synchronized with a sound track and that the mysterious business of movie making was in progress.[8] Since the prison guards had presented themselves as friends stopping by Wiseman's work place for a casual visit, they could do no more than ask general questions, to which they received friendly but vague answers from the filmmaker.

Wiseman's evasiveness—which was later characterized by the state as irresponsible—may also be explained, at least partially, on circumstantial grounds. Like so many other uncertainties in this case, there had never been an agreement between Wiseman and Gaughan as to *when* the project would be completed. One of the advantages for Wiseman of not receiving funding was that he did not have an editing deadline, yet the price of this independence was that he, like most free-lancers, had to support himself and the film while the work was in progress. Wiseman continued to hold his position as associate in sociology at Brandeis. The same spring (1966) that he began shooting the Bridgewater film, he and an associate, Donald Schon, formed a private consulting company, The Organization for Social and Technical Innovation, Inc. (OSTI), which conducted a variety of research jobs (an evaluation of the report of the National Crime Commission before it was published; the Model Cities proposal for Greenville, Mississippi; a study of urban transportation problems for San Diego) during the period that Wiseman was also working on the Bridgewater film project.[9] Wiseman would later refer to OSTI's efforts over a five year period, and to the work of most middle-level professionals who did policy research during the Johnson era, as a "grand boondoggle."[10] The OSTI projects paid some of the Bridgewater film bills but made it impossible for Wiseman to devote full time to the overwhelming process of editing forty hours of footage into an hour-and-a-half film.

In terms of sheer bulk, the physical material Wiseman had to manage was considerable: approximately two hundred boxes of four-hundred-foot reels of film, approximately two hundred boxes of the original one-quarter-inch audio tapes and then, after the transfer for editing purposes, approximately two hundred boxes of four-hundred-foot reels of magnetic tape. It "filled six or seven quite large bookcases."[11] Alyne Model, the only salaried staff member, was hired as an associate editor but she was essentially a cutter, making splices at Wiseman's direction. Marshall claims he played an active part early in the editing process, but Wiseman later "threw [him] out of the editing room."[12] Marshall has codirector's credit on the film itself:

Directed and Produced
by FREDERICK WISEMAN
Co-directed and Photographed
by JOHN MARSHALL
Editor
FREDERICK WISEMAN
Associate Editor
ALYNE MODEL
Associate Producer
DAVID EAMES

Recently published credits of Wiseman's films do not mention Marshall as codirector:

Producer: Frederick Wiseman
Director: Frederick Wiseman
Photography: John Marshall
Editor: Frederick Wiseman
Associate Editor: Alyne Model
Associate Producer: David Eames.[13]

To Wiseman, the process of editing soon became an entirely individual enterprise.

I don't believe in this whole business of testing out a film with an audience, or asking somebody else what they think, or even showing it to a small group and asking for their reactions. It's not that I'm not interested in their reactions, but after you've worked on a film for a year and have made the selections you have made, you are the one who knows what works and what doesn't work better than anybody else. Which is not to say that you are absolutely right about it; but if you've been at all hard with yourself about the material you really have a sense of what works and what doesn't and why.[14]

Yet at this beginning point in Wiseman's career as an editor, he was not quite so sure of "what worked" or "why." Although he had toyed with editing eight-millimeter films, and was somewhat involved in the editing of *The Cool World,* he had no training in the craft. His personal inexperience as a professional editor slowed down the process of editing; yet in many ways his missing apprenticeship also proved to be an advantage because it forced—and freed—him to experiment with the material unbound by traditional rules. The interest he developed in his eight-millimeter experiments "in trying to accumulate little reality episodes and trying to cut them together in a way that dealt with some of the complexities of the issues of a place"[15] remained a central concern in *Titicut Follies* and in his subsequent series of documentaries on American institutions.

The editing was a time of personal autonomy for Wiseman. Long before he finished editing the film, Wiseman began to act like a film-maker who had the right to make both artistic and business decisions. Although releases signed in the spring and summer of 1966 had run to the Bridgewater Film Company, the papers of incorporation were not drafted by Wiseman and signed by David Eames (president), John Marshall (treasurer), and Heather Marshall (secretary) until November 14 of that year. The company was run informally. It had no bylaws, no formal meetings, no minutes, no stock certificates, no balance sheet, yet it was organized to handle all commercial aspects of the film.[16] Wiseman assumed that the film and sound track taken at Bridgewater were the property of the corporation, although no formal documents were executed (Tr. 14:51). The company served as a medium of investment and also a means to protect the interests of the investors, a group that included the film crew. The papers of incorporation included provisions for the issuance of 1,200 shares of common stock, but no stock was ever issued.[17] Wiseman was not a stockholder himself and held no official position in the company.

Wiseman's experience as producer of *The Cool World* had taught him some important business lessons about introducing an independent feature.[18] Film festivals provide access to potential distributors and various opinion leaders in the film world. Beginning in April of 1967, Wiseman submitted the film in twelve international film festivals. Later, *Titicut Follies* was accepted at festivals in four cities: Florence, Mannheim, New York (all 1967), and Edinburgh (1968). It won awards at two: first place for the best documentary feature at Mannheim; the critics' prize and film best illustrating the human condition at the Festivale dei Popoli in Florence. Wiseman acted as a free agent, negotiating for the yet uncompleted film's exhibition. In a series of letters, Wiseman wrote that he "had complete independence" and "no interference" while making the film at Bridgewater, which he described as "about various forms of madness."[19] Writing to a festival committee on May 26, about the time he completed the final edit, Wiseman anticipated criticisms of *Titicut Follies* when he offered a series of disclaimers. "The Titicut Follies does not seek to judge or condemn; it is not meant as an expose of backward mental health or prison practices nor is it a circus freak show."[20] Even though Wiseman already sensed that motives he denied would be imputed, he was eager to have his film seen. No one was more eager to see it than Superintendent Charles Gaughan.

How Gaughan initially reacted to the finished film has been disputed. On June 1, 1967, the superintendent and approximately ten of Wiseman's friends met at a studio in Boston and saw the long-awaited documentary. Gaughan recalled that "when the film was completed there was almost complete silence for a period of minutes" (Tr. 4:51). When the silence was finally broken, it was by praise from Wiseman's friends, some of whom later testified in support of the documentary. Whether carried along by a general climate of praise or in response to a direct statement by the superintendent, Wiseman's impression was that Gaughan liked the film (Tr. 14:15). Gaughan testified that on June 1, he told Wiseman that he "was very surprised at the trend or the new theme that the film had developed . . . was amazed at the degree of nudity . . . questioned whether that degree of nudity was legal under state or federal laws . . . questioned the representativeness of a number of scenes that were used" and challenged whether the man being tube fed could be justified as representative (Tr. 4:52).

After considerable discussion with Eames, Wiseman decided in late May to call the documentary *Titicut Follies*. But the title and credits had not yet been added to the print screened on June 1, nor had the sound been mixed.[21] Otherwise, the film was complete. Gaughan later claimed that he did not raise more objections on June 1 because he did not realize that he had seen a completed film. The superintendent also testified that he had not asked Gavin to accompany him to the screening because he thought that he was going to see an unfinished film (Tr. 4:203). Given Gaughan's confusion about the "rushes," his total unfamiliarity with the editing process, and the highly innovative form of the completed film, this explanation is plausible. In addition, the tension between the superintendent and the commissioner regarding the documentary project from the outset would make Gaughan less than eager to involve Gavin at preliminary stages of decision making. The superintendent asked that the film be shown to Richardson, and Wiseman said he would take care of that as soon as possible.[22]

The screening Wiseman arranged on June 27 was attended by Gaughan, Elliot Richardson (then attorney general), Richardson's driver, and Assistant Attorney General Frederick Greenman. Again, reconstructions of reactions to the screening differ. Wiseman testified that "Mr. Gaughan said to me that, having seen the film a second time, he wanted to tell me again how much he liked the film and how powerful he thought it was" (Tr. 14:15). The filmmaker also recalled that Gaughan was pleased that Richardson also liked the film because the superintendent anticipated that he would need the attorney general's support. Wiseman's account of his conversation with Gaughan after the film screening is a poignant description of political vulnerability. "Mr. Gaughan also said that he didn't want to get into any difficulty over his job with Commissioner Gavin, that he had two sons, one of whom was in medical school or about to enter medical school, and a daughter in college; that he hoped that if Mr. Gavin was concerned and angry with him about the film that the attorney general's appreciation of the film would neutralize opposition that Mr. Gavin might have toward Mr. Gaughan for having allowed the film to be made" (Tr. 14:15–16). Wiseman recalled that Greenman "asked whether sub-titles or a narration would be of any value in explaining the film to people who were unfamiliar with Bridgewater and the Attorney General said he thought that the film would lose its impact if there were any sub-titles or narration" (Tr. 14:11).

Richardson later testified that either he or Greenman had suggested subtitles or narration (Tr. 12:139) and that the film he saw in June "did not appear to be a finished film" (Tr. 12:151). Almost a decade after the June 27, 1966, screening, goaded by the ugliness of a sensational trial, the two articulate, strong-willed attorneys were even more staunch in their disagreement over what was said and what it meant. Here is Wiseman in *Civil Liberties Review:* "Richardson thought the film was great. He understood it, understood what I was trying to do with it, and congratulated me warmly. The superintendent asked him whether I should show it to anybody else in the state government, and Richardson said no, not even the Governor, who was then John Volpe. The conversation took place in a sound studio. Unfortunately, it wasn't recorded."[23] Richardson replied, "When I first saw the film, I raised at once the problem of the rights of the individuals shown. I asked Wiseman whether he had obtained releases from all of these people, and he replied that he had. I reminded him the film would have to be shown to the commissioner of correction, and Wiseman promised me not to release it pending this review."[24] In this particular exchange, Wiseman had the last word. "Mr. Richardson is a man of intelligence and sensitivity caught in the conflict between his political career and his private reactions. Both he and I know what his reaction to the film was. It is too bad he doesn't have the courage to say in public what he said in private."[25]

In the summer of 1967, relations between these two men had not yet festered into bitterness. State officials seemed unaware that they were dealing with a filmmaker who would never succumb to compromise; Wiseman seemed unaware that he would not continue to have support in high places. Yet questions of liability surfaced when Richardson mentioned having Al Sachs of the Harvard Law School see the film. Gaughan later testified that the suggestion was made in Wiseman's presence at the June 27 meeting (Tr. 4:57), but in a July 5 letter to Wiseman, the superintendent wrote, "A day or two after the showing of the film to the attorney general, Fred Greenman called me . . . to tell me that . . . the attorney general had suggested that Professor Al Sachs should be invited to the next showing of the film."[26] Greenman called Gaughan about the film several times during the summer; he also met with Wiseman in July and they discussed a memorandum the attorney general's office was preparing about the superintendent's liability regarding the film. The attorney general's office was obviously aware of the completed Bridgewater documentary and alert to the potential legal problems its exhibition might engender.

The commissioner's office did not share this awareness. If we consider Gavin's early opposition to the project, the out-of-sight, out-of-mind posture of his office was somewhat surprising; but there were no inquiries regarding the progress of the Bridgewater film project from the department office and no information was offered. At the June 27 screening, Gaughan told Wiseman to try to show Commissioner Gavin the film (Tr. 4:58). The superintendent's July 5 letter cautioned, "Let us keep in mind that at some point the Commissioner will have to be drawn in."[27] The language of this letter may indicate that Gaughan's identification with Wiseman remained strong; in any case, the commissioner was not "drawn in" by Wiseman or Gaughan or Richardson that summer.

Wiseman proceeded as a filmmaker who had the right to make autonomous distribution and exhibition plans. Cinematographer Haskell Wexler was able to help at this point. He later recalled, "A friend of mine, Fred Wiseman, made a film called *Titicut Follies,* for which I arranged to get distribution with Barney Rossett, who now owns the Grove Press."[28] Wexler and Wiseman had both worked—Wexler as director of photography, Wiseman as cowriter—on a Hollywood feature, *The Thomas Crown Affair* (1968).[29] In 1967, Wexler was a well-respected cinematographer who had recently won an Academy Award for his camerawork on *Who's Afraid of Virginia Woolf?* (1966). A member of a noted and wealthy Chicago family, Wexler had long been associated with radical politics. He is best known for *Medium Cool* (1969), a fictional film about a news photographer's growing sense of political responsibility set in the real action of the Chicago Democratic National Convention of 1968, which he coproduced, directed, wrote, and photographed.[30]

Wexler was impressed with *Titicut Follies,* especially the camera work of John Marshall.

> It's a fantastic film, it makes you see what cinema-verite can do. John Marshall was the cameraman—I hadn't heard of him before. You see, the problems of shooting cinema-verite are so different. Not just the shooting but the cutting too. Ordinarily when you are shooting, when things stop happening you cut the camera . . . what really good cinema-verite guys do—or learn to sense—what John Marshall does—is when things seem to have stopped, you keep rolling, and move in a little on a face, and about four or five times in the film everything would stop, he would move in on a face and then you *see* the change happening, and then something would start again. When you get that moment, I don't think there is anything in films that I have ever seen, that can match it.[31]

Wexler called his longtime friend Barney Rossett, described the Bridgewater documentary as "extraordinary," and urged that the publisher see the film with a view to distributing it.[32] In 1967, Grove Press was distributing between 200 and 250 motion pictures and was expanding its 16mm line. As owner of the aggressively nontraditional Grove Press, Rossett had experienced the political harassment and litigation that could result from publishing and distributing controversial products. Grove had published Henry Miller's *Tropic of Cancer* when the book was banned in Massachusetts and elsewhere and had fought, successfully, all the way to the Supreme Court for its First Amendment rights.[33] In 1965, the cover of Grove's political magazine, the *Evergreen Review,* featured Che Guevara as a sort of "Man of the Year." Soon after, Grove's offices in Greenwich Village were bombed, supposedly by anti-Castro Cuban exiles. During the 1960s the FBI, the CIA, and the army kept Rossett and Grove Press under surveillance and maintained files on them.[34]

Rossett, a man accustomed to risk and a staunch supporter of the right of artists and journalists to take risks, met Wiseman at Grove's New York offices on August 16. Along with Edith Zornow, of Grove's film division, Rossett saw *Titicut Follies*. He told Wiseman that he liked the documentary very much and that he would get back in touch with the filmmaker. Rossett then consulted Wexler and still another influential mutual friend, attorney Ephraim London, about distributing *Titicut Follies*. Wexler and London both encouraged Rossett to proceed. It was Rossett's understanding that Wiseman "had permission to make the film and have it distributed."[35] Rossett later recalled under oath that "right from the very first time I saw it in August . . . [I assumed Grove was] dealing with something which the producer-director-owner had the right to sell."[36]

During this same period, Wiseman was also making other distribution plans. He hoped to introduce *Titicut Follies* at the Venice Film Festival in late August or early September. By midsummer, he still had not heard from the selection committee. (The film was not accepted.) During the third week of July, Wiseman submitted a print of *Titicut Follies* to the New York Film Festival, scheduled for late September. Wiseman informed the festival director by letter that he had secured releases from all the people in the film or from their authorized representatives. Within a month of that submission, festival codirector Amos Vogel notified Wiseman that his documentary was accepted in the "Social Cinema in America" division. Edith Zornow was a member of the festival selection committee; Rossett and Vogel were friends and colleagues. As founder of Cinema 16, a longstanding showcase for independent films, Vogel was one of New York's most influential champions of avant-garde film. Parts of a Vogel manuscript that would later appear in book form as *Film as a Subversive Art* were first published in the *Evergreen Review*.[37]

Richardson later claimed that he had never been told about the festival entries and characterized Wiseman's negotiations with Grove Press as deceptive.[38] He asserted that during the summer of 1967, "we were exploring possible compromises, such as the obscuring of identities and the adding of subtitles to explain various scenes."[39] It is not entirely clear what parties are included in Richardson's remembered "we," but filmmaker Frederick Wiseman was making no compromises that summer. Or later. One can interpret the director's intransigence and its consequences in a variety of ways, but the *Titicut Follies* Wiseman screened for Gaughan and Richardson, Rossett and Zornow, in the summer of 1967 was identical to the film that as of this writing rests impounded in the Suffolk County Court House, while its duplicates are shown, under unique restrictions, to Massachusetts audiences.[40]

Confronting the Paradox of "Reality Fiction"

In his proposal for a "Bridgewater film," Fred Wiseman predicted that the documentary technique he envisioned would "give an audience factual material about a state prison but [would] also give the film an imaginative and poetic quality that [would] set it apart from the cliche documentary about crime and mental illness."[41] There would be considerable debate regarding the "quality" of the imaginative and poetic dimensions of *Titicut Follies,* but the documentary that Wiseman first screened on June 1, 1967, provided an audience with factual material *shaped* by an individual who had created a product unlike others that had preceded it. On a variety of levels, *Titicut Follies* was and, less so, still is subversive and will always be paradoxical.

From the time Wiseman first approached Gaughan through all the litigation surrounding the subsequent film, attention has been directed toward the potential—then actual—content of the Bridgewater film. Henry Breitrose has observed that "it is an aesthetic of content that drives the documentarian, and the rule that for the audience a documentary is as good as its content is interesting is difficult to falsify."[42] In *Titicut Follies* Wiseman subverts conventional educational documentary expectations of content; he educates his audience by revealing what has previously gone unseen and unheard. No Wiseman film better fits the following Bill Nichols description than *Titicut Follies:* "Wiseman disavows conventional notions of tact, breaking through what would otherwise be ideological constraints of politeness, respect for privacy, queasiness in the face of the grotesque or taboo, the impulse to accentuate the positive. . . . Wiseman's 'tactlessness' allows him not to be taken in by institutional rhetoric; it helps him disclose the gap between rhetoric and practice. But this lack of tact also pulls Wiseman's cinema toward the realm of voyeurism."[43]

In *Titicut Follies* Wiseman shows a Bridgewater inmate in shots of full frontal nudity as he is tormented by guards into a rage of personal revelation; he includes footage of another nude inmate being carelessly force-fed; he presents an interview of a child molester, which reveals actionable information about the inmate's crimes. These are but three of the scenes in the film that have made the filmmaker vulnerable to charges of voyeurism. Wiseman foregoes the soothing, sensible, concerned voice of the authoritative narrator, common to most educational documentaries of the period, for the dark comedy of such passages as this soliloquy by an inmate:

> Charles Goodman, biddlegah, Volpe, Lt. Governor Richardson, biddlegah, McCormick, biddlegah and all members on parole. Biddlegah. I want all those men arrested biddlegah. Immediately. 168 pounds now down to 96 pounds, and all those known biddlegah. Deputy Brewer and all those known, John F. Powers, Volpe, Charles McCormick, Deputy Brewer all go back to von Braun. Palestine, give money sheckle. Biddlegah, biddlegah, President Johnson, biddlegah, all interest, Japanese, Japanese. We know the truth, biddlegah, twenty billion dollars, Charles Gaughan, biddlegah and now death. I point out to you I am Christ Jesus and I am called Borgia. Kennedy who is now biddlegah in truth Christ Jesus. I say in Mississippi niggers over to this fuckin part of the country. You no good John F. Kennedy. I say you stink. No good we send them back to England. We don't send them back to Mississippi back to prison. We put a sign up niggers we don't want to see your fuckin heads here. Finished.

Because Wiseman abandons the convention of a narrator's actual voice on the sound track, some have assumed that he consequently abdicates his own directorial "voice." In a second-order memory of the filming of *Titicut Follies,* French documentary pioneer Jean Rouch complained, "I would like [Wiseman] to say something, say what his thesis is. . . . In *Titicut Follies* there isn't any [commentary or 'guiding hand'], it's a certified report, which could perhaps be interpreted as a cynical and sadomasochistic report. I asked John Marshall . . . what was Wiseman's reaction in the face of all that, did he take pleasure in it, was he happy? And John Marshall said that there was a fascination with horror, which is a strange fascination and which should have been expressed."[44]

Beginning with *Titicut Follies,* Wiseman's work "represents a radical restructuring of the viewing experience."[45] He simultaneously challenges us not to look away, to experience life at Bridgewater, to see and hear what it "is," and also to figure out what it means, to us as individual viewers and to the filmmaker, by discovering the structure he has developed. This duality comes through even in rejections of the film. Judge Harry Kalus called the film "a nightmare of ghoulish obscenities" and "a hodge-podge of sequences," thus responding to *Titicut Follies* emotionally as a shocking dream and formally as an (unsatisfying) collage.[46]

In interviews, Wiseman has shown little patience with questions of influence, claiming he does not read social science literature because he is not good at foreign languages and that he reads the "usual writers"—naming George Eliot and Nathanael West.[47] He is especially fond of the density of characterization and situation in Eliot's work and recalls spending most of his time in law school reading novels in the Yale library. While in Paris for three years in the late 1950s, Fred and Zipporah (Chippie) Wiseman attended plays or movies five or six nights a week, so he was familiar with a wide variety of American and western European theatrical and cinematic material.[48] He has always been personally—and deliberately—isolated from the "film scene," but when he made *Titicut Follies* he had seen and admired many of the early direct cinema films of Robert Drew and Richard Leacock.[49]

Titicut Follies colleague and friend David Eames recalls, "I don't think Fred had any notion that this project, so vaguely conceived, so loosely defined, so fuzzy and wacky and chancy, would turn out to be, a long year later, a film called 'Titicut Follies.' Which is not to suggest he didn't know what he was doing. He did, after a fashion. 'There's a film there, there's a film there,' he would tell me. Part of his genius lies in his unilateral trust in his own instincts and his unswerving dedication to them."[50]

From the outset, Wiseman was inevitably confronted with a central dilemma of realist art: "The secret of art lies in betrayal."[51] Like every other contemporary filmmaker, Wiseman had access to technology that made him come to his own terms with a metaphysical paradox: he could produce something of his own making out of the physical material that had recorded the words and actions of other people. During the year Wiseman spent editing the Bridgewater footage and sound, he might have been ethically bound by a sense of fairness, or artistically bound by his own ability and imagination, or technically bound by footage shot with a single camera of unstaged action, but he was free to treat the material creatively. Keenly aware of this shaping function, Wiseman has always dismissed claims of cinema verite or film truth by documentarians as presumptuous at best and described his films as "reality fictions" or "reality dreams," thus calling attention to their paradoxical nature. "Your imagination is working in the way you see the thematic relationships between various disparate events being photographed, and cutting a documentary is like putting together a 'reality dream,' because the events in it are all true, except really they have no meaning except insofar as you impose a form on them and that form is imposed in large measure, of course, in the editing. . . . In that framework, you can make a variety of movies, and it's the way you think through your relationship to the material that produces the final form of the film."[52]

Wiseman realizes that the abstractions that emerge in the structure of the film are constructed. Wiseman gives himself two related, but quite different challenges: first, to structure understandable sequences and, second, to structure an understandable total film out of those parts. He allows himself great liberties in restructuring the time and space of the original material. Here is still another description by Wiseman of the freedom of the editorial process:

> So you are fiddling around with both the relationship between real time and film time or edited time, and you are fiddling around with the positioning and you are saying that these sequences happened in relation to each other when in fact they had no relation to each other either physically or temporally. You are creating a fiction based on non-fiction material that these things are related to each other, but they may be related to each other only in your mind. And the success of the film depends on the extent to which the whole film creates the illusion that these events have in fact some connection with each other. But it can create that illusion if in fact the process that led you to the conclusion that there is a relationship seems to have some validity in terms of the final form of the film.[53]

Although Wiseman has often said that the relationship between the pieces in his films "should be something other than a linear one,"[54] the tyranny of the projector dictates that his films move through real time, and so the most obvious connections are in images and sounds that directly follow one another. Wiseman has chosen not to work with split screen, multiple projection, superimposition, or various other flamboyantly obvious strategies to suggest simultaneity or relatedness. With some exceptions, which usually occur in the early films, he limits himself to the most austere and subtle ways of suggesting association. By various types of fragmentation—some ingenious and others quite routine—he manages to comment on the limitations of linear time progression and to suggest patterns of circularity and repetition.

John Marshall remembers that, during the early stages of editing, he, Wiseman, and Eames had long talks about how to structure the Bridgewater film and that together they worked out an editing outline of sorts. Wiseman disputes that recollection. "I never worked on an editing outline with Marshall."[55] Marshall, who now prefers sequence films "without bones," has recalled some of the "bones" or structuring principles in *Titicut Follies:* the idea of the follies, the movement from the front to the back wards (with progressively more helpless occupants), the return to various individuals.[56]

Assuming that Marshall was the primary decision maker, but seeing another anatomy, Nancy Ellen Dowd has written:

> I am aware of the argument which insists that Marshall has given a conventional structure to the film, selecting three or four major characters upon whom to focus (the foreign shrink, the head warden, the chinless psychologist, and Vladimir) and has even created a primitive plot (Vladimir's efforts to be released), in order to orient the audience, or to create a framework upon which to suspend the small isolated scenes. I do not believe this to be the case. . . . [Instead] Time encloses itself in a transparent and unsuspected framework as it proceeds in an overlapping stitch V-pattern from itself to itself. . . . The suicide itself [mentioned early in the film, the body seen on a television monitor] will never be spoken of again, and the victim will not appear until the middle of the film (the apex of the V) when the overlap stitch will be very tight and repetitive, cutting from the man being fed to the same man being embalmed. The structure loosens again; much later we see the burial of this same inmate and the movie ends with a scene from the Follies.[57]

Dowd's singular reading of the film as structured around one suicide indicates how seductive the "popular conventions" of character and plot remain for viewers, even when used "unpopularly."

Two scholars—Liz Ellsworth (Elizabeth Jennings) and Susan Heyer—have written detailed synopses of *Titicut Follies* and offer different interpretations of the structure of the film.[58]

Ellsworth mentions the "Follies" scenes in her interpretation of the film, but she does not treat these scenes as separate structural divisions. Ellsworth describes the film as moving through a display of institutional processes, from admission to release. Including the "Follies" scenes in the organizational matrix, as Heyer does in her more extended outline, results in a pattern that is not so much linear as

Figure 3-1.

Structure of *Titicut Follies* as Interpreted by Jennings-Ellsworth and Heyer.

JENNINGS-ELLSWORTH	HEYER		
Part 1: Admission	Act I		
Shots 2-35 (17:00)	A world of folly	Scene 1 Scene 2 Scene 3 Scene 4 Scene 5	Music Show Strip search Interview Inmate monologue Solitary confinement
Part 2: Free Time	Act II		
Shots 36-43 (3:11)		Scene 1 Scene 2	Yard montage "Chinatown" duet
Part 3: Routine Day	Daily activities	Scene 3 Scene 4 Scene 5 Scene 6	Daily confrontations Taunting Jim Guards' conversation Musical show insert
Shots 44-59 (15:50)			
Part 4: Who's Crazy		Scene 7 Scene 8 Scene 9	Role reversal Vietnam argument "The Ballad of the Green Berets"
Shots 60-73 (10:21)			
Part 5: Force-feeding	Act III		
Shots 74-97 (7:52)		Scene 1	Force-feeding Burial
Part 6: Birthday Party			
Shots 98-117 (6:46)		Scene 2	Birthday party
Part 7: Trying to Get Out	Contrasts in competence care, and concern	Scene 3	Psychiatrist's appointments Vladimir's review
Shots 118-134 (8:40)			
Part 8: Hopeless Cases		Scene 4 Scene 5	Al's bath Serious Problems
Shots 135-146 (3:40)			
Part 9: Getting Out		Scene 6 Scene 7	The Last Rites Inmate monologue Upside-down incantation
Shots 147-164 (10:13)		Scene 8	Funeral The final bow

spiral. Both writers comment on the systemic form of the film, yet it is difficult to describe the continuous loops in *Titicut Follies* in sequential prose. It is even more difficult to capture the patterns of thematic repetition and juxtaposition in outline form. Like other Wiseman films, *Titicut Follies* rejects the resolution of either narrative climax or expository argument. The resulting anti-climactic spiral seems to us the general shape of the film and one of the sources of its intrinsic despair.

Usually Wiseman has been reluctant to comment on why he included anything in his films, preferring that the documentaries speak for themselves and that his audiences do likewise. He is even more reluctant to discuss what he shot and recorded, but kept out of his films, and why. *Commonwealth v. Wiseman* provided the rare occasion when Wiseman discussed his artistic motives as evidenced in his editing decisions.

Wiseman testified that he "wanted to put the audience for the film in the state hospital"; he "wanted to put the audience in the midst of Bridgewater immediately" (Tr. 13:142, 148). The filmmaker emphasized that he intended to tap the experiential potential of direct cinema recording techniques. In other testimony, various individuals described footage that was shot and not used, footage that could have provided Wiseman with the material for a completely different style of documentary. Some of these outtakes are worth describing in detail, because they indicate that while at Bridgewater, Wiseman was still not yet sure of what would become the "Wiseman style," let alone sure of what particular pieces would be used in what final pattern. Wiseman and Marshall were keeping their artistic options open. Marshall recalled that he and Wiseman filmed many interviews. "We did that kind of like a safety net. If you couldn't hook things together with the pictures and the events and the follies as a recurrent theme, if that didn't work, you could always use an interview, but we didn't want to. We didn't want to make a talking heads movie."[59] Consequently, they had the material to construct another type of documentary about Bridgewater when editing began.

Much, although not all, of the unused footage could be grouped into three kinds of documentary material. The use of the first would have led Wiseman toward constructing a more traditional documentary; the second provided material for a more modernist or reflexive documentary; and the third could have been used in either style, but did not fit the rigorous direct cinema style Wiseman chose while editing the Bridgewater footage.

In contrast to fulfilling Wiseman's desire to put the audience in the midst of Bridgewater, each of these three kinds of unused material might have distanced a potential viewer. The first category—which would have filled the expectations of many typical documentary formats—consisted of several types of essentially expository footage: an interview of Gaughan by Wiseman (off camera) about the institution and its programs and goals; a speech by Gavin at the officers' training school across the street from the prison; a guided tour conducted by Eddie Pacheco for students from Whitman-Hanson High School in which the correction officer explained the funding problems of the institution and the subsequent picnic on the Bridgewater grounds; various scenes that established a general sense of perspective and context. Thus, Wiseman had the material to make his film "educational" in a more standard form or more bitterly ironic and personally damaging to Gavin and Gaughan by juxtaposing theory and practice in the most heavy-handed style of the expose film, had he so chosen.

The director-editor also had the footage to create a reflexive documentary, a type of film that by 1967 was common among avant-garde filmmakers. With footage of Vladimir turning to the camera in several different situations and saying that he wanted to use the film to get out of Bridgewater and of a guard repeatedly looking into the camera and saying, "We have failed, but it's not us in here who have failed, it is you out there," Wiseman could have made a camera-as-catalyst movie. There are several instances in the film of some acknowledgment of the camera's presence: the guard who is holding the inmate as he is force-fed looks directly at the camera, as if to indicate, "What can I do?"; the elderly man who sings "Chinatown" seems to be performing for the film crew. But the general style of *Titicut Follies* is observational and noninterventionist.

A third type of unused material could fit either of the two documentary styles mentioned. When Dr. Ross made his rounds, accompanied by the film crew, he would state for the camera the history of each individual and give a very brief statement concerning his condition. Because this footage conveys information in the authoritative manner of the expert or the typical television news reporter, it could have been used in the traditional educational format. The material would also have fit—but less easily so—in a documentary self-consciously examining documentary conventions and how people do imitations of media roles when they are filmed themselves.

Rejecting the possibilities of either a straightforward, "direct address" documentary in a traditional mode, or the aggressive introspection of the reflexive documentary, Wiseman depended upon various types of comparison for his organizational matrix. The director testified that a central motive in making the documentary was to discover for himself "what echoes of the larger world did one find at Bridgewater" (Tr. 13:141) and then to represent those echoes in his work. He "wanted to show something about the people that are confined [at Bridgewater] and their similarity or dissimilarity to people on the outside" (Tr. 13:141). Marshall has recalled that Wiseman was "very much into analogy" and frequently spoke of Bridgewater as a microcosm of the imposition of the state on individuals' lives.[60]

A last example of outtakes illustrates Wiseman's central organizing and thematic principle of comparison and his reluctance, for whatever reason, to move beyond the suggestive to blatant examples of role reversals in noting similarities between the keepers and the kept at Bridgewater. In a letter dated April 26, 1967, he described the Bridgewater film as organized around a skit from "The Titicut Follies" in which a psychologist and an inmate sentenced for murder reversed their roles (Tr. 15:80). Wiseman eliminated the skit from his final cut, but he retained the suggestion of similarities between the staff and the inmates and patients.

As finally edited, the documentary makes an issue of uncertainty. That theme is introduced immediately. The first sound we hear is a group of male voices singing "Strike Up the Band" and then, slightly later, we see, by a panning movement of the camera, a row of men singing in what seems to be a theatrical performance. They stand in front of the glittering letters "Titicut Follies" attached to a stage curtain. The audience is given no background information.

Throughout the film, we must figure out what is happening by clues within the text that are more similar to those planted in fiction films than in documentaries, but without any help from stars and stereotypical actions and consequences. Both the content and the form of the text suggest meaning, but the interpretive possibilities are vast. We gradually discover that we are watching the activities at a prison, then at a prison hospital for the mentally ill, but this information is never stated directly. Reading backward and forward, we note that some of the men in the opening chorus number are guards, some inmates; others we are never sure about.[61]

After the musical prologue, Wiseman compares two prison activities, using the obvious technique of crosscutting back and forth between two events, which are identifiable as separate and assumed to be simultaneous. A young man is interviewed by a prison staff member, presumably a psychiatrist (actually a "junior physician," a foreign doctor with a limited license); a group of men, mostly elderly, are stripped of their clothing and searched. Wiseman testified that here he was intercutting the material to compare "an emotional search with a physical search," both of which he considered violence against a person (Tr. 13:146). It is a juxtaposition many have noted, some in complaint for its lack of subtlety. Yet in the dialectical spirit that informs the entire work, Wiseman, according to his testimony, was also constructing a contrast here between youth and age, between a "young man being born into Bridgewater" (Tr. 13:147) and the old-timers, a contrast that has gone unmentioned by critics. Again, following conventions of fiction, Wiseman cuts on dialogue for emphasis:

INMATE: I want to get some help.   *Close-up of patient / inmate.*

DR. ROSS: I guess you will get it here.   *Close-up of Ross.*

Direct cut to the faces of old men presumably neglected for years.

In an example of the editorial irony that runs throughout the film, Wiseman suggests "the kind of help or the lack of it that this man might expect to get" at Bridgewater (Tr. 13:148).

In describing the interview scene, Wiseman pointed out one of the most frustrating limitations of this documentary style for the editor: the incomplete or technically unusable footage or sound track. After the interview, the inmate was confined to his cell, nude, because he was mistakenly described as suicidal. Yet the footage acknowledging that confinement error was too "jiggly" to use,[62] a consequence of shooting unstaged action on the run. Also dialectical is Wiseman's inclusion of the guard tousling the young man's hair in a gesture of friendliness, just before he locks him into his cell. In this crucial scene, the editor introduces the theme of isolation as the camera remains while the inmate stares forlornly out of his cell window. The next cut is dictated by narrative conventions: we see what the featured person supposedly sees while he looks out his cell window—activities in the prison yard. Again, conventionally, a sound bridge connects the two scenes. The innovation that Wiseman attempts and accomplishes in *Titicut Follies* is achieved through the unconventional use of the formal conventions of the illusionary narrative cinema.

Many of Wiseman's organizational principles are standard: the movement from birth to death, entry to exit. Wiseman recalled, "One of the things that provides a structure for the film is, in a sense, the range of activities from birth to death within the context of the institution" (Tr. 13:147). Since Wiseman's perception was that most men get out of Bridgewater in a pine box, he ended the film with a funeral sequence (Tr. 13:149). The actual last shots of the film are of "The Titicut Follies," but the variety show footage can be seen as a prologue and epilogue, framing the other events and commenting on them. The very last image is of a young inmate-patient performer in stage makeup and costume, smiling and clapping; we are left with the suggestion that he will waste his life in Bridgewater.

Some of Wiseman's metaphors are obvious. Later he would see them as weaknesses of the film.[63] Despite the obviousness that the "Follies" performances function metaphorically, they still have relatively open metaphoric meaning to various audiences. Some of Wiseman's intended associations are far less obvious. For example, he explained connecting a discussion between Pacheco and another guard about the past use of tear gas to quiet a violent inmate and an excerpt of Pacheco singing "Chicago" on the double associational level of reminiscence and violence. Wiseman explained, "Chicago, of course, has not only been a scene of considerable violence at one time, but it was also by way of a reminiscence of a life other than Bridgewater" (Tr. 13:162).

For Wiseman, as editor, the connections existed first emotionally and intellectually, then physically in the sense of joining the physical material. For the audience member, the process is reversed. The connections are physically there, as the projected film moves through actual time and space. Whether the viewer then approximates, matches, or negates the emotional-intellectual process that led Wiseman to join the pieces in the first place depends on a variety of factors, some of which Wiseman cannot control. Wiseman is well aware of the subjective nature of "rational" connections. "What's involved in the editing process is thinking your way through the material, and thinking not simply in a deductive way but in an associational way.

And trusting those little thoughts that pop up at the edge of your head about the possible connections between sequences. And then finally seeing whether it works. It's an interesting combination of the highly rational—or what you think is rational—and the highly nonrational in the sense of the associative."[64]

Provoked by Wiseman's connection of the filmic material, each viewer is challenged to construct associations, bringing to the film a personal and social history as perceptual context. All films operate this way to some extent, but because of the density of the images and sound track, their resemblance to the actual lives of the audience members at the level of social actions, and Wiseman's comparative nonintervention, the experience seems intensified in viewing Wiseman documentaries. *Titicut Follies* is particularly sensitive to "social" readings.

There are some sequences in *Titicut Follies* when Wiseman is obviously guiding the viewer through didactic editing. The most flagrant example of editorial point making occurs when an inmate being force-fed by a physician so unconcerned with the patient's well-being that he lets a cigarette ash dangle over the funnel is intercut with images of the same inmate, now dead, being carefully prepared for burial. The extreme contrast between the two kinds of treatment is made obvious by the crosscutting. It is an example of 1960s editing at its most obtrusive, a style Wiseman soon abandoned.

Although Wiseman did not mention this particular juxtaposition in his trial testimony about his thematic goals, he did describe at length the contrast he noticed between guards and the professional staff at Bridgewater in terms of their genuine concern for the inmates, and how he tried to convey that impression cinematically.

> One of the reasons that Mr. Pacheco appears so frequently in the film is because, in my view, he was one of the people at Bridgewater, more frequently found among the staff of correction officers than among the professionals, so-called, the professional staff of psychiatrists and social workers, who expressed genuine warmth toward inmates and treated them on an individual basis. And I was trying to use Mr. Pacheco in this film as an "everyman," as a touchstone, as someone who the audience would identify with, as someone who had reasonable standards of decency and who was generally concerned. (Tr. 13:156–57)

Contrast that proclaimed goal of identification with Pacheco to Elizabeth Jennings's comments, which are more extensive than most, but typical.

The "Star Guard," with a little help from Wiseman, comes off as the least sane of the "sane" characters. Wiseman allows him to return throughout the film with his compulsive lip movements and dramatic, egotistical gestures. In the middle *Titicut Follies* performance he sings "I Want to Go to Chicago" with a partner who is never identified as an inmate or employee. In isolation, the guard's expressions and gestures would make it hard to decide whether or not he's an inmate himself. In the birthday sequence he gives an encore of "I Want to Go to Chicago," then prances out of the room singing a line from "So Long for Now." In the last *Titicut Follies* shots, he gestures dramatically, looking diabolical in bottom lit extreme closeup. Wiseman allows the guard to build suspicion of his own sanity until we suspect that he really does belong on the same stage with the inmates. The final, diabolical shot convinces us.[65]

Jennings's comments suggest the viewer's dilemma that Wiseman provokes by using several types of quite different conventions in editing his films. Because he employs many Hollywood editing conventions, he invites the critics to look for clues like lighting and angle, which the fiction filmmaker usually controls, but which are often beyond the control of the documentary filmmaker.

There is also the reverse problem of underreading. Does Wiseman present a viewer with too much visual information to expect him or her to read the images "successfully" at the editing tempo he imposes? *Titicut Follies'* overall editing rhythm is much slower than the average fiction feature (32 seconds compared to 7.5 seconds average shot length for American features in the 1964–1969 period),[66] yet this average is skewed by five shots (out of 164) that are longer than two minutes. Exactly half of the shots are less than 20 seconds and 82 percent are less than 50 seconds, which is rapid for a film that provides no typical exposition. Even a sensitive critic who has gone through the extraordinary effort of creating a shot by shot analysis of *Titicut Follies* can "underread" its text. If Elizabeth Jennings considered Pacheco's partner "unidentified" as inmate or employee in the Chicago number, what possibility would the first-time viewer have of possessing the knowledge Wiseman presumes in the following testimony: "And the way the scene is shot, the camera is on the chest and face of Mr. Pacheco and the inmate and then the camera draws back and you see Mr. Pacheco's keys on his belt and you know that despite the friendliness that these men displayed toward each other, it is not Mr. Pacheco singing with another correction officer but he is singing with an inmate. . . . And that scene, to my mind, represented . . . a care and concern and an intimacy and a respect for the inmates" (Tr. 13:163).

Among the sequences in *Titicut Follies* that demanded particular "justification" from Wiseman is one that illustrates how a director's extrafilmic information about an event recorded might possibly blind the director-editor to meanings that seem obvious to some viewers who have no information on the situation filmed beyond the text. It also demonstrates how a film builds its own internal expectations. Very quickly *Titicut Follies* establishes an expectation of shock.

Under oath, Wiseman offered a benign description of the yard scene that occurs early in the film: Men are lined up around the walls of the courtyard. There is little activity in the middle of the yard, "no relatedness, no conversation." An elderly man plays "My Blue Heaven" on the trombone, "not to any audience, but to a hydrant." The song title strikes Wiseman as ironic, as does the fact that another inmate, some distance away, is "shaking his head" and "listening very attentively to the music" (Tr. 14:117–19).

Many viewers of *Titicut Follies,* including Judge Kalus, did not interpret this scene as a complex presentation of both isolation and attempts at connection among lonely men, but as prurient voyeurism. They assumed the "listener" was photographed while masturbating. Wiseman, and several guards, testified that this was not the case. Marshall said that this interpretation of the man's actions never occurred to him while shooting the film; Wiseman has claimed he did not edit with this characteristic in mind, since he was familiar with the "real" nervous habits of this particular inmate.[67] However, masturbation had been made an issue earlier in the film.

DOCTOR: You know what masturbation is. How often do you masturbate?
INMATE: Sometimes three times a day.
DOCTOR: That's too much. Why do you do this when you have a good wife and she's an attractive lady. She must not have given you too much sex satisfaction.

Left out of Wiseman's testimony about intentions were any references to material that dealt with political figures or religion, although both are part of the audio track and there is footage of the last rites being administered by the chaplain and also a funeral service. Eddie Pacheco tells a joke about Father Mulligan as part of "The Follies" prologue. Wiseman also omitted mentioning any interest in formal experimentation either as a goal in making the movie or as an art-for-art's-sake argument in defense of the completed work. And he certainly did not ever say—as he would several years later in an interview—that he himself considered *Titicut Follies* "often funny."[68]

The state also avoided mentioning the possible subversiveness of Wiseman's use of politics, religion, formal experimentation, and humor in *Titicut Follies*. It is not clear from the public record when Richardson and his staff decided to move against the film legally or exactly why they made that decision. If the film itself motivated this action, then the decision could have been made at any time after the screening on June 27. The *Titicut Follies* shown in late June was materially identical to the documentary that the Commonwealth would try to ban in late September.

In early September 1967, two bills attending to the plight of the forgotten men at Bridgewater, both of which had been submitted by Elliot Richardson, were near final passage in the Massachusetts General Court. This legislation would require: (1) legal civic commitment at Bridgewater; (2) periodic psychiatric and legal reexamination of inmates; and (3) authorization for the Massachusetts Defenders Committee to represent indigent inmates in these hearings. Although state legislators and journalists were still oblivious to the Bridgewater documentary, they once again expressed their shock and surprise and called out for reform, when, in August, a Superior Court hearing resulted in the transfer of fifteen men illegally confined at Bridgewater, some of whom had been held for decades.

Meanwhile, Fred Wiseman was negotiating with Grove Press on terms for distribution of *Titicut Follies*. Wiseman testified that during the first week of September he informed both Gaughan and Greenman that the documentary had been accepted at the New York Film Festival and that arrangements were being made to screen the film publicly there. Both Gaughan and Greenman denied receiving any such information.[69] Since Wiseman did not notify either office by letter, this detail was, like so many other details in the film's history, one man's memory against the memories of others. State officials claimed that the letter to them that announced the New York screening came from an unlikely source: a former state resident unconnected to production of the documentary.

By early September, film critics had previewed the films scheduled for screening at the New York Film Festival later that month. The first published review of *Titicut Follies* appeared in the September 9 issue of the *Saturday Review*. Critic Arthur Knight generally praised the film, but ended his piece by questioning its uncompromising frankness. *"The Titicut Follies* is, to be sure, a film of our times, a startling example of film truth. But, inevitably, it must raise the ethical question: Where does truth stop and common decency begin?"[70]

Knight was the first person to define the Bridgewater documentary publicly as a potential or actual "problem." Thus began a repetitious pattern, in which the press acted as mediator between *Titicut Follies* and a public drawn into vociferous support or opposition, without having seen the film. Soon after the publication of the *Saturday Review* article, Mildred L. Methven, a former Massachusetts social worker then living in Minnesota, wrote a letter of complaint, based on Knight's description of the film (which included the erroneous claim that hidden cameras had been used in the filming) to Commissioner Gavin, with copies sent to Governor Volpe, Senator Edward Kennedy, and the Civil Liberties Union of Massachusetts (CLUM). This letter was Gavin's first indication that the film had been completed; it was Volpe's first indication that a documentary had been contemplated or filmed at MCI-Bridgewater. Both Gavin and Volpe were angered by the situation and doubly insulted that their offices had been left uninformed. Volpe contacted Richardson, who said he had been unaware of plans for a public showing of *Titicut Follies*. Gavin called Gaughan to inquire about why he had been excluded from the screenings. Gavin later testified, "I felt that protocol would demand that they invite me to view the film in view of the fact that I was the one that [Wiseman] had all the dealings with to get permission to do this film" (Tr. 3:38). Gavin would later see advantages to his exclusion, but at this point he was irritated that his approval had not been sought.

Within days, Wiseman, too, had shocking news from an unexpected source. In a convoluted example of the press's feeding on itself, a reporter from the Quincy *Patriot Ledger* called Wiseman regarding a front-page article that had appeared in the September 16 *Ledger*. The author of the article, having been alerted by Knight's review to the existence of *Titicut Follies* and its scheduled showing, had interviewed several members of the Bridgewater staff about the documentary. The article quoted Gaughan as saying that the state's three censors would have to pass on the Bridgewater film before it could be shown at Lincoln Center.[71] Dr. Ames Robey, the former medical director at Bridgewater, was quoted as having said that he had a written agreement with Wiseman that gave Robey a right to review the portions of the film in which he appeared before the film was shown. Now it was Wiseman's turn to be upset. He claimed that he not only had never agreed to the state's right to censor the film, but that the topic had never even been mentioned before. When contacted by Wiseman, Gaughan denied making the censorship claim to the *Ledger* reporter.[72] Wiseman then contacted the attorney general's office and pressed Greenman to schedule a meeting of the attorney general, the superintendent, the commissioner, and the filmmaker "so that if there were any issues, they could be discussed openly and frankly."[73]

Obviously, there were some issues. The film still had not been shown publicly, but it soon would be. The *New York Times* had already carried an announcement for the Lincoln Center screening of *Titicut Follies* and a subsequent discussion of the film as part of the "Social Cinema in America" program on September 28. If there was going to be a frank and open discussion among these men it would have to be when they met at the attorney general's office on September 21.

When Fred Wiseman arrived at Richardson's office, he was accompanied by attorneys Alan Dershowitz and Gerald Berlin. Wiseman had originally hired Dershowitz, a member of the Harvard Law School faculty, to represent him. Since Dershowitz was then not a member of the Massachusetts Bar, he suggested they "bring in Gerald Berlin."[74] At that time, Berlin was serving as chairman of the Civil Liberties Union of Massachusetts. He had previously served as an assistant attorney general under Democratic Attorney General Gerald McCormack. Wiseman and his counsel met with Attorney General Richardson; Richard Ward, a legal assistant to the attorney general; Assistant Attorneys General Greenman and Levin H. Campbell; Commissioner Gavin; and Superintendent Gaughan. Gavin later recalled that Richardson did most of the talking, which seemed reasonable to the commissioner, since he assumed that Richardson had called the meeting (Tr. 3:153).

Beginning on fairly congenial terms, the meeting soon became a forum for all parties to express the feeling that each had been uninformed, if not deceived, about crucial matters. Attorney General Richardson and his staff claimed surprise—and dismay—regarding the New York Film Festival screening; Wiseman was concerned about censorship claims that had been reported in the state press; Gavin was extremely upset that he had not yet seen *Titicut Follies*. As Gavin later recalled, he "didn't want, from what [he had] heard of the nudity in the picture and so forth, the Commonwealth to be made a laughing stock nor the Commissioner of Correction" (Tr. 3:164).

Gavin said that he did not want to "compromise the governor."[75] Berlin noted that under Brooke's advisory opinion, there had been no necessity for showing the film to Gavin. The argument of protocol was then advanced as a counter. Assistant Attorney General Greenman later testified that at this meeting Gavin "said words to the effect that . . . simple dictates of common courtesy and protocol would have been to show him this film" and that "it had been the understanding" that Gavin had a right of approval and "the last word."[76] Wiseman later testified that, at this meeting, state officials made no claims of any censorship agreement, but argued from protocol and what seemed to them common understanding of the way the state operated.

To the lawyers present—seven of the nine men—it was not courtesy nor protocol, but rather the legal aspects of the arrangements that demanded close attention. Richardson spoke at length about responsibilities: the responsibility of the Commonwealth to protect the rights of the inmates and patients at Bridgewater and the responsibility of his office to advise Gavin and Gaughan as to the legal implications of their responsibilities. Often making reference to a legal memorandum that Greenman had prepared, Richardson voiced concern for the inmates' right of privacy. Dershowitz suggested that perhaps there might be some conflict of interest in the state representing both the Department of Correction and the individuals at Bridgewater. Consequently, he advised that individual guardians be appointed for each inmate shown in the picture before any determination was to be made as to what, if anything, should be done to protect them. Richardson said that he thought the law professor's analysis "ingenious," but felt the state should not evade its responsibility to the inmates.[77] While discussing the matter of liability, Richardson asked Wiseman for information regarding the releases that he and David Eames had obtained. On advice from counsel, Wiseman refused to give the attorney general the signed releases, to show him a blank release form, or to give him information about the contents of the form.[78]

If any one of these men had been optimistic about the chances of reaching some accord about the public screening of the Bridgewater documentary when the meeting began, they had much less reason for optimism one-half hour later when the meeting ended with Richardson telling Wiseman that he was "turning him down."[79]

Hours after the crucial meeting at the state house, Wiseman met with his colleagues Eames and Marshall. That same evening Commissioner Gavin, his three deputies, James Canavan (the public relations director for the Department of Correction), and the filmmakers saw *Titicut Follies* at a screening room in Newton. The next day, Gavin received a hand-carried opinion from the attorney general; he immediately wrote Wiseman to notify him that "in accordance with the agreement that you have with Superintendent Gaughan and me that it will not be shown without our approval . . . [you do] not have approval to show this film to anyone."[80] For the first time, censorship privileges were mentioned in writing; they were claimed as an a priori agreement. This letter to Wiseman, along with an enclosed copy of Richardson's letter to Gavin, was sent by registered mail to a Cambridge address that was no longer Wiseman's residence. It was returned, marked "unclaimed," approximately ten days later. Since a copy of the letter was sent to Berlin, Wiseman's attorney, there is little doubt that Wiseman eventually saw the commissioner's letter, but he did not receive the registered letter on September 22. That day the filmmaker was in New York negotiating with Grove Press for distribution rights to *Titicut Follies*. While Gavin was assuming that state administrators held veto rights regarding the exhibition of the Bridgewater documentary, Wiseman was assuming rights of his own. The Commonwealth of Massachusetts would need more than letters of disapproval to keep Fred Wiseman from showing the documentary that he had made. That would demand the support of the courts.

Chapter 4

The Conundrum of Competing Rights

On Friday, September 22, 1967, the attorney general's office moved with dispatch and force against *Titicut Follies*. In a single day, Attorney General Elliot Richardson sent an opinion to John Gavin; the Commissioner of Correction then wrote Wiseman that he did not have approval to show the film to anyone; Assistant Attorney General Frederick Greenman filed a bill of complaint in the Superior Court of Suffolk County (Boston) on behalf of the Commonwealth, Gavin, and Superintendent Gaughan to temporarily restrain Wiseman, his agents, and attorneys from entering into any contracts or agreements that would permit the showing of *Titicut Follies*. The bill also petitioned that Wiseman and his associates be permanently enjoined from "exhibiting, showing, or causing to be shown, or authorizing the showing of said film entitled 'The Titicut Follies' to any audience, group, person or persons without prior approval in writing by the plaintiffs."[1] The bill, filed and entered in the equity docket on September 22, included the signatures of plaintiffs Gaughan and Gavin. The commissioner later testified that he had not signed the complaint until around seven o'clock that night (Tr. 3:58). The following Monday, Greenman filed a motion to amend the bill in equity, adding the Bridgewater Film Company, Inc., as a party respondent.[2] The next day, September 26, counsel for the attorney general filed papers in the New York Supreme Court to halt the showing of *Titicut Follies* in that state. The Commonwealth sought both a temporary and a permanent injunction against the showing of the film in New York.

In retrospect it seems that the time for compromise between the Commonwealth and Wiseman—if indeed there ever had been such a time—had come and gone at the crucial meeting on September 21.

Once legal action commenced on September 22, the Commonwealth of Massachusetts and Frederick Wiseman became locked into adversarial positions that did not relax for two decades.

In a special night session of the Suffolk Superior Court on September 22, Judge Joseph Ford, without having seen the Bridgewater documentary, put a temporary restraining order on the exhibition of *Titicut Follies* in Massachusetts. The temporary restraining order was granted without notice to or presence of Wiseman's counsel.[3]

A motion also progressed swiftly through the New York Supreme Court. The Commonwealth filed the motion on September 26; New York Supreme Court Justice Francis T. Murphy, Jr., viewed the film the next day; Murphy heard arguments and reached a decision on September 28. During the hearing, with Murphy's knowledge and during a recess called for that purpose, counsel for the defendants (Richard Gallen representing Grove Press; Ephraim London on Wiseman's behalf) offered—as they had done two days before—a six week delay in further exhibition of the film if the Commonwealth would permit the New York Film Festival screening that evening.[4] According to Wiseman's later testimony, Justice Murphy advised counsel for the Commonwealth, Roger Hunting, to agree to the compromise so that parties might have time to resolve their differences outside of court.[5] Hunting called Richardson; the attorney general refused the offer, stating that he was responsible for the full protection of the privacy of the Bridgewater inmates.[6] The hearing continued. Its conclusion: Murphy denied the request to enjoin the showing of *Titicut Follies* in New York. In announcing his ruling, Murphy pointed out that both sides had agreed that the film "has social significance."[7] The Commonwealth responded with continued determination by filing a second motion for injunctive relief in New York, now naming two inmates—Albert Dagnault and James Bulcock (both of whom are shown nude in the film)—as co-plaintiffs. The second motion claimed that the defendants (The Lincoln Center for the Performing Arts, Inc.; The Bridgewater Film Company, Inc.; Frederick Wiseman; Grove Press, Inc.; and Barney Rossett) had taken advantage of the order denying the first motion for an injunction by then arranging for the commercial showing of the film. In the second New York hearing, the defense argued primarily on First Amendment grounds, claiming the widely recognized principle that freedom of expression was not diminished when a communication was sold for profit. On October 2, a second New York justice, Saul S. Street, denied the motion for injunction, arguing that insufficient evidence had been entered by the Commonwealth to exercise the drastic power of the restraining order. According to Justice Street, "The question as to whether there was an oral agreement is not for the court to decide at this juncture on this motion, the question as to whether or not the patients have any claims or rights remains. They are wards of the Commonwealth of Massachusetts. The Commonwealth could not surrender their vested rights, whatever they may be; they survive the showing of this film."[8] The Commonwealth of Massachusetts had failed in its legal efforts to block exhibition of *Titicut Follies* in New York state and thereafter abandoned the campaign to suppress the film through this route.

While the Commonwealth was petitioning Massachusetts and New York courts to enjoin the exhibition of *Titicut Follies,* Wiseman was equally aggressive in making immediate arrangements to protect the film. Directly following the critical meeting in the attorney general's office on September 21, Wiseman, Eames, and Marshall met at the Eames home in Cambridge. According to Eames and Marshall, Wiseman did not mention that earlier in the day Gavin had claimed a right to approve the film.[9] Wiseman did say that the commissioner was eager to see the film and, indeed, Gavin saw the documentary that very night in the presence of the filmmakers. At the screening in Newton (which was also the first viewing of the final cut for Marshall), neither Gavin nor his deputies said anything about censorship rights.[10] The night of September 21, Wiseman's colleagues must have been aware that state officials were not pleased with the Bridgewater film, but the trial testimony indicates that they had less than a full account of the meeting at the attorney general's office earlier that day. In preparation for negotiation with Grove Press executives the next day in New York City, Marshall brought Wiseman a copy of the contract that Marshall's parents had negotiated on his film *The Hunters,* to be used as a guide.[11] Eames and Wiseman seemed to have left for New York with the support, if not the active participation, of their cinematographer; however, according to Wiseman's testimony, on September 20, Marshall expressed concern about the absence of corporate bylaws and told Wiseman that he planned to consult counsel about his role as an officer in the Bridgewater corporation (Tr. 15:27).

Although Wiseman was not an officer of Bridgewater Film Company (BFC), which held all rights to the film *Titicut Follies,* he spoke on behalf of the film in the negotiations with Grove and signed contracts. The question of ownership was complicated for these three

colleagues. Exhibit 20, a letter to an investor, stated, "The ownership of the film is divided 50–50 between the investors who provide
the total $30,000 capital requirement and the above-listed incorpora-
tors [Eames, John and Heather Marshall] of the Bridgewater Film
Company." Eames was president, John Marshall treasurer, and
his wife, Heather, clerk. The state would later try to prove Wiseman
an untrustworthy associate and suggest that he held no corporate
office nor owned any corporate stock to avoid anticipated liability.
When questioned about his lack of corporate involvement with the
BFC, Wiseman offered an altruistic account:

> There were several reasons, the principal reason being that Mr. Eames
> and Mr. Marshall had put up a considerable amount of cash themselves
> and spent a lot of time working on the film without any compensation.
> And I was going to receive the principal credit for the film as the producer
> and director and editor. And this was the way that their interest in the
> film would be protected and the monies that they had advanced and the
> labor that they performed would be protected. In addition, the corporation
> was formed because we needed more money to complete the film and it
> was thought that we might be able to get some investors, which we subse-
> quently did. (Tr. 15:21)

Despite his lack of corporate status, Wiseman continued to take
charge of all negotiations when he and BFC president David Eames
went to New York. Wiseman asked Grove Press for fifty thousand
dollars for the exclusive rights to distribute *Titicut Follies* "in all sizes
and gauges of film for all purposes in the United States and Canada."[12] Grove offered fifteen thousand; they agreed upon twenty-five
thousand dollars. The film company was to receive 50 percent of theatrical gross receipts and 75 percent of any television sale, after
expenses were "taken off the top," which, according to Grove Film
Division head Edith Zornow, was "a standard industry deal."[13] On
agreement to spend at least ten thousand dollars in advertising,
Grove was to have "complete control of the matter and means of distribution."[14] There was no written contract signed that day with
Grove, but, according to all those present at the negotiations (Wiseman, Eames, Zornow, Grove president Barney Rossett, and Grove's
general counsel Richard Gallen), there was an oral agreement made
on Friday, September 22, to transfer distribution rights for *Titicut
Follies* from BFC to Grove, and all details of the Friday meeting
which were "commemorated" in the memo of September 25 were
agreed to on September 22.[15]

That Friday in the Grove offices there was no mention of the Thursday meeting at the attorney general's office or of any present or potential legal problem regarding exhibition.[16] Rossett later recalled, "I don't remember anything specifically, but the gist of the whole thing right from the very—right from the very first time I saw it [*Titicut Follies*] in August until then [September 22] was that we were dealing with something which the producer-director-owner had the right to sell that which he was speaking to us about."[17]

The meeting with Grove had been scheduled earlier in the week. It is impossible to know whether Grove's offer would have been altered or even withdrawn had the company known that the Commonwealth would petition for injunctions against exhibition in Massachusetts and New York. Grove Press was certainly no stranger to censorship problems; indeed, the company prided itself on its firm support of controversial publications, but litigation is always expensive and Grove was also a business. In the subsequent trial, the state would try to establish that Wiseman had deceived, among many others, the president of Grove Press. When questioned about whether Wiseman had indicated on or before September 22 that there might be a dispute about film rights, Rossett's reply suggests business-as-usual. "My answer is, unfortunately, a very vague one. It's entirely possible that he did, but if he did I do not recall it. However, in any endeavor that we are involved in, where we are dealing with creative people, I always take it for granted that there is the possibility of problems arising."[18]

The meeting concluded, Eames and Wiseman left a print of *Titicut Follies* with Grove. Wiseman immediately called Marshall to tell him about the agreement. According to Eames's testimony, the BFC treasurer was "extremely pleased" with the contract terms (Tr. 7:92). Wiseman, now alone, went to the offices of attorney Ephraim London for an appointment made earlier in the week. There, Wiseman made arrangements to retain London as his counsel. The distinguished New York attorney had earned an important place in film history with his successful defense in 1952 of the Italian import *The Miracle* (*Burstyn v. Wilson*).[19] The United States Supreme Court decision in *Burstyn v. Wilson* is commonly regarded as the beginning of First Amendment protection of film. In 1963 Arthur Mayer wrote, "Today we all turn to Ephraim London for advice on censorship matters."[20] Perhaps Wiseman would have been equally successful in the New York courts without the celebrated attorney as his counsel, but Wiseman doubtlessly had expert legal advice. In London's office, a letter to Du-Art Film Labs (the processor of all the Bridgewater footage) authorizing prints for Grove Press was prepared and signed by Wiseman. He returned to the Grove offices with this letter, met Eames there for his signature, then hand-delivered the order to the lab.[21] Still more arrangements were made over dinner with a representative of Springer Associates, the firm handling the public relations work for the Lincoln Center Festival. It had been a long, productive day for the producers of *Titicut Follies,* just as it had been for officials of the Commonwealth.

While Wiseman remained in New York, Eames returned to New England and discovered that all was not well. Over the weekend of September 23–24, the BFC president received a call from John Marshall, whose attorney had advised him to resign from the BFC. According to Eames, Marshall "said he didn't want to hurt the film in any way and he wanted what was best for the film and he hoped that his action or his contemplated action wouldn't affect the film adversely" (Tr. 7:85).

On Monday, September 25, the day that Wiseman and Eames signed what they would later term the "memo of agreement" with Grove Press, Marshall heard (on a local newscast) about the injunction against *Titicut Follies.* That day, John and Heather Marshall each wrote a letter of resignation to David Eames, president of Bridgewater Film Company, Inc. Notarized in New Hampshire, the letters protested the contract with Grove Press and the planned showing at Lincoln Center.[22] In telephone conversations with both Eames and Wiseman that day, Marshall allegedly claimed that he and his wife sent the letters on the advice of counsel, but he was "still with the film 100%" and hoped that they understood "he really didn't mean it [the protest] literally."[23] Not surprisingly, the state would seize upon the Marshalls' resignations to suggest that Wiseman at best had been a careless businessman, at worst that he had betrayed a friend and a colleague. In testimony, Eames and Wiseman presented the resignations as something akin to a legal technicality, which had no serious consequences and fostered no ill will. In private, according to Marshall, Wiseman was furious.[24] It is uncertain whether the resignations damaged Wiseman's ethos in the eyes of the trial judge, but they could not have helped it. Whatever the director felt personally about the resignations of John and Heather Marshall, he did not let their real or feigned protest deter his plans for the first public showing of *Titicut Follies* at the 1967 New York Film Festival.

Although Frederick Wiseman's work was not yet well known to the New York film milieu, there was probably considerable anticipation regarding the first public screening of *Titicut Follies* among this influential group. The Lincoln Center promotional material described the Bridgewater documentary as "explosive" and, as early as September 17, noted that Wiseman *and* Ephraim London would discuss the film after its festival screening, a sure clue of potential litigation.

Even before its first public showing, and before the Commonwealth began moving against its showing on September 22, *Titicut Follies* had been presented to audiences and viewed as a litigious film. Eight prints had been made of the film (Wiseman, Tr. 14:47), and by mid-September *Titicut Follies* was familiar to some members of the film community. The film had been shown at the Flaherty Film Seminar in Harriman, New York, in early September,[25] at three press screenings in conjunction with the festival, and had been reviewed in the national press. On September 22, 1967, it became known to a larger public when excerpts were broadcast on Channel 13 in New York. By September 27, *The New York Times* had reported the injunctive pleas by the Commonwealth. Justice Murphy reached his decision only hours before the scheduled 6:30 P.M. screening on September 28. A crowd stood in line for tickets to *Titicut Follies;* several hundred people "waited in the rain even after all tickets had been distributed."[26]

The advertisement that appeared in New York papers in early October announced *Titicut Follies* as a film "cleared by the Supreme Court of New York for showing at the Lincoln Center Film Festival."[27] Not only did the advertisement proclaim victory in a past legal struggle, but promises of public exhibition became part of the Grove Press defense in the second New York hearing, held on October 2. In his affidavit in opposition to the injunction, Grove counsel Richard Gallen, wrote, "It is impossible to calculate the damage to the film and to the reputation of the distributor that would follow if people who read the advertisements for the picture and come to the theater are unable to see the film."[28] Gallen presented a variety of arguments, mostly from the point of financial harm—the wheels of commerce were in motion and it was unjust to stop them. Gallen also denied the Commonwealth's claim that Wiseman had personally and contemptuously handled the commercial exhibition plans. "The negotiations for the theater and the arrangements for the exhibition of the film were made by the Distributor of the film, and Mr. Wiseman had nothing whatever to do with it."[29]

Injunctive relief was again denied to the Commonwealth, and *Titicut Follies* began a six-day commercial play on October 3 at the Cinema Rendezvous, a small first-run Manhattan theater, where it was shown six times a day to a total daily audience of approximately 300 people and grossed a total of eight thousand dollars.[30] The advertisements showed how a company protects itself financially and legally while marketing a potentially litigious product: The film was released by a newly formed corporation—the Titicut Follies Distributing Co., Inc. All references in the ads to the content of the film were quotations: "Relentless expose of a present-day snake pit, it deserves to stand with works like Upton Sinclair's *The Jungle* as an accusation and a plea for reform" (*Time*). "Makes *Marat/Sade* look like *Holiday on Ice*" (Vincent Canby, *New York Times*). A recorded message at the theater urged the caller "not to miss seeing the film which the state of Massachusetts attempted to keep from the public."[31]

Edith Zornow of Grove next placed the film at the Carnegie Hall Cinema, another small Manhattan movie house. It was advertised as an "engagement extended by popular demand."[32] Booked as a four-wall arrangement (whereby the distributor pays a sum for what amounts to theater rental and advertising control for a specific time and then keeps all profits, in contrast to a usual distributor-exhibitor split of admission receipts), *Titicut Follies* played seven times daily from October 14 to November 4. Attendance was comparable to that of the first run. From the commercial screenings in New York, Grove and Titicut realized gross revenues of $31,798.50 and, after payment of expenses, a net profit of $14,451.61.[33] The Carnegie Hall Cinema advertised the documentary by quoting Richardson, among others. The attorney general denied he had described the film as "superb" and requested that the theater remove his name from the marquee, which it did.[34] Grove had hoped to show *Titicut Follies* commercially in key cities throughout the country and to reopen it at the Carnegie Hall Cinema later in November, but those plans were canceled because of the continuing legal action against the film in the Massachusetts courts.[35]

Titicut Follies was among approximately one hundred films from the United States submitted to the Mannheim Film Festival and one of the five American entries selected to compete with sixty or seventy international films. On October 15, a friend of Ephraim London's attending the West German documentary festival notified London, who in turn notified Wiseman, that *Titicut Follies* had been awarded first prize for the best feature-length documentary. Immediately incorporated into the ad campaign, the international recognition was used as a credential of serious worth from then on. Other pretrial screenings during the fall of 1967 included a much publicized Boston showing to the Massachusetts General Court (a screening that required the passage of a special resolution), a private screening to some Massachusetts newsmen in Providence, Rhode Island,[36] a public showing at the Museum of Modern Art in New York City,[37] and an exhibition to three jointly assembled classes at Yale Law School, which was followed by a discussion with the filmmaker.[38] From its completion at the end of May through its public exhibition in the fall of 1967, probably fewer than ten thousand people worldwide had seen *Titicut Follies*.

The film's total audience as of the end of 1967 could have been easily multiplied tenfold by a single broadcast on National Educational Television (NET). Such a broadcast would have given Wiseman the opportunity to fulfill his proposal of educational broadcast to state officials and investors and to gather important supporters to the cause of exhibition. Of course, such a broadcast would also have added some opposition. Some time before November 10, Zornow had an offer to broadcast *Titicut Follies* on NET, but, unsatisfied with the financial bid, she refused.[39] In the closing days of the trial, Wiseman announced a pending NET offer to broadcast *Titicut Follies* (Tr. 15:141). Had a lawsuit against the film not been in progress, he has since claimed, the Public Broadcasting Laboratory would have run *Titicut Follies* as its first show.[40]

The Rush to Judgment outside the Courts

On the day that the attorney general's office filed the first request for an injunction against *Titicut Follies* in New York, the qualifying election for mayor claimed the attention of most Bostonians. School Committee Chair Louise Day Hicks and Secretary of State Kevin White were the victors; Beacon Hill Representative John Sears, the first Republican candidate for mayor in over twenty years, was a surprising third. All of the ten candidates had tried to appeal to the frustrations of the Boston electorate, but Hicks had tapped a particular discontent. "With a record turnout . . . she picked up the 'anti' vote. It was against a strong mayor, John Collins. It was against the

Boston concept of urban renewal. And it was against Negroes."[41] That last week of September, Boston's two favorite sports—baseball and politics—competed as excitements. A comment by a local journalist indicates the Boston habit of thinking of the two activities as comparable professional games, the attitude among the professional class that a Hicks victory would be regressive, and the common notion that Boston was in a period of transition and, therefore, under national scrutiny. "During the last two months the country has watched Boston, trying to determine whether the Red Sox had progressed enough to win, and whether the town had progressed enough for Louise to lose."[42]

That theme of "the whole country's watching" showed up frequently in remarks regarding *Titicut Follies*. Early on, various people defined the situation as one of national concern. At the critical meeting on September 21, Commissioner Gavin said he feared that the release of the Bridgewater documentary would result in the Commonwealth's becoming a national "laughing stock" (Tr. 3:164). In an October 3 letter to the editor of the *Boston Herald Traveler*, responding to a strongly negative editorial about the documentary, Representative Katherine Kane accepted Gavin's assumption of national interest, but turned his argument inside out, claiming that the documentary would offer Massachusetts an opportunity to show its public courage and sincere interest in reform. The only political figure to remain consistently supportive of Wiseman, Kane argued that suppression of the film would make Massachusetts a "laughing stock" and thus also appealed to the provincial desire to gain the respect of the larger world.[43]

Formed in February of 1967 and chaired by Democratic Senator John J. Conte, the Governor's Study Commission on Mental Health distributed a pamphlet to fellow lawmakers and the press on September 27. Its report described the grossly inadequate facilities at Bridgewater, outlined recommendations for the construction of a new 450-bed hospital there, and suggested changes in some mental-penal laws. The group generally supported the growing feeling among reform-minded legislators and citizens that the Bridgewater hospital for the criminally insane should be transferred from the Department of Correction to the Department of Mental Health. The special commission saw itself as a qualified, authorized fact-finding and advisory group and thus saw Wiseman as a usurper of their authority even if he were granted the role of reformer. Vice-chairman Robert Cawley claimed that the showing of *Titicut Follies* undermined the commission's three-year effort to recodify the state's mental health and commitment laws.[44] In early October, Representative Cawley, a Democrat from West Roxbury (a working-class section of Boston), announced his eagerness to conduct a legislative hearing regarding the conditions at Bridgewater and the circumstances under which the documentary was made. That interest was not shared by his co-chair and thus the decision to have a hearing became the first of a new round of political struggles. Like all the other disputes in this controversy, it had personal, partisan, procedural, and ideological dimensions.

Cawley's co-chair, Republican Senator Leslie Cutler, opposed the hearings, as did Attorney General Elliot Richardson. They both claimed that the hearings would quickly turn from an investigation of conditions at Bridgewater into a trial of persons involved in the film project and, since litigation against the film had begun, that action should proceed through the courts without the interference of testimony gathered elsewhere. While they had a valid point about due process, their reasons for making it were challenged by some Democrats as partisan and self-protective. They did not persist in their objections.

Four levels of conflict were obvious by the time the hearings began: (1) the struggle for control of *Titicut Follies;* (2) the struggle for control of MCI-Bridgewater; (3) the struggle for control of the legislative and executive branches of the Commonwealth; (4) the struggle for ideological control. The Bridgewater documentary, ostensibly connected only to the first, narrow struggle, became evidence and excuse for continuing and accelerating broader conflicts. The history of *Titicut Follies* is inexorably bound to the uses made of it.

Long before the trial verdict was issued in *Commonwealth v. Wiseman,* even before the legislative hearings began, the public judged *Titicut Follies.* By the first week of October, the editorial staff of the *Boston Herald Traveler* began assigning blame. A tone of vituperation was established quickly and never abandoned.

Responsibility for this debacle rests with the prison officials. . . . It is now up to the Attorney General to exhaust all legal remedies to right the wrong. And it is up to the Governor and the Legislature to consider whether the correction officials responsible should be allowed to go on making blunders without sharing in the consequences.[45]

> It is not possible for Gavin and Gaughan to escape responsibility for the astonishing incident, which is certainly without precedent in the commonwealth, and it will be surprising if there is not a clamor for their scalps by the families of the mental incompetents involved.[46]

> While some believe both Gavin and Gaughan should be fired for their parts in the incredible filming incident, it is the consensus that, at the very least, some kind of disciplinary action is in order.[47]

> One public official who has seen the film [The *Herald Traveler* writers had not] predicts that if members of the Legislature ever get a look at it "they will be out looking for a hanging rope."[48]

No legislator was looking for that rope more zealously than Representative Cawley. Using the Boston media, especially the *Herald,* as a willing tool, he made a series of accusations regarding the filmmakers' procedures and motives. He claimed that someone had invested $250,000 in the film, that it had been made entirely for commercial gain, that Wiseman had used hidden cameras, that *Titicut Follies* was anti-Catholic. All these claims were made before the co-chair saw the documentary. He then made a highly publicized trip to New York to see the film, after which he accelerated his resistance to its exhibition.

Before the hearings, a pattern of charge and countercharge was established. Once started, the accusations spread and infected everyone involved in the project. In response to Cawley's accusation of "deep personal involvement," Richardson charged that Wiseman had "doublecrossed the Commonwealth."[49] The attorney general further suggested that there may have been "a deliberate scheme" to exploit the banned-in-Boston theme for financial gain.[50] Wiseman, "shocked and dismayed at the intemperate, abusive and untrue personal attack made against [him] by the attorney general" said that Richardson acted "contrary to high professional standards established by the American Bar Association in that an attorney does not take his case to the media and personally attack the other party when the matter is pending before the courts."[51] Gavin wrote Volpe and blamed Richardson and Kane for influencing his decision regarding permission for filming.[52]

By the time the hearings began on October 17, "the prospect of massive damage suits against the commonwealth, possibly running into the millions of dollars,"[53] was widely discussed. Although there was blame enough to go around, the state and its officers would have been protected if they could pin the blame on Wiseman.

The *Titicut Follies* controversy was characterized as the "biggest political flap to hit the state since the wrangle a year [before] for the state medical school."[54] John Volpe chose to ignore the uproar, commenting only that he was "concerned with the looseness" in the handling of the documentary project.[55] At the request of the General Court, which had passed a special resolution for this purpose, the attorney general's office obtained a modification of the restraining order so that the legislature and the governor would be able to view *Titicut Follies,* but Volpe left for a national governors' conference in mid-October without having seen the film.

The majority of the 280 members of the General Court, however, eagerly watched at least some of *Titicut Follies* the morning the special legislative hearings by the State Commission on Mental Health commenced. Richard Gallen, counsel for Grove Press, hand-delivered a print of the documentary. Broadcast and print journalists, barred from the screening by armed guards, clustered outside Gardner Auditorium to question exiting legislators on their reactions to the film. Those who left early were interviewed first. All those who made an early exit, and many others, expressed outrage; a few praised the emotional power of *Titicut Follies* and felt the film, if edited, should be seen by the public. "Although they would talk only behind their hands, Republicans in the audience said that the Democratic majority would 'look for somebody to hang.' And the obvious target, they said, was State Attorney General Elliot L. Richardson."[56] Democrats found the *Titicut Follies* controversy a perfect excuse to level the general charge of "moral insensitivity" against the current Republican administration. It was a charge that had been successfully used against the former Democratic administration by the Republicans in the previous election campaign. This intensely partisan and extremely hostile environment was the context of the *Titicut Follies* hearings.

Testimony was taken under oath. Although never used—"invitations" sent to individuals were sufficiently persuasive—subpoena powers, at Representative Cawley's request, had been voted by the legislature. From the outset, Cawley seized the role of head prosecutor. Co-chair Cutler, who had, at Richardson's request, first opposed the hearings, now pushed to have state police assigned to an investigative detail connected with the hearings. A state trooper, sent to

New York, conferred with foundation officials regarding Wiseman's alleged grant proposals. State troopers questioned financial backers of the documentary at their homes, which Wiseman described as harassment. When asked at the hearing whether a trooper's visit to the Marshall home had frightened her, Heather Marshall replied that the officer's questions had not been more upsetting than those posed at the hearing in progress, and they were not bothering her.[57]

The hearings began on October 17 and ended on November 9, but were in session for only eight days. During the recesses, there was much speculation in the press regarding potential witnesses (for instance, Representative Katherine Kane and U.S. Senator Edward Brooke) and probable agendas. Disorganized at best, an abuse of power at worst, the hearings occupied the attention of the General Court for three weeks, then evaporated when the Senate failed to approve the House recommendation for a second probe of *Titicut Follies* to be conducted by a special committee on correctional problems.

First to testify was Commissioner John Gavin. He presented himself as someone only remotely connected to the documentary project and, therefore, not culpable of anything more serious than taking the suggestion of superiors (Richardson and Kane), assuming his subordinate (Gaughan) was responsible, and trusting that the filmmaker (Wiseman) would keep his word, which he claimed included a commitment to editorial control by the state. The second day of the hearings, October 18, Gaughan defended himself against Gavin's implication of mismanagement by attacking Wiseman for misrepresentation and duplicity. Here is an example of the style of questioning that was standard procedure throughout the hearings: "Asked pointblank by Sen. Francis McCann (D-Cambridge) if he felt that 'Wiseman and his production company tricked you and did not keep their agreement,' Gaughan answered, 'I very definitely do.'"[58]

After Gaughan's testimony, the commission called for a one-week recess, which led the filmmaker to complain that the press would have a week to feed off the correction officials' allegations, while he would have no opportunity for a rebuttal. The hearings were continued five days later, but behind closed doors, which brought another complaint from Wiseman's newly retained counsel. In one of many indications of the haphazard procedures of the hearings and their responsiveness to pressure, the testimony of three correction guards was then repeated in an open session that same afternoon. Officers

Gadry, Pacheco, and Banville claimed that they had also been misled by Wiseman. The following day, three members of the Bridgewater professional staff, Harry L. Kozol; his administrative assistant, Richard Boucher; and the chief clinical psychologist, Ralph S. Grafolo, appeared. Dr. Kozol, the director of the Treatment Center for the Sexually Dangerous and a faculty member at Harvard Medical School, had anticipated legal problems regarding invasion of privacy connected with the film making and, when the filmmakers would not agree to written safeguards and acceptance of liability, he denied them access to his unit. Hungry for a hero, many lauded Kozol's foresight and used this incident as proof that the hospital would be in better hands if administered by the Department of Mental Health. That some of Kozol's patients were included in the final film (in group scenes of the variety show actually shot before the directive was issued) was used as further proof of Wiseman's bad faith. Kozol himself claimed, "If the Department of Correction had adopted my attitude, there would have been no Frederick Wiseman and no film."[59] For some, blame was not enough.

On October 25, Fred Wiseman read a formal statement before the commission, a standing-room-only crowd of onlookers, and television cameras. He denied the charges against him that had accumulated over several weeks in and outside of the hearings. Under advice from his attorney that to do so would violate the injunction, he refused to turn over the unused footage demanded by Cawley. The following day, the commission asked that Wiseman, Kozol, Gavin, and Gaughan all return, so that they could be questioned together about their conflicting testimony. When asked if he objected to the multiple questioning, Wiseman's attorney, James St. Clair, replied, "This is an august body and should not be engaged in games. We have courts of law where conflicts can be tried before judge and jury."[60]

Tension between Cawley and Wiseman had begun weeks before. In reference to Cawley's prehearing accusations, Wiseman claimed that Cawley was exploiting the controversy for political gain and using the hearings as a platform from which to campaign for the secretary of state position, which would be vacated if Kevin White were elected mayor of Boston in November.[61] During Wiseman's testimony, Cawley's comments became so abusive that St. Clair objected to the legislator's exhibiting "personal animosity" toward the witness and to the "truth or consequences" tone of the questioning.[62]

But the low point in the hearings had not yet been reached. Testimony from David Eames, president of Bridgewater Film Company, Inc., predictably supported what Wiseman had said, yet the accusations of commercial exploitation continued. Representative Amelio Della Chiesa charged that *Titicut Follies* was produced "to make millions of dollars at the expense of the poor souls at Bridgewater State Hospital."[63] The BFC president's reluctance to accept Della Chiesa's offer to "give all of the film to the Commonwealth for the $30,000 it cost and forget the whole thing"[64] was interpreted as "substance" to the view that financial gain was the filmmakers' primary motive.

Richardson agreed with prison officials in claiming misrepresentation on Wiseman's part and denied Wiseman's contention that Richardson had told the producer that he need not show the film to anyone, including the governor. That denial was expected; what was unexpected was the discovery on November 2, during the testimony of cinematographer John Marshall, that Timothy Asch, a teacher in the Newton public schools, a lecturer in anthropology at Brandeis University, and a friend of Marshall's, had been audiotaping and filming parts of the hearings. Asch was directed to take the witness stand. When questioning revealed that he had briefly assisted John Marshall in filming part of the Bridgewater documentary,[65] commission members impounded the audiotapes and still- and moving-picture film that Asch and nine of his students from the Ethnographic Research Center at Brandeis had taken of the hearings. Asch requested legal counsel, and the hearings recessed in a state of confusion and suspicion.

The response to Asch revealed the depth of the fear and animosity some felt toward the members of the Bridgewater Film Company. Asch was immediately charged with deception by Representative Cawley. Asch claimed he had represented himself as being both from the *Brandeis Justice,* the university newspaper, and as doing freelance work.[66] Cawley's response was that the commission had been misled into thinking that Asch was a "member of the working press."[67] Early in the hearings, Wiseman had joked with reporters that some would try to make him into a Rasputin.[68] To those who claimed "Beatniks Aided, Insane Aren't"[69] and described *Titicut Follies* as a "montage of sex,"[70] Wiseman *was* a Rasputin. Rumors circulated that the footage taken at the hearing might be intercut into the documentary "to embarrass the legislature [*sic*] process or to exploit [the] committee."[71] To prevent this from happening, confiscation and destruction were suggested.

Based on a photograph of Asch printed in the Boston dailies, Cawley claimed that several legislators had identified Asch as a man who had "posed as a representative of Massachusetts House Speaker John F. X. Davoren's office,"[72] had accompanied a legislative tour of the Fernald School the previous spring, and had taken hundreds of photographs of retarded children. It was assumed that these photographs would now be used by Asch in an exploitative manner. Another flurry of accusations began. Attorney General Richardson said that he would "launch a full investigation and take action aimed at protecting the privacy of retarded children and other patients at the Waltham facility."[73]

A week later—November 9—Asch took the stand again to repeat a statement he had made several days before to the press. Asch claimed, "Prior to the story which appeared in Friday's newspapers, based on Rep. Cawley's statement, I had never had occasion to hear of the Fernald School. . . . Since the allegation that I took pictures there is false, the more serious allegation that I posed as a member of Speaker Davoren's staff is doubly false."[74]

People who considered themselves entitled to privileged information about *Titicut Follies* were disappointed and insulted when they learned what they considered important information directly affecting them at the same time as, or even after, the general public. Gavin (via a letter) learned of the documentary's release through a review written by an "out-of-stater."[75] Wiseman said he first found out that the state was claiming censorship rights through reading a news story in the *Quincy Patriot Ledger*.[76] Marshall discovered when watching a television news program that an injunction had been filed against the film.[77] Asch read in the Boston dailies about the allegation that he had posed as a legislative staff member on an inspection of a state facility.

From the outset, surprise and suspicion ran throughout the press accounts of the details that became the *Titicut Follies* "story." Quickly, media gatekeepers determined the importance of a cluster of details and seized the opportunity to define the situation: it was labeled a controversy. Two common metaphors—combat and theater—shaped the earliest discussions of the film and became self-fulfilling prophecies.

The Boston press played the *Titicut Follies* drama as tragedy, melodrama, slapstick, comedy of the absurd. The easy ironies suggested by the film title swiftly found their way into print. Circumstances surrounding the making of the documentary and then the investigation into those circumstances both became known as the Beacon Hill follies. A cartoon presented a hesitant hearing witness peeping through a curtain as "Titicut Follies, Act II."[78] A headline claimed, "Cawley Blooms as 'Follies' Star."[79]

During Wiseman's legislative testimony, Cawley challenged him to defend the "educational" worth of various sequences, which the legislator implied were sensationalized. Wiseman replied, "I am not going to review each scene with you on this occasion. The film speaks for itself."[80] But, because of the temporary restraining order, *Titicut Follies* could *not* speak for itself in Massachusetts. Instead, many spoke at great length about it. Since privacy invasion was one of several charges against the filmmakers and since their central defense was the public's right to know, descriptions of the film in the press created a journalistic dilemma. It was difficult—if not impossible—for a writer to discuss the film without becoming hypocritical or evasive. Wiseman's counsel attempted unsuccessfully to include issues of *The Beacon* (the MCI-Bridgewater newspaper) as a trial exhibit to establish that public identification of inmates and patients was routinely practiced by the state.[81]

The Boston media also fed, or even created, an appetite for information about Frederick Wiseman himself. Previously unknown to the general public, in contrast to the appointed and elected public officials involved in the controversy, Wiseman was especially vulnerable to stereotyping. The *Boston Record American* discovered and printed the lawyer-filmmaker's answer to the Massachusetts bar exam question about why he wanted to become a lawyer.[82] Eager to position Wiseman in an ideological camp, Boston dailies deemed as newsworthy that the Wiseman and Eames families had welcomed Benjamin Spock and Martin Luther King, Jr., into their homes,[83] that Wiseman's wife had signed a petition urging people to vote yes on the referendum to end the war in Vietnam,[84] that Wiseman wore his hair "cut long in back like an artist's."[85] It is difficult to see the following description of the Wiseman-produced *The Cool World* as anything but an attempt to tap pools of discontent: "The picture depicts all white people as evil, and all Negroes as good."[86] There was considerable comment about Wiseman's coolness and his wit.[87] A portrait emerged of a liberal intellectual, a Cambridge radical; the same evidence was thus used for and against Wiseman as an individual. Some who formed judgments of the man bypassed the press and made direct contact with Wiseman. The director said he personally received many letters and calls of support. He also received a large amount of hate mail, much of which he classified as "anti-kike letters," and calls threatening him and his family.[88] Gavin also received death threats, which were headlined by the *Record,* unreported by the *Globe.*[89]

The Boston press served as the locus and the prime participant in the debate regarding the film. Often functioning as press agent for unreliable informants, the Boston dailies printed accusations and later retractions as central components of news stories. The *Titicut Follies* controversy thus fed on itself. Exploiting the media's insatiable need to know, Richardson and Wiseman both called prehearing press conferences. On October 13, Wiseman distributed a folder to members of the press with his press release, copies of the New York court decision, reviews of the film, and letters of praise from various citizens and mental health organizations. Both Wiseman (October 22) and Richardson (October 29) were interviewed about *Titicut Follies* on Boston radio station WEEI's "Bay State Forum." Gaughan, previously known for his candor with the press, did not follow the suggestion that he, too, have a press conference. Attacked on all sides, Gaughan withdrew from the challenge to manage press impressions and to control some of the information flow.

Undaunted by not having seen *Titicut Follies,* citizens of Massachusetts used letter-to-the-editor sections in Boston papers as an arena for debate regarding the documentary and what they perceived to be related issues. Often the controversy surrounding *Titicut Follies* functioned as a springboard from which to launch a discussion of a related topic. The letters expressed a considerable range of attitudes, often presented with cynicism or anger. Definitions of the problem varied significantly. The contradictions in consensual values evident in the letters illustrate how problematic the legal notion of "community standards" was in connection with obscenity in the late 1960s. The privacy issue confounded the presence of nudity in *Titicut Follies.* Considerable opposition to the film seemed to come from a constituency that would have been offended by any public exhibition of nudity, or any use of what was considered offensive language, and thus saw nudity and profanity themselves as issues. Amid the diversity, two clearly defined positions emerged and rigidified as the controversy continued. The arguments and judgments in the letters often echoed the editorial voices of the Boston papers, which, in turn, had followed the legal pattern of advocacy and judgment.

Both sides argued that the villainous opposition was hiding behind a legitimate civil right to cloak the real situation and personal deviousness. Advocates of general exhibition claimed the state had raised the privacy issue and moved aggressively against the film, not to protect the inmates as it claimed, but to protect itself from the political embarrassment of being shown defective both in its management of Bridgewater and in the handling of the film. Advocates of the ban claimed that the filmmaker had raised a false free speech issue to conceal a serious violation of the state's trust in which he had misrepresented himself and exploited the helpless inmates of Bridgewater for financial and professional gain.

The three Boston dailies—the *Globe,* the *Herald Traveler,* and the *Record American*—all devoted substantial attention to the *Titicut Follies* story, but there were appreciable differences among the three in the character of that attention.[90] Each set a tone immediately, a tone in keeping with the general position of the paper, and remained fairly consistent throughout the coverage.

Of the three newspapers, the *Globe* was the calmest, most disciplined voice. Still in September, a *Globe* editorial acknowledged a civil rights dilemma in the *Titicut Follies* case and called for a compromise "to clear up these cross-purposes between the right to privacy and the public's right to see the film."[91] In subsequent editorials, the *Globe* staff supported the film (October 18), spoke of the unfairness of the legislative hearings (October 19) and, during the trial (November 20), speculated that the zeal exhibited in the investigation of *Titicut Follies* flowed "less from civil libertarian sentiment than from a collective guilty conscience concerning conditions at Bridgewater."[92] Ray Richard's "The 'Titicut Follies' Film: Anatomy of a Controversy"[93] is an example of the analytic journalism that the *Globe* prided itself on. The *Globe* was the only Boston paper to follow the litigation concerning the film through the 1970s.[94]

The *Boston Record American* formed an early judgment regarding exhibition of *Titicut Follies* and consistently maintained its position. An editorial on October 19 argued that the film was an exploitative invasion of privacy and advocated corrective and punitive action. A tabloid with a predominantly working-class readership, the Hearst-owned *Record* practiced what is sometimes euphemistically known as New York-style journalism. Emotional, politically conservative, the *Record American* aggressively played the role of assistant prosecutor against Wiseman and the Bridgewater Film Company.

Also extremely accusatory of Wiseman and strongly dependent on emotional appeals, the *Boston Herald Traveler* did commission a lengthy guest commentary written by an academic who would later appear as a witness for the defense and a long, analytic piece that included a positive review of the film.[95] The characteristic *Titicut Follies* piece in the *Herald Traveler* was a liberal-baiting commentary by Thomas C. Gallager. No single journalist set himself up as a judge more than Gallager. Wiseman was not the only person involved in the documentary project whom Gallager found guilty, although he condemned the director-producer of *Titicut Follies* with particular fury.

Gallager and others were strongly critical that *Titicut Follies* was being shown commercially in New York. Several assumptions seemed to underlie the protest of commercial exhibition: that all films exhibited commercially made vast sums of money; that no one would pay to see a film for "educational" reasons; that broadcast on ETV would somehow not have been public exhibition. The fact that a single ETV broadcast would probably reach a much larger and more juvenile audience than a year of exhibition on the art theater–film society–university classroom circuit was lost on the *Herald Traveler* writers. Both the *Herald Traveler* and the *Record American* picked up the double-bind logic that Representative Cawley used against the films of Wiseman and Marshall. If they made no money, they were "flops"; if they made money, they were exploitations.

Although *Titicut Follies,* in this early period, had no commercial public screenings in the United States outside of New York—and exhibition ended there on November 4, 1967—the film was much discussed in the national press through the fall and into 1969.[96] Some critics found the film a violation of norms of privacy, responsibility, fairness, or technical skill, but the majority of reviewers considered it powerful social criticism. *Titicut Follies* became a national cause célèbre, attracting interest and support rare for any documentary, especially one made by a heretofore unknown filmmaker. A witness for the defense in *Commonwealth v. Wiseman,* critic Richard Schickel, stated in cross examination, "I do not think that this film would have been reviewed in *Life* had not it become a subject of controversy in the courts" (Tr. 16:97).

Counsel for the plaintiffs tried to hold Wiseman responsible for whatever critics had said about the film. It was a responsibility that Wiseman firmly and consistently disclaimed, yet he was willing to use reviews as evidence in support of the film. In the "Answers of the Respondent Frederick Wiseman to the Petitioner's Original Bill in Equity," Wiseman attached reviews from *The New York Times, Newsweek, Cue,* and *The Christian Science Monitor.* He or his counsel wrote, "The Respondent says that . . . the film has been consistently recognized as a powerful document of vast social sweep and artistic integrity. A sampling of critical reviews and commentary by social scientists dealing with the power, quality, and truth of the film are annexed hereto and marked Exhibit B."[97] During the fall of 1967 and the winter and spring of 1968, *Titicut Follies* became a rallying point for various publics. Wiseman has claimed that he received letters and calls from many inmates and their families expressing their support of the film and its exhibition.[98] There were no organized prisoners' rights groups that defended or opposed *Titicut Follies* in 1967–68, nor were any such groups active inside Bridgewater. The *Titicut Follies* Defense Fund, headed by the Reverend Harvey Cox of Harvard Divinity School, reflected support for the film at its most organized. Predominantly, but not exclusively, composed of individuals involved in professional, academic, and artistic work in the New England–New York area, this group provided a number of trial witnesses for the defense and also discussed the film in a national forum, which, in turn, broadened the support. Various organized groups, such as the Playboy Foundation, joined the defense cause. But there were constraints on the effectiveness of such support. It was of minimal value legally since the trial judge would not hear arguments in defense of the film as a social document or as art. It was probably counterproductive, emotionally, among some publics. People like Cox, an active and outspoken leader in draft-resistance counseling, were perceived as part of a general conspiracy by a substantial Massachusetts constituency. For this group, the fact that much of the national press responded positively to the Cox pro-exhibition position became not proof of its validity, but proof of an attitude that a handful of liberals controlled the national media.

A decade after the trials, Superintendent Gaughan recalled the film's supporters with bitterness:

> The "Hippy group" who were so supportive of Wiseman at the time were widely in vogue. I felt that my position, based on the truth and capable of substantiation by various documents, did not require great vocalization. Our testimony was given to the courts, as required by law, and we came out very successfully.

I felt that Wiseman's Titicut Follies and other items of that sort are now part of modern history. They were part of the breakdown of the morality and convictions of the great mass of Americans. Today, one wonders what moral obligations and duties the average American has. We are bombarded by a highly prolific variety of media, anxious to make a dollar, which caters to our most jaded sensibilities. To rationalize these events with constitutional interpretations belies the farcical. Regrettably, this type of interpretation appears most prevalent in the academic group who are the group most divorced from normal American reality.[99]

It would be a mistake to characterize all judgments regarding exhibition of *Titicut Follies* as clearly and cleanly halved, with each unit possessing established markers of social/economic class and political/ ideological attitudes. No group better belies such facile division than the American Civil Liberties Union (ACLU) and its state affiliate, the Civil Liberties Union of Massachusetts (CLUM). With a membership mostly drawn from the political left-of-center, the organization is dedicated to the preservation and full implementation of the Bill of Rights.

Frederick Wiseman was a member of ACLU-CLUM in September 1967 when Mildred Methven sent the CLUM office a copy of her letter of complaint regarding *Titicut Follies*. That same week, Wiseman engaged Gerald Berlin, the CLUM chairman, as his personal counsel, an arrangement obviously unknown to the Boston journalist who wrote in early October that "despite this invasion of privacy of the patients involved, [*Titicut Follies*] has produced only silence in the ranks of the liberals, and the civil libertarians. In fact, one of their number, Rep. Katherine D. Kane (D-Beacon Hill), has staunchly defended the film. There have been no cries of outrage from the Civil Liberties Union of Massachusetts, or its articulate chairman, Atty. Gerald A. Berlin. . . . The only individual who has come to the defense of these sick people is Republican Atty. Gen. Elliot L. Richardson."[100]

The beginning of the legislative hearing coincided with the appearance of these claims and observations in the *Herald:*

. . . the controversy has damaged the image of the Civil Liberties Union . . . [which] appears to harbor less concern for the demented patients at Bridgewater than for the beatniks in Cambridge. It has chosen to stand mute in the "Titicut Follies" controversy.

Moreover, its chairman, Berlin, has turned up as the lawyer for the producer of the film. . . . [Rep. Cawley] sought to contact Luther Macnair, the executive director of [CLUM], to suggest he view the film.

Where was Macnair?
Over at the Boston Common, watching for any violations of the civil liberties of the draft card burners.[101]

Even without Gallager's public baiting, even without the introduction of a partisan struggle regarding responsibility for the film, the position of the CLUM on the *Titicut Follies* case would have been complicated. On October 20, a cartoon appeared on the *Herald* editorial page entitled "Titicut Follies-Another Act." It featured "Attorney-Chairman Berlin" astride two white horses (labeled "Attorney for Titicut Follies Producer" and "Chairman of Civil Liberties Union") racing in opposite directions. That same day, Berlin resigned as Wiseman's counsel. Berlin has said he withdrew because of "personal disagreement over management of the case."[102] Wiseman recalled that Berlin "told me that he could no longer represent me because the CLUM would lose contributions if he did so, and besides he now thought that I didn't have a good case and suggested that I give it up. I left the office furious because his primary obligation was to me, his client, and not to CLUM. I then retained other lawyers who were not professional civil libertarians."[103]

Berlin has declined to respond to Wiseman's accusations, but others have attested to Berlin's scrupulousness in handling the case and in avoiding any possible conflict of interest.[104] Plaintiffs' counsel took Berlin's deposition in preparing *Commonwealth v. Wiseman* for trial, but did not call him as a witness.[105]

By late October, CLUM had not taken a position regarding exhibition of *Titicut Follies*. The CLUM Executive Committee explained its silence in a press release on October 28 that included the following statements:

The versions as to what actually happened, and under what agreements, are contradictory and confused, and until these facts have been clarified in a dispassionate forum, resolution as to the relative weight to be accorded to competing civil liberties are premature and indeed harmful. This in short is the reason, and the only reason, for the failure of the [CLUM] to add its voice to the hue and cry concerning the film. . . .
The termination of [Berlin's] relationship with Mr. Wiseman is in no respect the result of criticism of his conduct within the Union. On the contrary, we endorse his participation as a lawyer, and we are in total disagreement with suggestions in the press that it has been inconsistent with the purposes of our organization.

The CLUM board had not seen the documentary, and therefore stated, "Under these circumstances expression of a judgment on our part at this time would be highly presumptuous. . . . The decisional process can be entrusted only to the judiciary." CLUM suggested that it might take a position in an *amicus curiae* brief, if the case were later filed with an appellate court. It presented its carefulness as superior to the haste of other judgments: "We do not believe that we, or the public generally, are in a position to render judgment at this time."[106]

CLUM did file a friend-of-the-court brief in the appeal of *Commonwealth v. Wiseman* before the Supreme Judicial Court of Massachusetts in the spring of 1969.[107] Signed by CLUM counsel Henry Paul Monaghan and prepared by the five-member board, the brief continued in the cautionary tone of the 1967 press release: there were competing civil liberties claims; the union board had still not seen the film; the court, after having seen *Titicut Follies,* would have to be the judge. The brief objected to the extremity of the injunctive relief entered in the superior court and suggested that—if the supreme judicial court found that there were specific privacy invasions—the film itself should be altered or audiences be limited to specialized groups in order that competing civil liberties might be balanced. The truth or falsity of the oral contract question was not considered critical.

In 1974, Wiseman characterized CLUM's "Solomon-like solution" as a position "against the film" and recollected with considerable bitterness, "The moral insensitivity and cowardice of CLUM and its chairman were for me the worst part of the *Follies* case. . . . The national ACLU stayed out of the case. All I could get at the New York office were a few stale ironies from the staff general counsel."[108]

A chain of letters appeared in the *Civil Liberties Review* following the publication of Wiseman's remarks: Richardson claimed that concern for the privacy of the inmates had led CLUM "to file its *amicus* brief supporting the state."[109] Wiseman answered that CLUM never supported the state's position that *Titicut Follies* should be banned and that, since the board of CLUM had just voted unanimously (on May 8, 1974) to support an action to be brought in the state and federal courts to have the film shown without restriction, he hoped that Richardson would "support this CLUM postion so that they can continue to have a comity of interests."[110] Ellen Feingold (then president of CLUM) criticized Wiseman's discussion of the role of CLUM in the legal struggle over *Titicut Follies*. "[His] statements oversimplify just where his films excel—in showing an issue objectively in its complexity." She outlined the CLUM position: "It is clear in retrospect that the court's attempt at balance resulted in prior restraint. . . . The Union is still trying to find a balance among competing issues, but we have shifted emphasis and are working actively to lift the ban on public showing. The problem posed by violation of the patients' privacy still troubles us."[111]

Executive Director John Roberts said that the major reason for the shift in CLUM's position regarding *Titicut Follies* was that the privacy concern had waned with age.[112] By 1984 even Elliot Richardson saw no reason why exhibition should continue to be restricted.[113] Yet the privacy concern has also intensified with age, since some of the inmates and patients pictured in the film have since been released from Bridgewater. Alan Reitman has called the right of privacy "the new zone of civil liberty" and has wondered how the ACLU might help "to rein in technology's power to surveil, record, and disseminate the details of a person's life . . . yet [use] that power for positive purposes."[114] In 1976, the CLUM board established a policy regarding direct representation. "Staff lawyers may accept any case in which there is a clear civil issue and no competing civil liberties interest."[115]

On November 1, 1967, while the legislative hearing involving *Titicut Follies* continued, four Bridgewater guards (Charles J. Cullen, Carlton G. Shaw, Edwin F. Spencer, and George L. Parent) filed a defamation suit in federal court in New York against Titicut Follies Distributing Co., Inc.; Grove Press, Inc.; and F and A Theaters. They sought an injunction to prohibit current and future distribution and exhibition of the documentary, then playing at a commercial movie house owned by F and A Theaters, and claimed damages of eight hundred thousand dollars (one hundred thousand dollars for each officer on each of two counts). *Cullen* invoked a New York privacy statute that provided grounds for such action if "a person, firm or corporation . . . uses for advertising purposes, or for the purposes of trade, the name, portrait or picture of any living person without having first obtained the written consent of such person."[116] The guards claimed they had not signed releases and had been deceived by the filmmakers about the type of film being made and the plans for its future use. *Cullen v. Grove Press,*[117] although certainly having much in common with previous and subsequent litigation involving *Titicut Follies,* nevertheless presented some legal questions not posed in other cases. Here was (1) a defamation suit (2) filed in Federal Court (3) against three New York firms engaged in the distribution and exhibition of *Titicut Follies* (Wiseman and BFC were *not named* as defendants) (4) seeking damages for state employees pictured in the documentary because (5) their privacy had allegedly been invaded by their presentation with nude inmates. Obscenity was not stated as grounds for action, but implied by a description of the film as a "montage of sex" by counsel for the plaintiffs, Robert F. Muse, and by the filed claim that Grove Press "is engaged principally in the sale and distribution of salacious printed materials that have an overbearing emphasis on the carnal aspects of sex."[118]

Federal District Judge Walter R. Mansfield heard the case only two weeks after the November 1 filing and announced his decision by the end of the month. Prepared in some haste, the case for the plaintiffs set for itself the formidable task of proving libel and/or invasion of privacy not only sufficient to realize damages for the guards, but also injunctive relief. That the case failed should come as no surprise, especially after previous petitions for injunctive relief had been denied by two New York supreme court justices.

Cullen's suit responded to predicted and actual comments such as those of NBC-TV "Today" reviewer Judith Crist, who, questioning the possible bias of *Titicut Follies,* asked "Are all the attendants sadistic morons?"[119] The guards claimed that the documentary holds them "up to ridicule, contempt and scorn in all respectable segments of our society and community," because (among other reasons) inmates are presented as "indistinguishable from the guards" and the film "has been edited . . . to emphasize certain erotic aspects of nudity and overtones and suggestions of indifference and brutality on the part of the Correction Officers as a class of which your plaintiffs are members."[120]

Neither the complaint nor the other pleadings offered any proof that the filmed events were false or distorted, let alone proof of the defendants' knowledge of the documentary's alleged falsity or reckless disregard of the truth, thus failing to comply with the holding of the U.S. Supreme Court decision reached earlier that year in *Time, Inc., v. Hill.*[121] Faced with *Time,* the plaintiffs made the general claim in oral argument that "the film does not give a true and balanced impression of conditions at Bridgewater but distorts conditions thereby emphasizing the bizarre and failing to show other aspects that would explain the scenes that are portrayed and thus put them in proper context."[122]

Based on the trial judge's own viewing of the film, the testimony of the producer-director (whose academic and professional experiences the judge found relevant), Wiseman's offer (declined) to show the court the balance of the eighty thousand feet of film shot at Bridgewater, the "imposing array of affidavits" from experts in various fields and film critics, Mansfield found *Titicut Follies* not a false report. Mansfield, the son of a former mayor of Boston, wrote, "By its very nature the subject matter is such that a chronicle of it must to some extent be gruesome and depressing in character, and in this case the picture fulfills such anticipation." He found the allegation of invasion of privacy, based on the guards' appearances in scenes (for example, and most particularly, the "skin search") in which inmates or patients are pictured nude, not worthy of consideration. No proof to support the allegation of inflammatory advertising was offered. Because of the nature of the filming (at such a close physical distance), the judge assumed consent at all times on the part of the guards.

Responding to the questions of obscenity, "at best hinted at in the plaintiffs' reply," Mansfield found that "the nudity appears in each instance to form an integral part of an episode that is of legitimate public interest. . . . There are no commentaries or actions that could be construed as an appeal to any prurient interest in sex, and this Court does not believe that the material is so patently offensive as to affront community standards."

The judge further found the contentions (sharply disputed by the filmmakers) that the film crew suggested actions or scenes for the film, that the guards participated in scenes with naked inmates subject to an understanding that only the "upper extremities" of inmates would be photographed, and that the film would be exhibited only for "educational purposes," even if true, not grounds for injunctive relief or damages. Mansfield held that "The conditions in public institutions such as Bridgewater for the care of the criminally insane, including the physical facilities, conduct of employees, and type of treatment administered to inmates, are matters which are of great interest to the public generally. Such public interest is both legitimate and healthy." Mansfield found the distribution and exhibition of *Titicut Follies* protected by the First Amendment.

Although the federal judge emphatically denied the guards' motion, Mansfield kept the judicial door open to further considerations. "This conclusion does not, of course, constitute an adjudication of rights of non-parties, such as individual inmates claiming violation of their own personal rights or state officials suing for breach of contract, if any, with respect to conditions for exhibition of the film."

Several weeks before the Bridgewater guards filed their damage suit against the distributors and exhibitors of *Titicut Follies,* there had been speculation in the Boston press that the Commonwealth would be sued for damages. Journalist Thomas C. Gallager reported that Representative Cawley had been "advised by legal experts" that there was a "prospect of massive damage suits against the Commonwealth, possibly running into the millions of dollars, by patients whose rights of privacy have been violated, and members of their families."[123] Legal scholars later claimed that releases were only for the filmmakers' protection, since the state was immune from tort liability (invason of privacy itself),[124] but that the state, as guardian, also has a duty to protect the rights and interests of its wards—failure to do so is grounds for suits for money damages. A sensitivity to the legal vulnerability of the state was one of several reasons that Dr. Harry Kozol objected in the spring of 1966 to filming at the division under his direction. During the summer of 1967 and into September, the question of the state's liability, through Gaughan, had been raised at meetings between Wiseman and the attorney general's office.

Announcing the preparation of *Cullen v. Grove Press,* the *Herald Traveler* further stated that "it was understood from one reliable source that 'perhaps 100, perhaps even more' libel and other suits would be brought in Massachusetts on behalf of the inmates."[125] As of this writing, only one such case has gone to trial. The suit, entered on behalf of thirty-five inmates pictured in *Titicut Follies* against Wiseman and Bridgewater Film Company, Inc., sought five million dollars in damages for alleged invasion of privacy and breach of contract. The action was taken technically through guardians appointed to represent the inmates, thirty of whom were no longer at Bridgewater. Assistant Attorney General Donald Wood was counsel for Charles W. Gaughan, guardian of one of the patients. Attorneys Paul Tamburello and Neil Chayet represented the others. The 210-page statement of the case, filed November 3, 1969, was the lengthiest entered to that date in Suffolk Superior Court.[126]

In a seventy-two page decision, Judge Robert Sullivan rejected all 560 claims made on behalf of the inmates. He ruled in Wiseman's favor on First Amendment grounds, finding that conditions at

Bridgewater were "all matters of news and of great public concern."[127] Sullivan refused to grant the inmates a share in the profits of the film (then twenty-seven thousand dollars) since there was no evidence of any contract or any agreement that subjects in the film were to be paid. To the claim made on behalf of the inmates that the film's public showing had added "psychological harm" to the subjects, the judge responded, "This court has been asked to place a dollar value on an almost imperceptible change in degree of insanity. Such a task is impossible."

Legal scholars point out that definitions of privacy are "necessarily subjective, abstract, elusive," but "whatever its form, an invasion of privacy is presumed to have an adverse effect on an identifiable person's psychological well-being."[128] Sullivan's decision provokes the basic question: Could a person judged legally insane be found (legally) to have had his or her privacy invaded under *any* circumstances? In *Commonwealth v. Wiseman,* the defense argued against the state positions that inmates (a) were incompetent to give consent and (b) had suffered an invasion of privacy, claiming that if competent to give consent, then the subjects' privacy had been waived; if incompetent, then the subjects could not suffer the mental anguish claimed by privacy invasion.

The next legal question regarding damages would seem to be whether a person, presumed sane and released from Bridgewater, would suffer current mental anguish when his past condition is made public. So far no damage suit filed by a former inmate or patient himself has gone to trial. In the spring of 1977, approximately ten days after *Titicut Follies* was shown at the University of Massachusetts-Boston, through the sponsorship of a civil liberties class, a member of the student body came to the class to protest the then-new practice of showing the film on Massachusetts campuses. The student had been an inmate at Bridgewater in 1966, and although he claims he tried to avoid the camera and did not give his consent to be filmed, he is clearly identifiable in the documentary.[129] As of this writing, he has not filed suit for damages.

A month after the Commonwealth filed its first papers petitioning for an injunction against the exhibition of *Titicut Follies,* Suffolk Superior Court Justice Joseph Ford ordered the suit "first case out" on the list for hearings the following month and thus moved *Commonwealth v. Wiseman* to trial in slightly less than two months.[130] Normally, the Commonwealth would have been represented by its

attorney general, but, since Attorney General Elliot Richardson was a
potential witness in the case, all early motions and other legal papers
were signed by Assistant Attorney General Frederick Greenman,
chief of the Division of Health, Education, and Welfare. Two attorneys from Ropes and Gray, Richardson's former law firm—Edward
B. Hanify (the son of a former superior court judge) and George C.
Caner, Jr.—were appointed as special assistant attorneys general,
and they acted as counsel for the Commonwealth in the trial.

James D. St. Clair and Blair L. Perry of Hale and Dorr represented
Wiseman and BFC. In 1967, St. Clair was remembered as Joseph
Welch's assistant in the Army-McCarthy hearings; he would later be
known as Richard Nixon's Watergate lawyer. He is highly regarded
within the legal community; a lawyer's lawyer, St. Clair has been
described as "all case and no cause."[131]

Grove Press was represented by John Larkin Thompson, whose
first major task was to disengage his clients (Grove and Titicut Follies Distributing Co., Inc.) from the state court proceedings. In a pretrial conference, Thompson argued that the case against them should
be tried in a federal court. St. Clair argued against the removal, saying that it would be a burden for the Commonwealth to conduct two
trials.[132] The plaintiffs, eager to move to trial against Wiseman, did
not oppose the separation petition. The trial judge allowed the severance; however, U.S. District Court Judge Francis J. Ford later
remanded the case against Grove back to the Suffolk Superior Court,
where it was heard in the spring of 1968.

Oliver Wendell Holmes's century-old reminder remains worth con-
sidering when one tries to understand *Commonwealth v. Wiseman:*
"The life of the law has not been logic: it has been experience. The
felt necessities of the time, the prevalent moral and political theories,
intuitions of public policy, avowed or unconscious, even the prejudices
which judges share with their fellow-men, have had a good deal more
to do than the syllogism in determining the rules by which men
should be governed."[133] The controversy that swirled around *Titicut
Follies* outside the courtroom reflected serious divisions regarding
what might be called necessities and substantial differences in moral
and political theories. Those tensions found their way into the court
presided over by Judge Harry Kalus. Born in Russia, raised in three
different working-class neighborhoods of Boston, Kalus worked as an
upholsterer while he attended Suffolk University Law School. He
was later elected to the General Court (Democrat, Ward 12), served

as an assistant corporation counsel for the city of Boston and then as legislative counsel to Governor Maurice J. Tobin before Tobin appointed him a district court judge.[134] In 1962, he was elevated to the superior court by Governor John Volpe. Hardworking and conservative, Kalus was "a real Commonwealther," a man dedicated to serving his state.[135] Throughout the *Titicut Follies* trial, Kalus played an active role, not just in making determinations regarding evidence and procedure, but also in questioning witnesses (for example, posing forty-one sequential questions to witness for the defense Richard Schickel; Tr. 16:82–91). At one point, counsel for the defendants would raise an objection to one of the judge's questions; at another, Kalus would apologize for his intrusions.[136] Two decades after the trial, in an interview with Charles Taylor, Wiseman recalled, "It was all in the hands of this judge . . . and it was clear that he hated me and hated the movie, from the first day. The moment the thing started, I knew I was cooked."[137]

During the pretrial conference on November 17, 1967, which was mostly dialogue between St. Clair and Kalus, St. Clair defined the situation as a case "without any substantial precedent . . . [in which] substantial issues are going to get resolved . . . [and thus] the case has significance beyond the parties themselves" (Tr. 1:36). St. Clair's interest in the case came through in his description that "there are many, many issues. It is a very unusual case and I find it very fascinating. . . . I have a feeling that this case is going to grow more complicated rather than less" (Tr. 1:33). Later in the conference, Kalus remarked to the defense counsel, "Well, you said this was going to be a thorny trial, it certainly is" (Tr. 1:59). These men of the court seemed to agree that legal dilemmas would confront them; at that point in the trial, they seemed eager to meet the challenge.

The first confrontation was a decision regarding the screening of the documentary itself. All agreed that the trial judge should see *Titicut Follies,* but Kalus wondered if the injunction against the film did not also apply to him. St. Clair assured him that the court did not enjoin itself. He also claimed that it would not be an open and public trial if the screening were private and that the issuance of the temporary injunction by another judge who had not seen the film had been not just inappropriate, but unconstitutional. Throughout the lengthy trial—eighteen trial days, sixty-four exhibits, 2,556 pages of proceedings (plus another two days of nontranscribed oral arguments)—counsel for Wiseman and BFC would maintain the position contained in their pretrial request for an open screening of *Titicut Follies*.

THE COURT: Then for the benefit of the public only?

MR. ST. CLAIR: For the benefit of the integrity of the judicial system, as I view it. (Tr. 1:65)

The judge denied the request.

Because of the litigation in New York and federal courts, the legislative hearings, and the extensive press coverage of the controversy, the entire trial of *Commonwealth v. Wiseman* was, in a nonlegal sense, a series of rejoinders or second pleadings. For example, the first witness, Commissioner John A. Gavin, was questioned about his answer to a question asked in the legislative hearing based on an attribution in a newspaper based on an interview. For the plaintiffs and the defendants, *Commonwealth v. Wiseman* covered a great deal of old ground, but it was not the same legal ground.

Commonwealth v. Wiseman was not a defamation case and it was not filed as an obscenity case. The plaintiffs (the Commonwealth of Massachusetts, with Superintendent Gaughan and Commissioner Gavin in their official capacities, and James C. Bulcock, through Gaughan as his guardian) alleged that the defendants (Frederick Wiseman and Bridgewater Film Company, Inc.) had breached an oral contract and invaded the privacy of the named inmate. The petitioners claimed that all receipts from the film should be held in trust for the inmates, but there was no plea for damages per se. Rather, they sought to enjoin exhibition of *Titicut Follies*.

A description of the *Titicut Follies* project by Edward Hanify in his opening remarks serves as an outline of what the state claimed were promises unkept. "The project then . . . [promised to be] an educational film about the Massachusetts Correctional Institution at Bridgewater, probably financed by the support of a national foundation, the ultimate film to use only the photographs of inmates and patients who were legally competent to give releases, with the film maker bound to obtain written releases from each inmate and patient whose photographs were used in the film, and the final film, prior to public release, to be subject to the approval of Superintendent Gaughan and Commissioner Gavin" (Tr. 2:10).

The general defense position regarding the allegation of breach of contract was that there were no conditions actually agreed upon that had been breached, that there had been no agreement regarding censorship by the state, and that, even if there had been a censorship agreement, it would be unconstitutional and, therefore, legally unenforceable.

Let us consider each subpart of the charge. Since Wiseman did not obtain foundation funding and since *Titicut Follies* had been exhibited theatrically in New York, the state's position was that Wiseman and BFC "attempted to engage in commercial traffic with tragedy in violation of Wiseman's basic agreement with the Commonwealth and petitioners Gavin and Gaughan."[138] The state argued not only that *Titicut Follies* was a sensational, exploitative product of dubious educational value, but also that Wiseman and his associates had intended, from the outset, to create such a product. Because of the nature of the allegation, questions regarding motives were allowed and became central to the arguments of both sides. David Eames, the associate producer and president of BFC, was called as a witness for the state and was presented as someone lacking the academic and technical credentials necessary for educational film making who had been misled by Wiseman—a characterization Eames strongly denied. John Marshall, whose deposition had been taken by the state, was not called to the witness stand by the state or the defendants.[139] Still, the resignations of Marshall and his wife were much discussed during direct examination of Eames and cross-examination of Wiseman. Counsel for the state implied that these resignations cast serious doubt on the integrity of the enterprise. Marshall, an articulate, well-educated member of a wealthy Cambridge family devoted to anthropological research, was not present to claim or disclaim allegiance to the educational worth of the project.

Wiseman, the central witness for the defense, naturally asserted the legitimacy of his motives, the BFC procedures, and the final film. The producer-director was on the witness stand for almost three full days. Unshaken by the aggressive cross- and recross-examination, Wiseman maintained that he had met all contractual agreements. He claimed that, along with the "loneliness and isolation and despair at Bridgewater," he also wanted the film to disclose "the tenderness and the concern and the genuine interest that was expressed on the part of people like Superintendent Gaughan and the correction officers" (Tr. 13:141–42). His answers were usually direct, often extremely detailed. A response to his counsel's question regarding his editing strategies lasted for twenty-five minutes.[140]

The defense argued that, although foundation support had been denied, the investors and crew continued to see the project as an educational endeavor. Arrangements with Grove Press were necessary to recover the expenses of making the film and to guarantee its exhibition. The defense was in the delicate position of presenting *Titicut Follies* as essentially a noncommercial project, according to the terms of the agreement, and also arguing its First Amendment protection for any commercial use or intent. The defense presented a group of witnesses with established academic credentials, all of whom contended that *Titicut Follies* had considerable educational value—a university dean (Gerhart D. Weibe), a professor of psychiatry (Leon Shapiro), and a professor of social psychology (Morris Schwartz).

The agreement to film only competent persons was a matter of written contract and went undisputed as a condition by the defense. The state, therefore, tried to prove that some individuals in the film were incompetent at the time filmed and thus conditions were violated. Lengthy expert testimony by Samuel Allen, the director of clinical psychiatry and acting medical director at Bridgewater State Hospital, and Samuel Tartakoff, a retired physician who had been director of the Division of Legal Medicine for the Massachusetts Mental Health Department, was entered by the state to support its contention that the BFC had filmed incompetents, including the named plaintiff.

The defense offered the evidence, also in writing, of Wiseman's proposal that competency would be determined by state personnel, who would accompany the filmmakers at all times. Wiseman's defense sidestepped the burden of proving that the subjects were, in fact, competent by referring to the consent procedures in which competence was assumed by the BFC crew unless the superintendent or his staff said otherwise, which was never the case. Eames and Wiseman both testified that they were not sure of the definitions of competency or sanity before they went to Bridgewater and became increasingly unsure of them after their time at the institution (Tr. 6:160–66; 15:136). Cross-examination of the doctors in reference to the subjects' mental reports revealed how rarely the men at Bridgewater had received psychiatric examinations. One of the men filmed had not been given a psychiatric examination for more than eight years, and it had been more than six years since his last physical exam.[141] St.

Clair stated that "Bridgewater is a prison; whether or not it is a hospital is a question of fact for the Court" (Tr. 8:14). The defense questioned the particular credentials of the expert witnesses and the general capacity to determine sanity. St. Clair quoted the venerable Justice Frankfurter: "Only one proposition seems certain, that is, that sanity and insanity are concepts of incertitude" (Tr. 8:12).

The discussion of sanity also pertained to releases and indicated how intertwined the legal, medical, and ethical questions are in the *Titicut Follies* case. In cross-examination, Dr. Tartakoff acknowledged that insanity is essentially a legal, not a medical description (Tr. 8:5). Yet he was willing, at the request of state counsel Caner, to apply that term to individuals pictured in *Titicut Follies*. Since, by law, a contract made by an insane person is voidable, releases signed by incompetent inmates and patients could be set aside. Caner also challenged the legality of releases made out in the spring and summer of 1966 to a corporation (BFC) not legally organized until the following fall. Even if no releases were voided for such reasons, the state introduced the evidence that only eleven or twelve of the sixty-two identifiable inmates had signed releases.[142] Staff members had signed the balance of the 106 releases, but their releases were not questioned or discussed.

The defense claimed that since Attorney General Brooke had not explicitly mentioned releases in his opinion (releases were mentioned in the Gavin request that was part of the correspondence from Brooke) and since no release form had been offered by the state, there had been no agreement regarding releases. St. Clair argued that the state "cannot have it both ways" (that is, to argue as *parens patriae* on behalf of the inmates and to have a right protectable by a release, which assumes a position antagonistic to that of the releasor; tr. 8:33). The defense maintained that all who were pictured gave their consent, albeit unwritten in many cases. The BFC attorneys introduced canteen receipts and cash account records as evidence that MCI-Bridgewater officials assumed that the inmates were sufficiently competent to allow them to make these kinds of contractual agreements. The records were not accepted as exhibits, but were marked for identification.

The most heavily argued section of the breach of contract allegation was the contention by the state that Wiseman had agreed to state approval prior to the release of the Bridgewater documentary. Much of the testimony of Charles Gaughan and John Gavin spoke to the point that Wiseman had agreed to this condition. Elliot Richardson and Frederick Greenman firmly and forcefully testified that they, too, had assumed that *Titicut Follies* would not be shown publicly without state approval and that Wiseman was well aware of that condition. Thirteen correction officers, including two who had been named plaintiffs in *Cullen v. Grove*, testified that they had, at some time in the presence of the BFC crew, heard state approval as a condition of film making mentioned by Superintendent Gaughan, the crew, or both. The defense argued "the complete lack of any objective conformation [*sic*] of any right of censorship" (Tr. 2:35) and that this condition, although consistently claimed untrue by Wiseman and Eames, would be unlawful, if true.

The allegation of invasion of privacy was filed in the name of one inmate, James Bulcock, who is shown nude with his genitals exposed and is provoked by guards into revealing personal information about himself. The scene involving this man and his interaction with the guards, who shave him and return him to his cell, lasts for six minutes and forty-five seconds and is one of the lengthiest in the film.[143] Bulcock, who was known in the trial as No. 3, had been confined to Bridgewater for twenty-five years and had no known living relatives. Around October 1, 1967, Superintendent Gaughan signed a petition to be made the man's legal guardian; they never met. Inmate No. 3 did not sign a release form. Based on his records, an examination by Bridgewater staff members prior to the trial, and his observed behavior in the film, he was classified by Allen and Tartakoff as incompetent at the time of filming. In arguing invasion of privacy, counsel for the plaintiffs implicitly emphasized two areas of the privacy tort—intrusion and public disclosure of private facts—but did not explicitly refer to a privacy tort. Although only one individual inmate was a named plaintiff, Hanify's opening remarks indicated that the privacy invasion would be argued in plural terms. "It is the view of the Commonwealth that essentially [*Titicut Follies*] displays nude and incompetent inmates at Bridgewater in the process of manifesting their hallucinations, their abberations [*sic*], their mad ravings and their basic mental diseases in circumstances depriving them of spiritual and physical privacy" (Tr. 2:21). Both Gaughan and Richardson testified that they had registered complaints about privacy invasion with Wiseman as early as the previous summer.

The defense pointed to case law that found that confinement itself limited privacy. St. Clair and Perry argued that filming introduced no invasions of privacy substantially greater than those routinely experienced by the men at Bridgewater. Although not allowed in evidence by the trial judge, footage taken by the BFC crew showed a high school tour of the facility in which students observed nude inmates. The footage included students looking into No. 3's cell, which had a name plate over the door. Here is the defense co-counsel attempting to present the defense argument:

THE COURT: Would you state that again?

MR. PERRY: That the right of privacy, your Honor, is often stated in terms of a right to be let alone. It is our position that those people so unfortunate as to be at Bridgewater have a right not to be let alone, in other words, that they have been abandoned by society, in effect, and—

THE COURT: That would be the most monstrous proposition I have ever heard. (Tr. 15:157)

Continuing that argument, the defense claimed that inmate No. 3's medical treatment had actually improved considerably after the release of the film and that the acceleration in attention was not coincidental. Thus, they argued, disclosures of such deplorable conditions would be in the inmates' and patients' best interests. Bulcock did not appear as a witness. He had been sent a notice of deposition by the defense, but there is no Bulcock deposition filed with the case records.[144] No family member served as a witness for the plaintiffs or the defense.

Counsel for the defense accused the Commonwealth of hypocrisy in the case in general and in particular details like the use of numbers rather than names in the trial testimony. St. Clair argued that "it is the privacy of the Commonwealth that is being sought to be protected here, not the privacy of these poor, unfortunate individuals" (Tr. 2:23).

The main defense, of course, was on constitutional grounds. St. Clair and Perry invoked the First Amendment. "It is our position that under the law of this Commonwealth, there is no recognized right of privacy; that to the extent that one ever would be or could be recognized, it is subordinate, as the Court has indicated in the Themo case, if recognized, to a right of people to know or a right of disclosure in a matter of public interest" (Tr. 15:156). Defense counsel argued that the public has a right—and a duty—to know what transpires in a public-supported institution. They contended that public scandal cannot be revealed without scandalous revelation.[145]

Although the case was not filed on an obscenity charge, St. Clair anticipated obscenity claims when he said in his opening statements that "this is not a case . . . that involves any pornography. There is not even any suggestion that this would attract any prurient interest on the part of anybody. This is a factual film" (Tr. 2:34). There was a shadow charge of obscenity throughout the trial. Obscenity originally meant beyond the bounds, offensive. In the *Titicut Follies* case, two vague terms—privacy invasion and obscenity—often blurred into a general complaint of offensiveness. Witnesses for the plaintiffs made frequent reference to the general amount of nudity in the film (correction officer Lepine testified that there are at least seven inmates shown nude who are clearly identifiable and about eleven others shown nude, but not easily identifiable); to an interview in which an inmate discusses his sexual behavior (some of which is actionable); and to a scene in which an inmate is allegedly shown in an actual or implied act of masturbation. Wiseman was asked to write out a description of an outtake considered too offensive to be discussed aloud in the courtroom. The description, from a Wiseman affidavit in previous action in a New York court, states, "For example, there is the line-up for showers. Approximately fifteen or twenty men at a time are taken naked from their cells, many of them with their genitals in various states of erection."[146]

Defense witnesses attesting to the value of *Titicut Follies* as news (Louis Lyons, print journalist, director of the Neiman Fellowships at Harvard, and WGBH-TV [Boston NET] news commentator), social document (experts from the fields of sociology, psychology, law, and medicine), and art (Richard Schickel, author and film critic for *Life* magazine, and Willard Van Dyke, documentary filmmaker and director of the film division of the Museum of Modern Art) followed the pattern of First Amendment defense in many obscenity cases. Between 1967 and 1971, the U.S. Supreme Court reversed obscenity convictions in thirty-nine cases in which a majority of the Court, applying separate tests, decided that the material in question was not obscene. What became known as the LAPS test was the "test" whether a work, taken as a whole, lacked literary, artistic, political, or scientific value and could, therefore, be denied First Amendment protection; however, Kalus stated that *Commonwealth v. Wiseman* was not an obscenity trial and refused to let a social psychologist continue testimony, ruling that "the question of whether the film has any value as a social document is irrelevant to the issues in the case."[147]

When questioned about the necessity of having subjects identifiable in the film, Wiseman did not call upon poetic license as his defense; he defended his choices on informational/educational grounds. Schickel's testimony in cross-examination sounded a great deal like that in an obscenity case, yet the *Life* critic avoided an explicit art-for-art's sake position (Tr. 16:44–98). Willard Van Dyke, the last witness in the trial, made a distinction, which he claimed to be a commonly held one, between instructional and educational documentaries. The filmmaker said instructional films were didactic and did not challenge a viewer to think. Van Dyke described *Titicut Follies* as an educational documentary, because, rather than telling, it helps "someone to understand" (Tr. 17:26).

Before the attorneys presented their final arguments, the trial judge mentioned "certain issues of law and fact and mixed law and fact issues" that they might wish to address: (1) the question as to the status of the plaintiff parties; (2) "almost a threshold question and a fact question"—whether there were any conditions imposed on Wiseman concerning the privilege or permission to make the film; (3) the question of representation by Wiseman as to the purpose for which the film was to be used; (4) whether commercial use of the film allowed the defendant to claim free speech; and (5) whether anyone could sign a release for the persons filmed who were mentally ill.[148]

Final arguments were presented before the court on December 14 and 15, 1967; briefs and memoranda of law were filed December 22. It now became Judge Harry Kalus's responsibility to render a judgment. Don Pember describes the considerable power given to judges in cases under equity: "The rules and procedures under equity are far more flexible than those under the common law. Equity really begins where the common law leaves off. Equity suits are never tried before a jury. Rulings come in the form of judicial decrees, not in judgments of yes or no. Decisions in equity are (and were) discretionary on the part of judges. And despite the fact that precedents are also relied upon in the law of equity, judges are free to do what they think is right and fair in a specific case."[149] It did not take the court long to consider its judgment. On January 4, 1968, Judge Harry Kalus issued his "Findings, Rulings and Order for Decree."

Kalus found that Frederick Wiseman and Bridgewater Film Company, Inc., had breached an oral contract with the Commonwealth of Massachusetts and invaded the privacy of James C. Bulcock. Kalus wrote:

> The film product which Wiseman made . . . constitutes a most flagrant abuse of the privilege he was given to make a film. . . . There is a new theme—crudities, nudities and obscenities. . . . It is a crass piece of commercialism—a contrived scenario—designed by its new title and by its contents to titillate the general public and lure them to the box office. The film is 80 minutes of brutal sordidness and human degradation. It is a hodge-podge of sequences, with the camera jumping, helter-skelter, from the showing of an inmate in an act of masturbation to scenes depicting mentally ill patients engaged in repetitive, incoherent and obscene rantings and ravings. The film is excessively preoccupied with nudity, with full exposure of the privates of these persons. There is no narrative accompanying the film, nor are there any subtitles, without which the film is a distortion of the daily routine and conditions at the Institution. Each viewer is left to his own devices as to just what is being portrayed and in what context.[150]

Regarding the issues that he had mentioned before final arguments, Judge Kalus found that (1) the Commonwealth and Gaughan as guardian had status; (2) there were conditions imposed on Wiseman by the state; (3) Wiseman had misrepresented his purposes; (4) no free-speech claim was legitimate here; and (5) the men at Bridgewater had a right to be left alone. Writing the first decision in Massachusetts legal history based on the right to privacy, Kalus said that "this right of privacy rests upon the most elementary principles of natural law. . . . The true rule is that equity will protect the personal and intangible rights of an individual just as it will enjoin the violation of a person's property rights."[151] He dismissed the First Amendment claim. "No amount of rhetoric, no shibboleths of 'free speech' and the 'right of the public to know' can obscure or masquerade this pictorial performance for what it really is—a piece of abject commercialism, trafficking on the loneliness, on the human misery, degradation and sordidness in the lives of these unfortunate humans."[152]

Kalus not only found for the Commonwealth, but the outraged judge exceeded its demands for injunctive relief. He modified the bill of complaint by deleting the words "without prior approval in writing by the plaintiffs" and ordered the respondents to deliver to the Commonwealth "the balance of the film footage (the original negative and any and all prints thereof), together with sound tapes, taken by them at Bridgewater."[153]

On December 28, 1967, the Commonwealth had filed a motion for enlargement of the injunction, to force Grove/Titicut to discontinue distribution of the documentary. Judge Kalus reserved judgment on the Commonwealth's petition concerning the disposition of the income and profits from the commercial exhibition of *Titicut Follies* until the conclusion of the suit against the respondents Grove Press, Inc., and Titicut Follies Distributing Co., Inc.

A hearing regarding the disposition of income was held on May 23, 1968. Daniel Mahoney, attorney for Grove and Titicut, was the only witness. Kalus ruled against the trust requirement, stating that it would be "inappropriate, if at all legally permissible, for the Court to order that any and all of the inmates at Bridgewater share in any profits made by the several respondents in the showing of a film" (Tr. 18:39). Kalus went on to state that there could be no pooling of a fund, since each person "is entitled to recover for himself, and alone, for such damages he has proved he has sustained and suffered" (Tr. 18:40).

Kalus ordered a permanent injunction against the showing of *Titicut Follies* in Massachusetts, directed the Commonwealth to destroy the unused Bridgewater footage, and dismissed the bill without prejudice to the petitioner (the guardian of Bulcock) to bring an action at law for damages. The final decree of the Suffolk Superior Court, entered on August 6, 1968, by Judge Harry Kalus, was a clear and almost complete victory for the Commonwealth.[154]

The same day that the final decree of the superior court was entered, denying the petition that the receipts and profits from *Titicut Follies* be held in trust for the men at Bridgewater, the Commonwealth appealed the decree to the supreme judicial court (SJC). Yet certainly the respondents, Frederick Wiseman and Bridgewater Film Company, Inc., had been more—to use the language of the Commonwealth appeal—*aggrieved* by the Kalus decree. Within the week, Blair L. Perry had claimed an appeal for his clients. The appeal was scheduled for the May sitting of the supreme judicial court.

As cross-appellants, the petitioners (the Commonwealth) argued: (1) The showings of *Titicut Follies* by Grove and Titicut were illegal; (2) Grove and Titicut should account for the profits made by the film to the inmates whose rights of privacy were violated by its showings (the brief listed gross revenues of not less than $31,798.50 and net profits of not less than $14,451.61); and (3) the petitioners had standing on behalf of their wards to reach the profits from the film. The Commonwealth claimed that "the constructive trust remedy is peculiarly appropriate in the case at bar because of the difficulty incompetents are likely to encounter proving compensatory damages in a tort action."[155] The petitioners suggested that the court should determine how the profits would be distributed to the inmates or their representatives.

The brief for the respondents (Wiseman, et al.) raised questions of both fact and law. Counsel for Wiseman and BFC argued: (1) The findings upon which the decree was based were not supported by the evidence and were misleading (twenty-one detailed challenges to the court's findings were listed); (2) there was no material breach of contract by Wiseman; (3) the petitioners had no interests that were entitled to equitable protection; (4) no right to privacy is infringed by the film; (5) the film is protected by the First and Fourteenth Amendments to the U. S. Constitution; (6) any restrictions imposed upon Wiseman as a condition of his being permitted to make the film are void and unenforceable because of the First Amendment; (7) article 16 of the constitution of the Commonwealth of Massachusetts [which protects freedom of speech] prohibits any injunction against showing of the film; (8) the basic principles of equity and public policy compel that *Titicut Follies* be permitted to be shown to the public, regardless of the conditions under which filming was permitted; (9) the Commonwealth should be barred from relief in this case by reason of its unclean hands and inequitable conduct; and (10) the evidence did not warrant the relief granted by the trial court in the final decree.[156]

As appellees, the petitioners (the Commonwealth) argued: (1) *Titicut Follies* violated the conditions on which permission was granted; (2) the conditions of the contract (as found by the trial court) were constitutional; (3) showings of the film were properly enjoined as a continuing invasion of the rights of privacy of the inmates shown; (4) the injunction against the continued showing of the film is not an invalid prior restraint on First Amendment rights; (5) the Commonwealth had standing to obtain an injunction enforcing the contract and protecting the inmates' rights of privacy; and (6) the Commonwealth should not be barred from relief by "unclean hands."[157] In other words, they supported the trial judge's finding of fact and law.

In addition, three organizations—the American Sociological Association (ASA), the American Orthopsychiatric Association (AOA), and the Civil Liberties Union of Massachusetts (CLUM)—filed *amicus curiae* briefs with the supreme judicial court. Writing for the ASA, Sherwood B. Smith, Jr., argued that the film is an important document that can be effectively used by professional groups for research, instruction, and discussion; and that any asserted right of privacy on behalf of the inmates does not preclude, as a matter of law, professional viewing and use of the film.[158] A broader argument in support of exhibition was entered by counsel for the AOA, Martin Levine and Harold S. H. Edgar, who claimed: (1) The interests of the patients at Bridgewater, and of the mentally ill elsewhere, require that *Titicut Follies* be widely shown; (2) the interests of society in free discussion prohibit the enjoining of the film; (3) the Commonwealth and its officials have a clear conflict of interest in claiming to act for the patients in initiating censorship of a film critical of a state mental institution; and (4) the supposed contract cannot constitutionally authorize prohibition of the film.[159] The third brief filed by a friend of the court presented an abstract discussion of the issues, but gave limited support to the Wiseman appeal. On behalf of CLUM, Henry Paul Monaghan argued that (1) The rights to personal dignity and privacy of the inmates of Bridgewater may be violated by unlimited distribution of this film; (2) some injunctive relief may be appropriate on the facts of the case; but (3) even if some injunctive relief were appropriate in this case, the decree entered in the superior court was too broad.[160] The Massachusetts Supreme Judicial Court had indicated its willingness—if the proper case presented itself—to consider whether and, if so, to what extent any nonstatutory right of privacy existed within the Commonwealth. Court watchers assumed that *Commonwealth v. Wiseman* was such a case.

Appeals were heard on May 6, 1969. On June 24, the Massachusetts Supreme Judicial Court issued its decision. All five justices agreed to modify the final decree, so that the injunction prohibited the showing of *Titicut Follies* to the general public, but allowed specialized audiences (legislators, judges, lawyers, sociologists, social workers, doctors, psychiatrists, students in these or related fields, and organizations dealing with the social problems of custodial care and mental infirmity) to see the documentary. The court regarded the film as a "collective, indecent intrusion into the most private aspects of the lives of these unfortunate persons in the Commonwealth's custody."[161] Still, it acknowledged the value of the film as a social document and allowed that "the film may indirectly have been of benefit to some inmates by leading to improvement of Bridgewater."[162] Preservation of the unused footage by BFC was allowed.

For the first time in its 277-year history, the SJC recognized a legally enforceable right of privacy in Massachusetts; however, the court explicitly stated that the right was recognized only to the extent of the factual situation presented in the particular case. Therefore, the court itself refused to define the situation as one of legal precedent. Justice Cutter, who wrote the decision, explained the modification as an attempt to balance conflicting public and private interests, probable good and possible harm. The court required that Wiseman add a brief explanation to the film that "changes and improvements have taken place in the institution since 1966."[163] The court held that a constructive trust based upon receipts for past showings of the film was unwarranted, since it was not an appropriate basis of recovery for any individual inmate who may have suffered ascertainable damage.

A number of legal scholars writing about *Commonwealth v. Wiseman* have seen the SJC modification as a legal improvement over the lower court decision, but they question the arguments the higher court used to explain its solution to a legal dilemma. David L. Bennett and Phillip Small wrote in the *Suffolk Law Review* that "It is difficult to comprehend how the court could have decided the *Wiseman* case without resolving the underlying problems raised by the First Amendment. . . . It appears illogical to dismiss First Amendment considerations in one part of the case by merely relying on the breach of contract, and then balance the private interests of the inmates against the public interest in another part of the case. . . . The court appears to have achieved the best of both worlds in its ultimate result, but neglects the need for rational consistency in reaching this result."[164] The *Harvard Law Review* noted:

> Although the Supreme Judicial Court specifically disclaimed giving any weight to the interests of the Commonwealth . . . it seems likely that the state had an undue influence upon the final decision. A preliminary question never reached by the court, for example, was whether the government should have been permitted to act as legal guardian for the prisoners. . . .
>
> [The required announcement regarding improvements] is a pernicious and, understandably, unique requirement. Such an announcement would in no way benefit the inmates, for whose sake the suit was supposedly brought, and would serve only to improve the image of the Commonwealth

and the Department of Correction. Indeed, insofar as the audience takes the announcement to mean that conditions at Bridgewater are now acceptable, the inmates would be harmed.[165]

And, finally, a comment in the *Columbia Law Review* states that "ironically, [the] first judicial recognition of a right to privacy in Massachusetts is designed to protect the sensibilities of the criminally insane from the effects of a disclosure which can only improve the squalid circumstances of their lives. The only interests clearly protected are the dignity of the Commonwealth and the public image of her agents. . . . 'Titicut Follies' is an unfortunate case."[166]

Certainly Grove Press and Titicut Follies Film Distributing Co., Inc. considered *Commonwealth v. Wiseman* an unfortunate case. In the summer of 1971, the same day that the U.S. Supreme Court announced its decision to allow the publication of the Pentagon papers, a Boston paper also announced that Titicut and Grove had filed a civil suit in federal court against the attorney general of Massachusetts (then Robert H. Quinn), Judge Harry Kalus, the SJC judges, Gavin, and Gaughan for "an impermissible prior restraint on free expression."[167] The defendants filed a motion to dismiss the case, a dismissal which Judge Frank J. Murray allowed the following spring.[168] As of this writing, no individual who does not fit into one of the specialized groups allowed to see *Titicut Follies* has filed a suit against the Commonwealth, protesting the elitist position of the current regulations.

Hardly any dispute ever goes to trial unless there is real fervor pushing at least one side forward. In the litigation involving *Titicut Follies*, strong feelings motivated all parties to the original argument. That passion continued for two decades, during which the Commonwealth of Massachusetts and Frederick Wiseman remained consistent in their claims, tenacious in the willingness to initiate or resist litigation.

In the spring of 1980, the office of still another Massachusetts Attorney General (Francis X. Bellotti) moved for a supplemental order to enjoin Wiseman from exhibiting *Titicut Follies* at the Saxon Theater as part of the "Boston Jubilee 350" (an event organized by a deputy mayor of Boston, Katherine Kane). U.S. District Judge Rya W. Zobel denied the motion for supplemental relief.[169]

Wiseman has been denied two petitions for *certiorari* to the United States Supreme Court. In 1983, his attorney, Blair Perry, was preparing a third appeal.[170] The first request, based on several First

Amendment issues, was filed in the fall of 1969. Wiseman claimed that the Massachusetts decision limiting showings of the film to professional audiences is "a unique pernicious form of censorship"; he asked whether a state can "ban the showing to the public of a documentary film revealing conditions in a state institution on the theory of enforcing restriction imposed upon the filmmaker by the state as a condition of permitting the filming." Finally, the appeal claimed the *Wiseman* decision conflicted with the principles established in *Time, Inc., v. Hill.* [171]

Twice Wiseman has been just one vote short of the needed four for review of *Commonwealth v. Wiseman* by the U.S. Supreme Court. [172] Justices Harlan, Douglas, and Brennan voted to hear the first Wiseman appeal. Justice Harlan explained the reasons why he voted to grant *certiorari* and set the *Wiseman* case for plenary consideration:

> The balance between these two interests, that of the individual's privacy and the public's right to know about conditions in public institutions, is not one that is easily struck, particularly in a case like that before us where the importance of the issue is matched by the extent of the invasion of privacy. . . .
>
> A further consideration is the fact that these inmates are not only the wards of the Commonwealth of Massachusetts but are also the charges of society as a whole. It is important that conditions in public institutions should not be cloaked in secrecy, lest citizens may disclaim responsibility for the treatment that their representative government affords those in its care. At the same time, it must be recognized that the individual's concern with privacy is the key to the dignity which is the promise of civilized society. . . .
>
> [The conclusions of the Massachusetts Supreme Judicial Court] represent a measured and thoughtful attempt to grapple with a difficult and important problem. Yet they demonstrate the importance of review by this Court for they sharply focus the dimension of the question presented by this case. The question at this juncture is not whether the Supreme Judicial Court was correct or incorrect in striking the constitutional balance, but merely whether this Court should grant certiorari. I fail to see how, on a complex and important issue like this, it can be concluded that this Court should withhold plenary review. The case for review is strengthened by the fact that a distinguished federal judge refused to enjoin in New York the showing of this very same film. This is not of course the traditional conflict that requires this Court to step in, but it underscores the difficulty and importance of the issues that are apparent both from reading the decision of the Massachusetts court and a viewing of the film.
>
> I am at a loss to understand how questions of such importance can be deemed not "certworthy." To the extent that the Commonwealth suggests

that certiorari be denied because petitioners failed to comply with reasonable contract conditions imposed by the Commonwealth, that question itself is one of significant constitutional dimension, for it is an open question as to how far a government may go in cutting off access of the media to its institutions when such access will not hinder them in performing their functions.[173]

The second petition for *certiorari* was filed for October term 1970 and denied December 7, 1970. National Educational Television was allowed to file an *amicus curiae* brief in support of the petition for rehearing. Again, Wiseman had three favorable votes (Justices Harlan, Brennan, and Blackmun). Justice William O. Douglas, who had previously voted in favor of review, withdrew from consideration because excerpts from his book *Points of Rebellion* had appeared in the *Evergreen Review,* a Grove Press publication, and he wished to avoid any possible conflict of interest.[174] Wiseman argued for a rehearing on the grounds that the important free-speech issues should be considered in the initial stage by a full nine-man bench, but to no avail.[175] *Wiseman v. Massachusetts* was never heard by either the Warren or the Burger Court.

In July of 1987, Wiseman returned to the Suffolk Superior Court, filing a motion to permit showing of *Titicut Follies* to general audiences. Wiseman's attorney, Blair Perry, argued that the motion should be allowed because (1) the applicable law had changed (regarding prior restraint) and (2) the facts had changed (few of the inmates shown in the film and identifiable were still living; attitudes of society toward public disclosure of conditions in an institution such as Bridgewater had changed; officials of the Commonwealth who sought to suppress the film were no longer in office; the original release of the film was credited with resulting in significant improvements at Bridgewater).[176]

The Commonwealth responded that it supported the showing of *Titicut Follies* to the general public "as long as a procedure is first imposed and followed to its conclusion to locate the inmates and patients depicted in the film, notify them of the pending motion and provide representation, as needed and separate from the Commonwealth to protect their privacy rights."[177] According to the state, consent by subjects or their guardians should be a prerequisite of public release. After twenty years, the Commonwealth moved to the position that Alan Dershowitz held during the crucial meeting at the attorney general's office on September 21, 1967, before any litigation had begun against *Titicut Follies*. During the fall of 1987, the attorney general's office attempted to locate the inmates and patients who appear in *Titicut Follies*. By mid-December, representatives of the Commonwealth determined that "of the 62 inmates so identified as appearing in the film, 28 are deceased; two are in custody at M.C.I., Bridgewater; one is in custody at M.C.I., Concord; four are in other institutions operated by or licensed under the Department of Mental Health; four are in nursing homes and six are believed to reside in private residences. The remaining seventeen have not been found despite diligent efforts, and all or some of them may be deceased."[178] The Commonwealth requested that a guardian *ad litem*—a guardian appointed for the purpose of a suit—be appointed to represent the interests of persons whose photographs are included in the film and who may be under some present disability. In a hearing on August 27, 1987, Blair Perry stated that he was not convinced that the appointment of a guardian was "appropriate or necessary." Later, Perry and the attorney general's office agreed to nominate Mitchell J. Sikora, Jr., as guardian. Sikora, who had served in a similar capacity in a number of cases, was a former state assistant attorney general and a partner in a Boston law firm, with experience teaching in several Massachusetts law schools. Judge Andrew G. Meyer appointed Sikora as guardian *ad litem* on December 17, 1987.

Early in January 1988 newspapers throughout the Commonwealth ran the following announcement:

Titicut Follies

Legal proceedings have started again on "Titicut Follies," a film made at M.C.I. Bridgewater in 1966. Exhibition of the film is enjoined to anyone other than certain specialists or professionals. The film's producer has asked the Suffolk County Superior Court to permit the film's showing to the general public.

The Court has appointed a guardian ad litem to represent the interests of certain persons whose photographs are shown in "Titicut Follies." If you believe you or someone you know is shown in the film, please immediately call or write Stephen A. Jonas, Deputy Chief, Public Protection Bureau, Department of the Attorney General, One Ashburton Place, 19th Floor, Boston MA 02108, (617) 727–4878.[179]

The Commonwealth's announcement led to the discovery of two or three men who had not been found by the earlier search of state records.[180] In April 1988, Sikora began to prepare his report, to be based on a review of parts of the trial transcript (the testimony of correction officer George J. Lepine, Jr., which described the appearances of each of the identified persons in the film), a viewing of the film, interviews with the men pictured, and a search of state departmental and agency records. Men found competent by the guardian *ad litem* would make their own decisions, with the aid of counsel if they desired, regarding general exhibition of the documentary. Sikora was directed to report to the court on behalf of anyone he considered incompetent and to determine whether public exhibition of *Titicut Follies* would harm or benefit each person. Meyer's order made it clear that the report, recommendations, and opinions of the guardian *ad litem* would be advisory only. Meyer also ordered that the guardian "shall not disclose the names and addresses of the named persons to any members of the public (including, without limitation, the press or media) without further order of the Court. In his report to the Court, the GAL [guardian *ad litem*] shall refer to named persons by initials or other means appropriate to avoid public disclosure of their names and addresses."[181]

During the spring and summer of 1988, Sikora traveled throughout the Commonwealth, interviewing each former or present inmate or patient pictured in *Titicut Follies* whose whereabouts was known. On several occasions, the men he spoke with gave him information that led him to still other men who appear in the film. Most of the men were living in Massachusetts, many in halfway houses or nursing homes.

Sikora's first task as guardian *ad litem* was to determine the competency of each man on the narrow question of his present competency to decide for himself whether he wished to consent or object to the general release of *Titicut Follies*. Sikora followed the general legal doctrine that a person is competent until proven otherwise. Although all the men were living in 1966 in what was then called a hospital for the criminally insane, Sikora did not assume any former incompetence. He introduced himself to those he interviewed by saying that he had "been appointed by the court to come to see them."[182] To aid Sikora in making his determination as to whether each man was presently competent to represent himself in the motion before the court, Sikora talked with each man pictured in the film individually; he consulted the person's state records, going back to the beginning of the file, but with a special emphasis on recent psychological evaluations; as necessary, he sought psychiatric consultation and considered additional information furnished by attorneys associated with the case. Sikora did not use behavior pictured in *Titicut Follies* as evidence in the issue of competency in 1988. Using these standards and procedures, Sikora considered ten of the men he interviewed incompetent. Three men believed to be in the film and to be residing in Massachusetts were unavailable to Sikora. In one instance, the guardian believed that family members were preventing him from interviewing their relative until someone in the family was permitted to view *Titicut Follies.*

To aid the guardian in his next task—a judgment as to the effect of the general exhibition of *Titicut Follies* on each of the men judged incompetent—Sikora interviewed the men themselves and any family or friends he was able to locate. He asked the men and their friends and relatives to recall and to speculate as to the past and future effects of *Titicut Follies* on the inmates shown in the film: "whether they have felt any sense of an invasion of privacy or embarrassment or emotional distress about the existence of the film or any prior showing of the film" and "would they or will they, in the future, in their estimation, feel any embarrassment."

He asked each man if he remembered the filming at Bridgewater and if he knew about the controversy surrounding the film. Memories varied greatly, as did the mental abilities of the men. "Some men remember it vividly; others need prodding; others don't seem to remember it." If the men did not remember the filming or know about the controversy, Sikora attempted to "fill them in to try to refresh their memories." He found that the most competent men were aware of the controversy surrounding *Titicut Follies.* Despite their general incompetence, some of the incompetent men seemed "to have a good focus about this particular issue." Sikora noted that some incompetent men "showed an awareness and at least some prior memory and viewpoint about it and expressed that viewpoint. That viewpoint, for the most part, was that the film should be shown." Only two of the people Sikora interviewed had seen *Titicut Follies.*[183]

The men pictured in *Titicut Follies* did not typically have any friends or family members to watch out for them. Sikora's search indicated that most of the men, many of them quite elderly in 1988, had been abandoned and forgotten by whatever families they once had. Still, Sikora received telephone calls from persons who claimed to be relatives or friends of men in *Titicut Follies.* "They're concerned and want to hire attorneys and get into the proceedings." Usually the callers had not seen *Titicut Follies* but had developed strong opinions about it. On checking these leads, Sikora very often found that the person mentioned did not appear in the film or was dead. In Massachusetts, the right of privacy dies with an individual and thereafter cannot be claimed by a relative on behalf of another.

In March 1989 Sikora submitted his written report to Judge Meyer. Before delivering his report to the judge, Sikora had sent copies of it to the attorney general's office and to Wiseman's counsel. Sikora advised the court that exhibition of *Titicut Follies* would not harm the incompetent men pictured in the film. Sikora recalled that, "for the most part, I came to the conclusion that in their circumstance, the sheltered circumstances of state institutions or homes for the elderly or nursing homes or sometimes protected circumstances of relatives and families, that the showing at this juncture in time would not cause them harm. But each case I described in its own terms. In some cases, that view was easy to reach, and, in some cases, a little bit more difficult." According to Sikora, most of the incompetent men appear "almost glancingly in crowd scenes" in the film. "People who appear most prominently, continuously, and visibly and who have changed the least physically are ironically the competent individuals."

Sikora's fifty-four page report was constructed as a series of individual evaluations of seven competent, ten incompetent, and three unavailable men pictured in *Titicut Follies*. To preserve the confidentiality of each person's identity, the guardian used initials and the numerals that had been used in *Commonwealth v. Wiseman,* rather than names. With some slight variations, each individual report included a description of the person's (1) appearance in the film; (2) past and current living circumstances; (3) physical characteristics; (4) family connections; (5) memories of Bridgewater and attitude, if any, toward exhibition of *Titicut Follies,* either by the individual or his legal guardian. Sikora then assessed the person's (6) abilities; and (7) awareness of publicity; and, finally, determined (8) the person's competence to make a decision about the exhibition of *Titicut Follies.* In the ten evaluations of men considered incompetent, Sikora speculated as to the probability of harm or benefit of exhibition for each person individually. He advised that general exhibition of *Titicut Follies* would not harm any of the incompetent men. Sikora also reported on the views expressed regarding exhibition by the competent men in their interviews with him, while making it clear that he was "not deciding" on their behalf, as he had done for the incompetent men.

Three of the seven competent men seemed indifferent to the showing, another expressed mixed feelings, two supported general exhibition, and one man strongly opposed its general release. Sikora concluded his report with this additional recommendation:

> The incompetent individuals, or at least those designated as incompetent for the general conduct of their affairs outside an institutional setting, should receive continuing shelter from publicity about the film. A number of them exhibited painful feelings and memories about their time at Bridgewater. They were reluctant to be reminded about it and sometimes became emotionally upset or despondent as a result of our discussion. Upon that observation, I recommend that their anonymity be carefully perserved and that they not suffer any intrusion from publicity which may accompany the present litigation phase or from any ultimate decision. In particular, I note that a number of representatives of the print and electronic media are following the litigation. Several have informed me that, if at all possible, they would wish to interview any appropriate subjects of the film. I believe that the majority of incompetent individuals and their families should receive continuing protection against involuntary communication from the media.[184]

Sikora considered seven of the men he interviewed competent to decide for themselves regarding the general exhibition of *Titicut Follies*. Those men were invited to attend a showing of the film in a screening room at public television station WGBH, located outside Boston in Brighton, on April 11, 1989. As the court order stood in 1989, most of the men pictured in *Titicut Follies* were not members of any of the professional groups allowed to see the film. Judge Meyer entered an order to allow the special showing for these men. Four of the men pictured in the film were present at the screening, which was followed by a discussion; one man was represented by counsel, another man by his brother. One of the former patients had previously seen the film, or at least parts of it, in connection with a university course he had taken.

On May 19, 1989, Judge Meyer saw *Titicut Follies* at Zipporah Films in Cambridge. Soon after this screening, a hearing date of June 7 was set for discussion of Wiseman's 1987 motion to open the film to general exhibition. At the Commonwealth's insistence, on May 31 Wiseman's attorney sent each of the men present at the April 11 screening a notice announcing the scheduled hearing and describing what would happen if the motion were allowed. In some respects, the hearing provoked another layer of concern. It was imperative that all the men who appeared in the film and were considered competent know about the hearing so they could have an opportunity to voice their opinions about general exhibition; it was also important for the hearings to be public so that the issue could be debated openly. Assistant Attorney General Stephen Jonas considered the procedure of using initials rather than names of individuals a satisfactory way to "honor the First Amendment" by keeping the procedure "open, but also [to] try to protect these folks." Sikora described both the incompetent and competent men pictured in the film as "fragile" and said that the "seven competent individuals vary in their capacities to withstand a flood of publicity."

Although open to the public, the hearing on June 7, 1989, in Suffolk Superior Court was not listed in the court docket, and few members of the press knew that it had been scheduled. A camera operator from the Boston ABC affiliate, WCVB, videotaped the proceedings, but no flood of publicity surrounded the hearing. One ex-patient, W. W., spoke on his own behalf; a former inmate, M. K., was represented by counsel.[185]

The hearing itself included arguments but no testimony. Blair Perry, whose legal involvement with the case began in 1967, reviewed the legal history of the film and argued on behalf of his client's motion. Perry claimed that the Suffolk Superior Court had the power to modify the injunction. By tradition, an injunction may be or should be modified if, since the original entry, there has been some change in the law or some change in circumstances. Perry argued that both the law and the circumstances had changed since *Titicut Follies* was originally enjoined from general exhibition. Perry pointed to six U. S. Supreme Court cases, four of which had been heard after the original *Titicut Follies* case. Perry submitted that "if the Pentagon Papers case had been decided before *Titicut Follies,* the Supreme Judicial Court would not have ordered any injunction against the exhibition of the film. If it had not, the Supreme Court would surely then have taken a review and reversed on the basis of that case."[186]

As to the circumstances of the case, Perry claimed that many of the inmates pictured in the film were now deceased; that Sikora's report assumed "there would be no harm for those not competent to represent their own interests"; that the Commonwealth no longer relied on any contractual limitations on showing the film, nor did it object to allowing the motion; that Wiseman was now recognized as "the most eminent documentary filmmaker in the United States, perhaps even in the world"; that the film itself was recognized as "as a very important film"; that the film had been given at least partial credit for some of the improvements at Bridgewater. Perry argued that despite improvements to the physical plant at Bridgewater State Hospital, treatment conditions at the hospital continued to be inadequate and that general showings of *Titicut Follies* would serve the public interest by focusing attention on the needs of the facility.

Perry anticipated the objections of the former inmate who was represented by counsel at the hearing by presenting to the court a copy of a release signed by the objecting inmate, designated as M. K., on June 6, 1966 (Ex. 1).[187] Perry entered an additional affidavit by Fred Wiseman, describing the circumstances under which he had filmed the inmate. Perry claimed that M. K. was competent at the time of the filming in 1966 and reminded the court that the guardian *ad litem* had considered M. K. competent when he was interviewed in 1988. Perry argued that not only had M. K. signed a release in 1966, but that "the film has been available to at least substantial segments of the public for twenty-two years more or less," and that M. K. never protested the showing of the film until the spring of 1989. Since M. K. was, at the time of the June 1989 hearing, in prison in another state, "serving a sentence for an offense not unlike that for which he found himself in Bridgewater in 1966," argued Perry, showing *Titicut Follies* would be "nothing beyond the record of the crime for which he now serves."

Perry presented Judge Meyer with a form of order containing the modifications suggested. As designed by Perry, the order would continue to shield the names and addresses of incompetent men and would preserve the right of any of the men in the film to seek damages or other relief at any time after the film was released to the general public.

Stephen Jonas, representing the Commonwealth, took the position that the state no longer opposed the general showing of *Titicut Follies;* however, Jonas emphasized that, in recognizing the "First Amendment interests in a full and fair showing of an important film on an important subject," the state did not presume to speak for the competent men pictured in the film, since it was "legally appropriate" for these men to represent their own interests. Jonas said he was "not sure" that the changes in the law were "as radical as [Perry] would put them, but there are certainly substantial changes in the factual circumstances." Jonas claimed that the state was always interested in balancing First Amendment rights with the right of privacy, but "the balance that was struck twenty years ago in favor of arguing for an injunction over that film has changed." Jonas reviewed the procedures that the Commonwealth had insisted upon, including the appointment of a guardian *ad litem* to represent the interests of the incompetent men pictured in the film. "We did not feel that we could simply step aside and allow the general showing of the film. We felt that more was necessary for us to fulfill that duty. And we think that more has been done."[188]

Objections to allowing the motion to remove restrictions on general exhibition of *Titicut Follies* were presented by Michael Sullivan, a privately retained attorney representing M. K., and by a former patient, who acted as his own counsel.

The man identified as M. K. is clearly seen in *Titicut Follies* discussing with a doctor the charges that had brought him to Bridgewater. Sullivan advised the court that his client had not seen *Titicut Follies,* but that Sullivan had seen it at the WGBH screening. In telephone conversations with his client, Sullivan relayed his observations of the film. Based on his attorney's descriptions, his family's residency in the Boston area, and his own intention to move back to the area, M. K. "strongly objects to the injunction being removed." Sullivan argued that even though the court was taking precautions to shield the names of those pictured in *Titicut Follies,* "many of these people [including his client] will be easily recognizable and will be identified in the film." Sullivan reminded the court that Jonas and Sikora spoke only on behalf of those considered incompetent when they said they had no objections "to the film being released for general public purposes. . . . They have not rendered an opinion as to whether or not irrevocable harm would come to those inmates or patients who are presently competent."

Sullivan had not filed a formal memorandum of opposition to the motion before the hearing. He explained that he had not received notice from Blair Perry until "on or about June the second" and had been engaged in another filing. Meyer granted Sullivan more time—until the end of June—to complete his written memorandum, but the judge was not willing to give Sullivan another opportunity to present an oral argument.

A former patient at Bridgewater State Hospital, W. W., speaking on his own behalf, expressed mixed feelings about the restrictions on *Titicut Follies.* The man, who had been illiterate when first sent to Bridgewater, had earned two master's degrees after his release from the hospital. In the film he is clearly identifiable in several scenes of the rehearsal and performance of "The Titicut Follies." His full name is mentioned in the film by a correction guard and by a nurse, who, he said, had referred to him, without basis, as a schizophrenic.[189] The man said he had refused to sign a form that would have released to Wiseman "our rights to this film, factual or fictional, for two dollars."

Currently employed as a counselor, the former patient claimed that he had "lost many jobs behind this film." He recalled that he had previously objected, without success, to the dean when he learned that *Titicut Follies* was scheduled to be shown to a class in which he was a student at the University of Massachusetts at Boston. He argued that the showing of the film was an embarrassment to his children and a stigma to himself. Although he admitted that he was ambivalent about whether the film should be shown freely and granted that it might have contributed to what he considered great improvements at Bridgewater State Hospital (which he continues to visit as a volunteer), he complained repeatedly that Wiseman had made the film for profit, had become famous because of *Titicut Follies,* and had "walked on me and the others . . . to make that name." He described what he saw as an essentially ethical dilemma: Wiseman "did very good by showing us the ills of that institution, but, by the same token, he still deprived me of my rights, as an object for others to notice about me. And yet still, he will reap the benefits financially."

After the former patient had presented his complaints, Blair Perry added "just a footnote." He said he would have "considerable sympathy with [the ex-patient's] point of view if, in fact, Mr. Wiseman had made a great deal of money from this film." He reminded the court of the substantial costs of litigation and said he was "sure that Mr. Wiseman has not ever recouped his expenses and probably never will." Meyer and Perry agreed that financial gain was not the immediate issue of the case, but Perry succeeded in not allowing the accusation against Wiseman to go without challenge into the record.

During the hearing, Meyer made it clear that he found the public interest argument compelling, and clearly seemed to place documentary film within the general protections granted to speech and writing. He spoke of the treatment of the mentally ill as "a very important subject. . . . Some people will write books about it, some people will make films about it, and some people will teach or lecture about it." Nevertheless, Meyer stated that he did not subscribe to Perry's contention that the film needed to be shown to citizens of the

Commonwealth to provide needed information for the current debate about conditions at the state hospital. From the vantage point of 1989, Meyer considered the value of *Titicut Follies* to stem primarily from its contribution to history. "I think *Titicut Follies* is now about history, more than the present day, and this really has nothing to do with present day conditions, but is historically of interest."

As the June 7, 1989, hearing ended, there was a general sense in the courtroom that Judge Meyer was sympathetic to Wiseman's request that the film be released for general exhibition without any restrictions. All that remained was to wait for the Sullivan brief, due at the end of June, and Meyer's eventual decision. But the dilemmas of the *Titicut Follies* case were not resolved so easily.

Blair Perry had argued that if M. K. had not objected to *Titicut Follies* in the more than twenty years since its first release, he had lost any claim to do so in 1989. Sullivan's brief in opposition to Wiseman's motion, filed on June 29, 1989, began by arguing that the relief Wiseman sought was not being made in a reasonable time. Sullivan then presented a series of claims countering those Wiseman's counsel had presented in the July 1987 motion and the subsequent public hearings on that motion. Sullivan claimed circumstances had not substantially changed: "Since the production of the film and the Order of the Court only two things have changed that affect this film, the public's more general acceptance of nudity and violence in film and the death of some inmates depicted in the film. Certainly privacy rights have not eroded and Wiseman's conduct around the production of the film has not changed."[190] In response to Perry's contention that the law had changed since the SJC rulings of 1969 and 1971, Sullivan challenged the assertion that the U. S. Supreme Court's decision in the Pentagon Papers case was relevant to the Wiseman motion.

As to his client's complicity with the filming, Sullivan claimed that M. K. was not competent when he signed a release in 1966. Sullivan said that M. K. would be irreparably harmed by a general release of the film in 1989. Sullivan's conclusion spoke to the dilemma of *publicly* objecting to an invasion of privacy:

> While it appears only two objections have been raised concerning the release of this film this Court should not assume that other objections under normal circumstances would not be present. M. K. by all accounts, including the opinion of the Guardian Ad Litem, would be harmed by the general showing of the film. Therefore he requests this Honorable Court to deny the Petitioner's request. Absent an outright denial of the

Petitioner's motion then M. K. would request this Court order Petitioner to either remove or conceal M. K. so that his rights continue to be protected before any showing to the general public. Such relief could be made with minimum harm if any to the Petitioner while at the same time insuring that the rights of M. K. are protected.[191]

Sullivan's argument for M. K., and his request that, if the film were to be released, M. K. should be removed from the film or his identity concealed, echoed a line of argument that had first been introduced with respect to this same inmate in the 1967 trial. In 1967, it was the Commonwealth of Massachusetts that had used the case of M. K. as part of its consideration of Wiseman's motives and methods, and that had suggested the possibility of finding a way of concealing his identity. But in the 1989 hearing, Stephen Jonas, the deputy attorney general, did not argue on behalf of M. K., or any other inmate or patient appearing in the film. The Commonwealth's position in 1989 was that the guardian spoke for the incompetent men; the competent men spoke for themselves (or, in the case of M. K., through private counsel); and that the Commonwealth recognized Wiseman's First Amendment rights. Jonas said: "We are no longer in the same place we were twenty years ago. . . . At this point the Commonwealth does not have any objections to the granting of the motion." Jonas's position in 1989 sharply contrasted with the position taken by the Commonwealth at the 1967 trial. To understand the Commonwealth's position in 1989, both in general and as it concerned the case of M. K., consider the following excerpt from the *Commonwealth v. Wiseman* trial (Tr. 14:146-51) in which Edward B. Hanify, co-counsel for the Commonwealth, cross examined Frederick Wiseman about his procedures in filming M. K., his motivations for including certain scenes in *Titicut Follies,* and, by implication, the consequences of those choices on the privacy of the inmate and his family. In the section of the 1967 trial transcript that we quote here, Hanify is cross examining Wiseman; at various points Judge Harry Kalus interjects questions and has side conversations with Wiseman and his attorney, James St. Clair.

Q Now, I direct your attention to an interview between a young man and a doctor which takes place in an early sequence of the film and in which, in the course of the interview, the young man reveals to the doctor that he has violated his own daughter and has been masturbating through the years. Do you recall that scene?

A I recall the scene to which you are referring. I don't accept the characterization of it but—

THE COURT. In what way don't you accept the characterization?

THE WITNESS. I think the man admits to abusing his daughter—I don't remember precisely what he says about masturbation—but I don't think he talks about masturbating through the years. There is a reference to masturbation.

Q Now, when this scene was filmed, did you come in with your tape recorder?

A Yes, sir.

Q And did you have a release in the form that has been admitted in evidence here?

A Yes, sir.

Q And did you give this man the release before the filming started?

A I don't remember whether it was before or after the filming started.

Q It might have been before the filming started?

A It might have been.

Q And did you give the doctor the release before the filming started?

A I don't remember with respect to the doctor.

Q Wasn't it your general practice to have a release there and get the signature on it before the filming started?

A Sometimes it was and sometimes it wasn't.

Q And that may have happened in this case, may it not?

A It may or may not have.

Q Now, what did you tell this man about your purpose in filming this interview?

A I told this young man that we were making a documentary film at Bridgewater, that we would like to take his picture. In fact, we had photographed this young man the night before on his admission to Bridgewater and had spent a considerable amount of time with him when he first came into the institution, which are sequences which are not part of the film but are part of the out-takes.

Q Well, at that time and in those pictures, did you ask permission to film him?

A Yes, sir.

Q But nevertheless, you say you renewed the request prior to the filming of the interview.

A Well, I remember explaining to him in some detail the night before and I remember asking him the morning of the interview that is shown in the film whether it was all right to continue to photograph him, and he said "Sure."

Q Now, what did you tell him the night before?

A I told him in essence what I had told the others, that we were making a documentary film and it might be shown on educational television like Channel 2 but it was going to be a film that would get wide distribution about Bridgewater. And he expressed great interest in the film—

THE COURT. What did he say?

THE WITNESS. He said he was interested in the film, that he had been at Bridgewater before and it was a horrible place, and he said that he hoped he wouldn't get sent to F Ward but he was afraid that he would get sent to F Ward because people were always sent to F Ward when they first came to Bridgewater, no matter what they had done and no matter what their behavior had been.

Q So then you proceeded after that discussion to film him?

A Yes, sir.

Q And you recorded the admissions which he was making to the doctor about his conduct with his daughter and his other sex conduct, did you not?

A Yes, sir.

Q And you told the Court yesterday that you thought the doctor's questions to this man evinced a prurient interest by the doctor, did you not?

A That is correct, sir.

Q Now, when you placed that episode in the film, sir, did you think that it would have an appeal to the prurient interest of certain members of the public?

A No, sir.

Q Did you tell this young man in any form of words that his features would be clearly identifiable in this picture?

A Yes, sir. The man signed a release.

Q Did you tell this young man in any form of words that his features, identifiable in connection with an admission of molesting his own daughter, would be shown in a commercial movie house?

A I didn't put it in those words, sir, but the man knew that his features were going to be shown in the film and he encouraged us to take his picture.

Q And indicated that he was willing to have his own daughter see him making that confession?

A He didn't say anything about that, sir.

Q Was it possible, sir, for you to have depicted whatever condition you wanted to depict in that interview without the man's features clearly identifiable?

MR. ST. CLAIR. I object.

THE COURT. Stenographer, please.

(Last question read.)

THE COURT. From the point of view of the physical and technical, I suppose the answer is yes.

A It was possible physically and technically, yes.

Q And you later photographed him in the nude in his room?

A I think in the film he only appeared—he was in the nude but—

THE COURT. Well, whether later or before, I don't think is of any consequence. Is he depicted in the film in the nude at some time?

THE WITNESS. Yes, he is, from the rear.

THE COURT. A rear view of him?

THE WITNESS. Yes, sir.

THE COURT. Full length?

THE WITNESS. In his cell it is not full length. Well, I am not sure whether it is full length as he was walking down the corridor or not. I don't believe it is but I am not sure.

This passage from the 1967 trial makes it clear that the court was willing to consider, in some detail, ways in which Wiseman might have concealed the identity of inmates shown in the film, and to imply that his failure to do so was an indication of bad faith.

In 1989 former inmates pictured in *Titicut Follies* took three different positions on its possible release to the general public.[192] M. K., through his attorney, was unyielding in his opposition to general exhibition. W. W., who appeared in his own behalf at the June 1989 hearing, and complained that Wiseman had grown famous and made money at the expense of the inmates, was nevertheless ambivalent about whether the film should be released. There was a third response by men who appeared clearly and prominently in the film and were considered competent by the guardian: support for exhibition.

Several key sequences in *Titicut Follies* focus on the futile attempts of a young inmate to be released from Bridgewater and returned to the state prison at Walpole. It was this young man, Vladimir, who sought to be filmed, yet refused to sign a release, perhaps hoping to negotiate his transfer as a condition of signing the filmmakers' consent form. Later, during the trial, according to Wiseman, Vladimir did send his consent in a letter to the producer-director. More than twenty years later, when interviewed by Sikora, Vladimir said that he had never seen *Titicut Follies,* but that he supported its release to the general public and was eager to see it. Vladimir attended the special showing on April 11, 1989, and then reaffirmed his support for unrestricted exhibition.[193]

To many who had followed the *Titicut Follies* case closely, the decision rendered by Judge Andrew Gill Meyer on September 22, 1989, came as a surprise. Meyer had appeared, even as late as the hearings in June, to be prepared to end the two decades of restrictions and half measures that had plagued the film. Instead, Meyer ruled that, for the first time since the Massachusetts courts had issued an injunction against the film more than twenty years before, *Titicut Follies* could be shown to general audiences—but only if the identities of some men pictured in the film were blurred. Twenty years after the compromise decision of the Massachusetts Supreme Judicial Court to allow *Titicut Follies* to be shown, with a disclaimer, but only to specialized audiences, superior court judge Andrew Meyer ordered another compromise when he decided that the film could be shown, but only with alterations, to general audiences. The SJC had directed Wiseman to make one alteration to *Titicut Follies* as a condition for showing it to specially qualified audiences: "In view of the lapse of time since the film was made, the modified decree should fairly require including in the film, for all permitted showings, a brief explanation that changes and improvements have taken place in the institution since 1966."[194] The court's requirement that Wiseman add this "explanation," which has nothing to do with protecting the privacy of the inmates and patients, and everything to do with protecting the reputation of the Department of Correction and the Commonwealth of Massachusetts, has for two decades added support to Wiseman's charges about the real motives of the Commonwealth in its actions against the film.[195]

Meyer anticipated the attention his decision might engender. In a tone more teacherly than argumentative, he wrote, "Because of the serious issues raised by the plaintiff and the public interest in the court's ruling on the Motion to Amend Final Decree After Rescript, a rather detailed analysis of the court's reasoning in support of its order is warranted."[196]

Meyer accepted—as was his obligation—the facts of the case as described by fellow superior court judge Harry Kalus in Kalus's 1968 opinion. Thus, Meyer characterized the permission Wiseman received to film as "conditioned upon [Gavin's and Gaughan's] viewing the film and approving it before its release. Wiseman agreed to those conditions." Meyer recalled that Kalus was outraged by the film, and that Justice Cutter, speaking for the SJC, and Justice Harlan, of the U.S. Supreme Court, both considered *Titicut Follies* an invasion of the privacy of the inmates filmed. Meyer also recalled the praise many had expressed for the film's power. His own reactions embraced that duality of response:

I have viewed the film and agree that it is a substantial and significant intrusion into the privacy of the inmates in the film. However, I also regarded *Titicut Follies* as an outstanding film, artistically and thoughtfully edited (some 80,000 feet of film reduced to 3,200 feet and requiring 84 minutes running time), with great social and historical value. . . .

Another observation about the film: it is true.[197] It accurately depicts the conditions of Bridgewater in 1966.

Meyer then considered the plaintiff's argument that changed circumstances should permit a public showing of *Titicut Follies*. Because of a "careful and painstaking investigation" by the guardian *ad litem*, the court knew that of approximately sixty-two inmates pictured in the film, twenty-eight had died. Twenty men were located. Seven of those men were considered competent by the guardian. Meyer quoted from Wiseman's 1987 affidavit in which the filmmaker stated that, in almost twenty years of showing the film to specialized audiences, he had never received any complaint from any inmate shown in the film or from family or friends of those pictured in the film. But during the consideration of Wiseman's motion some former inmates did register concerns with the court. The judge wrote, "As of today, several competent former inmates favor the showing of the film and several oppose the showing." Meyer elaborated on some of the objections. In addition to M. K., who had been represented by counsel at the June 1989 hearing, W. W., who had appeared on his own behalf at that hearing, was characterized by Meyer as unambivalent, and as one who "strongly opposes public showings because, he says, they would harm him and his children." The judge noted that he had received a phone message from another former inmate "who strongly objects to the film being shown publicly" and he stated that two other inmates, "both apparently competent, are concerned about public showing."

In his advisory report to the judge, Mitchell Sikora had reviewed the case of each of the ten incompetent men and in every case advised that he found no grounds for opposition to general exhibition of *Titicut Follies*. But in his decision, the judge, instead of citing the guardian's recommendations regarding each of the ten incompetent men, as individuals, quoted from Sikora's concluding, general recommendation that the incompetent men should receive continuing shelter from publicity about the film:

A number of them exhibited painful feelings and memories about their times at Bridgewater. They were reluctant to be reminded about it and sometimes became emotionally upset or despondent as a result of our discussion. Upon that observation, I recommend that their anonymity be carefully perserved and that they not suffer any intrusion from publicity which may accompany the present litigation phase or from any ultimate decision.

In his motion before the court, Wiseman had argued that both changed circumstances and changes in the law warranted a dismissal of restrictions on the public exhibition of *Titicut Follies*. In the motion and at the hearings on that motion, Wiseman's counsel, Blair Perry, cited a number of cases heard since 1971 in which the Supreme Court had been sympathetic to First Amendment arguments. Judge Andrew Meyer acknowledged that the First Amendment and Article 16 of the Massachusetts Declaration of Rights "guarantee the public's right to know matters of public concern. Any system of prior restraints on expression bears a heavy presumption against its constitutional validity." Still, he considered the claimed precedent in cases like *Smith v. Daily Mail Publishing Co.* and *Cox Broadcasting v. Cohn* not entirely applicable:

> In contrast to these two cases, the present case involves information obtained by a special agreement with the Bridgewater authorities. We are not talking about information in the public domain or ordinarily available to the media. Frederick Wiseman had no fundamental right to go to Bridgewater and film inmates. He did so only with permission of the authorities and that right was qualified. Judge Cutter stated that "[Wiseman] violated the permission given to him, reasonably interpreted, and did not comply with valid conditions . . . that he obtain written releases."[198]
>
> Furthermore, Bridgewater is more than a hospital or treatment center; it is also a prison managed by the Department of Correction. In fact, in many respects it is more of a prison than a hospital.[199] Its prison characteristics raise another interesting point not yet discussed: the right set forth in Article VIII of the United States Constitution and in Article 26 of the Massachusetts Declaration of Rights which assure protection from "cruel and unusual punishment."
>
> I find no free speech or freedom of the press case which warrants completely vacating the restrictions imposed in 1971.

Meyer saw the greatest changes in the relevant legal standards since 1971 not in the right of freedom of the press but in the right to privacy: "Since *Wiseman* the Massachusetts legislature has enacted several laws pertaining to a patient's privacy. . . . If anything, the commitment of Massachusetts' courts to the individual's right to privacy, since 1971, has been strengthened not weakened."

> Permitting uncensored viewing of this film would, in effect, be granting permission to any cameraman admitted to a public institution under agreed-upon conditions, to ignore such conditions, break his promises, film any patient undergoing medical or psychiatric treatment without the

patient's consent and then show the film for profit anywhere, anytime and justify all such acts on the basis of an overriding public interest in the matter. . . . I doubt very much that the citizens of Massachusetts wish to allow film makers to enter their hospital rooms at any time, film patients in any situation, and then exhibit the film in public movie theaters throughout the nation. . . . Does a prison superintendent have the right to say to a film maker, "Feel free to go into my prison and film the inmates in their most intimate moments?" I believe our Supreme Judicial Court, at least implicitly, has wisely said no to this question.

Releases signed by incompetents are meaningless and the consent of an official to invade the privacy of his charges, without a compelling state interest, is meaningless. Our government officials, instead of invading an individual's privacy, must protect it.

Meyer claimed to champion the right of the free press as well as the right of privacy, arguing that the best way to support both of those rights was through compromise:

When the unqualified exercise of a fundamental right by one individual results in destroying a fundamental right of another, a compromise solution is desirable. After much reflection, I conclude that in this case both rights can be protected. Since "Titicut Follies" requires the balancing of the constitutional right of privacy against the freedom to publish, I believe some precautionary measures, short of total prior restraint, will still protect the inmates' privacy. The solution is an order requiring the blurring of faces of those shown in the film, still alive, and either incompetent or competent and objecting.

Those who have died will not complain. Privacy is personal and ends with death.[200]

Those who are living and incompetent must be protected under the doctrine of "parens patriae," as stated by Judge Cutter.[201]

Those who are living, competent and objecting must be protected by the privacy doctrine. It is especially important to protect this group since many are reintegrated into society and leading happy and productive lives. They must not be punished twice by having their identities revealed and their faces shown in films exhibited in every neighborhood theater throughout the nation.

The blurring of a few faces may affront the artistic standards of the film maker but if he is sincere in his stated goal of bringing about changes in conditions at M.C.I. Bridgewater,[202] such an objection is trivial in view of the difficulty of resolving the conflict between the right of privacy and the social benefit ensuing from the public showing of the film.

I suggest the following resolution: the film may be shown provided that the faces are blurred of those individuals (1) who have refused to give their consent (2) who are incompetent to give their consent or (3) who cannot be located. . . .

By this compromise, Wiseman's First Amendment right is left substantially intact, as is the privacy of those portrayed in the film. Any right to artistic freedom which may be impinged upon by this order is far outweighed by these inmates' right to privacy while in embarrassing and degrading situations. The public's right to be informed of issues of public concern, such as the conditions at a state mental hospital, is protected as well. Bridgewater is fully exposed; only the faces of unconsenting inmates are concealed.

Judge Andrew Meyer's 1989 decision in the case of *Titicut Follies* was surprising because, during the hearings, he had appeared sympathetic both to Wiseman's general First Amendment claims and to the state's abandonment of its objections to the film. Why did Wiseman's motion to remove all restrictions from the exhibition of *Titicut Follies* fail?

Not for lack of expert counsel on Wiseman's behalf. Blair Perry was both professionally skilled and personally committed to the case. Perry began his law career by earning the highest score on the Massachusetts bar exam in 1957. At the time Wiseman's motion was under consideration Perry was recognized by his peers as one of the most outstanding attorneys in the nation. At Hale and Dorr, the second largest and arguably the most prestigious law firm in Boston, Perry became a senior partner in 1968. He was popular and admired, especially among young attorneys in the firm who looked to him for guidance in trial law.[203] Perry shared with Wiseman a wry sense of humor, a love of baseball—in 1987, Perry's business card was a mock Boston Red Sox baseball card—and a long-standing friendship. They had met as undergraduates at Williams College, where Perry's father was a professor. Both Perry and Wiseman graduated from Williams in 1951; both then entered law school—Perry to Harvard, Wiseman to Yale. Perry was James St. Clair's assistant when *Commonwealth v. Wiseman* went to trial in 1967. Perry continued as Wiseman's counsel thereafter, representing his friend not only in the continuing *Titicut Follies* litigation, but also handling all legal matters for Wiseman's distribution company, Zipporah Films.

The motion did not fail because Meyer was personally outraged by the film, as fellow superior court judge Harry Kalus had been. Meyer not only recognized Wiseman's strong First Amendment right, but also expressed his admiration for the worth of *Titicut Follies* as a social document in the public hearings and in his final, written decision. Andrew Meyer's family life and education resembled Fred

Wiseman's more than Harry Kalus's. Andrew Gill Meyer was born in a Boston suburb in 1923; his father was an investment counsel, his mother a housewife. Meyer earned a bachelor's degree in government from Harvard, a master's in American history from Columbia, and a law degree from Harvard. He had taught at Girard College and served in both the army and the navy before he applied to the Massachusetts bar.[204] Meyer worked as a trial attorney, then served as a district special justice for two years. Known for his integrity, intelligence, and fair-mindedness, Meyer was appointed an associate justice of the superior court by a conservative Democrat, Governor Edward King, in the summer of 1979.[205] On August 27, 1987, in an early hearing in response to Wiseman's motion, Wiseman's counsel, Blair Perry, requested that Meyer continue as presiding judge on the case, under the condition that Meyer himself agreed and that representatives of the attorney general's office supported the request, which they did.

The motion did not fail because of continued opposition to exhibition by the Commonwealth. Neither the office of the attorney general nor administrators at Bridgewater State Hospital opposed the general showing of *Titicut Follies* in 1989. After Meyer's decision, Stephen Jonas said that the office of the attorney general supported the withdrawal of restrictions on exhibition: "We feel that 20 years after the fact that the First Amendment issues weigh heavily in the balance" over privacy issues.[206]

The motion did not fail because the guardian *ad litem,* speaking on behalf of the incompetent men, objected to the general release of the film. Mitchell Sikora's report could be used to argue for or against the general exhibition of *Titicut Follies.* In his consideration of the incompetent men one by one, Sikora said he found no justification to oppose general exhibition of the film. In the conclusion of his report, Sikora stressed the vulnerability of the men to publicity, but there was nothing in the conclusion that directly opposed the general exhibition of *Titicut Follies.* However, in his individual evaluations of the competent men, Mitchell Sikora reported that some of the competent men indicated in their interviews with him that they had objections to the general release of the film. Meyer praised the thoroughness and the carefulness of Sikora's report in the formal hearing of June 7, 1989, yet, from the outset, Meyer had been clear that the guardian's report was advisory only. Meyer chose not to follow Sikora's advice regarding the presumed effect of general exhibition of the film on each of the incompetent men who appeared in the film. Instead,

Meyer concentrated on Sikora's caution regarding potential *publicity* surrounding the showing of the film, to support continued restrictions on exhibition of *Titicut Follies*.

The motion did not fail because there would be no legal recourse for men who claimed privacy invasion if the film were shown without restriction. In the June 7, 1989, hearing, Blair Perry suggested to Judge Meyer, both orally and in writing, a procedure by which individuals could file for personal damages resulting from exhibition of the film.

Meyer had little reason to think that Wiseman would compromise on the blurring of identities. It is difficult to know how much Meyer understood the technical or financial complications of following his order to blur some faces in the film, but there were clear indications that Meyer was aware of Wiseman's unwillingness to alter *Titicut Follies* to accommodate privacy interests. In public hearings on Wiseman's motion on August 27 and September 3, 1987, the possibility of obscuring faces was mentioned.[207] On September 3 Perry said that he knew his "client would not agree" to an expurgated version of the film. Meyer responded: "It looks like all or nothing."

Thus, Judge Andrew Gill Meyer must have considered the privacy argument legally and ethically compelling, so compelling that he ordered a compromise that, in its probable effect, was not a new compromise so much as a continuation of the status quo regarding the restricted exhibition of *Titicut Follies*.[208]

The compromise that Judge Meyer "suggested" in the fall of 1989 was a new solution to the dilemma of competing rights in the *Titicut Follies* case, but only in the sense that Meyer was the first judge to order such a compromise as a condition of exhibition. The suggestion of blurring identities was made, according to Elliot Richardson, before the film's first public showing in 1967 and it was offered as a solution by various parties once litigation began. In direct examination during the *Commonwealth v. Wiseman* trial, Elliot Richardson recalled the June 27, 1966, screening of *Titicut Follies*. The attorney general claimed he raised the issue of privacy that night and mentioned reservations he had regarding exhibition of the film: "This led to a discussion of the kinds of editorial revisions that might be made in the film, in order to avoid these problems, that is, the matter of obscuring the identity of individuals, the obscuring of parts of the person which would raise problems of decency or obscenity for communication standards" (Tr. 12:114).[209]

In the CLUM *amicus* brief filed before the SJC in the spring of 1969, blotting out identities was a suggested compromise to the dilemma that faced the court: "To the extent that the inmates are shown in a degrading fashion, respondents should be given an opportunity to eliminate the offensive scenes by blotting out the personality and identity of the actors."[210] The following spring, in a comment on recent cases, the *Harvard Law Review* criticized the SJC compromise that allowed only an elite audience access to the film. Instead, the *Harvard Law Review* argued, it would be better to let everyone see the film, "covering the identities of prisoners unwilling to be so exhibited."[211] A *Columbia Law Review* piece, published in the same period, argued *against* blurring, on the grounds that "a blacked-out face, or a figure filmed from behind allows the viewer a sense of detachment, or unreality, which lessens the outrage."[212]

Years later, shortly after Wiseman filed his 1987 motion, the desirability of such a compromise was "debated," in an extremely abbreviated form, on a *Nightline* episode devoted to *Titicut Follies*.[213] A first "exchange of opinion" was presented in a pair of taped interviews edited to simulate a debate between former Assistant Attorney General George Caner and Frederick Wiseman. Caner was shown saying, "The state suggested, before the thing erupted into litigation, that Wiseman might block out the faces of the individuals involved—there could be a black spot that obliterated the features—and the state would have been willing to have allowed the film to be shown on that basis, if the people were not identifiable." Wiseman, in supposed response to Caner, but more clearly in response to an ABC question, was then pictured covering his face and remarking, "How would this interview look if I talked to you like that? Would you be interested in broadcasting that?" Later in the broadcast, during a "live-by-satellite" interview section, Ted Koppel asked Wiseman, "Why can you not understand that the state of Massachusetts would be concerned about the privacy not only of the individuals that you showed but also members of their family, and why could you not take them up on their offer to say, 'Go ahead and show the film, as long as you not include segments in which the faces of the individuals being mistreated are recognizable?'" Wiseman, in Montreal, responded, "Well, I think it's impossible to show—make any film in which you can't see people's faces, just as you wouldn't have much of a broadcast tonight unless you see the faces of the participants. So when I make a documentary movie, I think people's character, their emotions, their feelings are registered in their faces." In this exchange with Koppel, Wiseman seemed to accept the presumption that an "offer" of general exhibition in exchange for blurring identities had been made at some time by the state and that it was an offer he had refused.[214]

Since their invention, still photography and motion picture film-making have been considered instruments of revelation. The history of photographic images as visual evidence is a long and complicated one. That history also includes social traditions, professional conventions, and technical procedures that have blocked "revelation" by purposefully obscuring parts of mechanically reproduced images. The reasons for making parts of images unclear are numerous, and include motives such as artistic experimentation, but the most abiding reasons connect with notions of public decency and propriety and personal privacy and security. Social attitudes and legal constraints against the public display of nudity had film processors blocking out not just faces, but also body parts, of participants in stag movies. The privacy of victims of violence and the safety of individuals serving as police or news informants have encouraged print and electronic journalists to block a face, or electronically scramble an image in newspaper and television investigative reports. There has also been a tradition of blurring identities in educational films prepared for the training of physicians and psychologists. An earlier practice of filming actual interviews of patients (often filmed from the back or with their faces obscured) in films produced for future clinicians has in some instances been replaced by a procedure in which professional actors impersonate patients suffering from mental illnesses, with the hope that the manifestations of the various illnesses can still be displayed, as can appropriate interview procedures by an actual psychiatrist or psychologist, while protecting the privacy of individuals. Litigation involving privacy rights has played a part in these decisions by publishers and producers to temper full disclosure.

A variety of technical procedures make it possible to obscure parts of a filmed image after its orginal photographic processing. Most of these techniques require expensive technology and are labor-intensive, thus making them extremely costly; all of them are visually damaging, which, in one sense, is the point of the process. If Wiseman were to follow Meyer's order, several processes might be used. The least expensive would be to have the film transferred to video, and then electronically scramble the images that need to be blurred. This is a relatively simple and inexpensive procedure, but it would be made much more expensive in practice because someone familiar with the identity of every man in every frame of the film would have to advise the editor shot by shot throughout the entire film. The transfer to video (and back to film) would visually degrade all of the images in the film, even those not obsured. The most sophisticated process for obscuring images on 16mm film is called rotoscoping. Mattes would be made for each frame in which some part of the image had to be obscured. In a sound motion picture, such as *Titicut Follies,* there are 24 frames per second of projection time. Each frame of the film that was to be altered would have to be blown up to 35mm film. A lab technician would have to put each frame (assuming that the images to be obscured are constantly moving, which is possible, but not probable) into an animation stand, project it down, locate the area needing masking, draw that outline on a piece of paper that has been pre-punched, cut out the black representation of the area to matte out, and then assemble all of these in sequence. Then each matte is put on the animation stand and photographed on 35mm film. The original film and the film containing the mattes are then combined to create a composite print. Then the 35mm composite is reduced once more to a 16mm print. If 35 minutes of the 89-minute film had some parts that had to be obscured, that would necessitate 50,000 drawings, at a cost of approximately $600,000 in a union lab using 1989 prices.[215] This final price is an extremely rough estimate, but it indicates how infeasible the procedure would probably be, on financial grounds alone, for an independent filmmaker like Fred Wiseman. Although Meyer expressed his concern about *Titicut Follies* being exhibited in neighborhood theatres throughout the nation, it is unlikely that the film, if unrestricted, would be screened in many commercial theatres. Beyond a possible PBS broadcast, the film would probably continue to follow its exhibition profile of twenty years: mostly screenings in various educational environments. In 1989 Zipporah films booked *Titicut Follies,* usually at a rental fee of $150 per screening, for approximately 105 screenings. Assuming that rental prices and demand for the film remained constant, and not allowing any funds for replacement prints, office maintenance, interest, or other overhead, all predictable and quite considerable costs, Wiseman would have to rent *Titicut Follies* for forty years to pay the hypothetical $600,000 lab bill for blurring faces.

Beyond economics are questions about whether following such an order would actually accomplish its stated intention. Do the various devices used to blur identities "work?" And behind that question is a prior assumption. Meyer's order implied that the identities of the men were fully, or at least sufficiently, protected at the time of his 1989 decision. Is that so? Had the modified decree of 1971 protected the identities of the men for twenty years? A core irony in such situations is that once privacy becomes an issue considered by the courts, the possibility of complete anonymity is destroyed. During the *Commonwealth v. Wiseman* trial great pains were taken to disguise the identities of the men pictured in the film. All references to inmates and patients were by number, not name or initials, in the trial. Exhibit 17, which fully identified the men for the use of the court, was impounded by Judge Kalus. Yet papers filed by the Commonwealth on May 10, 1968, as part of its brief for the SJC appeal (and thus part of the public record) listed the last names of the inmates and patients pictured and described their activities in the film.[216]

In the "Dialogue of *Titicut Follies*" compiled in transcript form by Wiseman's company and distributed on request for some years to scholars researching Wiseman's films, inmates and patients are identified by name in two ways: as part of the transcription of the words heard on the sound track of the film itself and as identification of the speaker in "script" format. Names are usually first names in both forms, but last names are also present in both forms and, in a few rare instances, a full name is transcribed from the sound track.[217]

In his September 1989 ruling Meyer approved the release of the Sikora report in which men are identified by initials, and in which, by necessity, their current living conditions are quite fully described (although addresses are never given). Hence, the detailed report of the guardian, a mechanism created to help Meyer arrive at his opinion, could work against anonymity, in that an energetic and curious person could use it to help identify the former inmates. Similarly, the heightened attention to who is pictured where and whether the man has been located, deemed competent, and given consent could contribute to making anonymity less possible than it might have been otherwise. Even the restricted viewing conditions in effect since 1967 had not protected all men pictured in the film from recognition. In his report the guardian recalled that several men had mentioned to him that they had been recognized when friends of theirs had seen *Titicut Follies* under the conditions of the modified decree; in the June 1989 hearing a man pictured in the film complained that his daughter experienced such a recognition. There are a variety of ways in which the identity of the men shown in *Titicut Follies* could fairly easily be established. As the judicial system continues to consider ways to protect the privacy of the former inmates, its own processes inevitably create further leakages in the vessel of privacy.

Meyer issued a deliberative opinion, in the sense that it not only judged a past set of events but that it also predicted and attempted to bring about an effect. It is a decision that establishes a policy. Policy decisions, usually in the realm of the legislative sphere, are typically subject to evaluation as to their effects. But in Meyer's order, as in most judicial orders, there was no mechanism provided to monitor the effect and no provision for change if the solution proved ineffective. It is hard to see how an evaluative scheme could have been built into this sort of decision, since the directive Meyer issued in his attempt to protect the privacy of the objecting, the incompetent, and the unlocated men, if followed, could be evaluated only if it failed. A successful protection of privacy is presumably invisible, and therefore in a fundamental sense not capable of being periodically proved. The effect of the decision on the First Amendment rights of the filmmaker and the public's right to know is even harder to measure.

Immediately after Meyer's decision was announced, there was a flurry of interest in the New England press about the decision, but that interest was short-lived. Early headlines in print and on radio and television broadcasts in New England on September 29, 1989, were misleading: an AP story in the *Springfield Union News* read "Judge Lifts Ban on *Titicut Follies*"; the *Boston Herald* headline claimed "*Titicut* Ban Lifted after 22 Years"; the *Boston Globe* ran the headline "Court Eases 22-year Ban on *Titicut Follies*"; a *New London Day* story carried the headline, "22-year Documentary Ban Lifted"; radio and television broadcasts also announced a "lifted ban." On September 30 the *New York Times* ran a story on the film under a somewhat tentative headline, "Judge Proposes Compromise on Banned Film." The *Times* story, a special report from Boston, dated September 29, included information on Wiseman's unwillingness to blur identities as a condition of general release and his plans to appeal, plans that were relayed in the Boston press accounts of September 30.

Within the Boston civil liberties community, reactions to the decision were mixed. Some saw in Meyer's responsiveness to the objections of M. K. and others an ethically admirable example of support for the privacy rights of the most powerless and a correct legal reading of the state privacy statute. Inmate/patient advocate Roderick

MacLeish praised the decision: "It's a reasonable balance between the patients' privacy and the public's right to know." Apparently assuming that Wiseman would accept the compromise situation, MacLeish said, "I just wish it had happened when the film was made because there might have been more public outrage about what was going on at the facility." Alan Dershowitz strongly criticized Meyer's ruling: "This is just preposterous. The fact that the nation's most liberal state is the only state in the history of the United States ever to censor a non-obscene film continues to be a shame on the commonwealth. I hope myself that Fred Wiseman does not blur out the faces. This is not a film about faceless people. If they think they're protecting the rights of the mentally ill, they're wrong."[218]

Wiseman told the *Boston Herald* that he refused to blur faces in *Titicut Follies:* "It would make the film meaningless. I know of no way that faces can be blurred out. Even if that were technically possible, I wouldn't do it, because it would totally destroy the film. . . . I appreciate the judge's thoughtful decision. It is not one that I agree with, and I intend to appeal it."[219] In an interview reported in the *New York Times,* Wiseman said, "The whole point is that these are not faceless people. Their faces reflect the lives they've lived and how they've been treated." In the same interview, Wiseman reached back to an argument he had often used in the past twenty years: "The state has a conflict of interest. It asserts that it wants to protect the inmates' privacy rights, but it really doesn't want the public to know how these people are treated."[220] But in 1989 the Commonwealth of Massachusetts, through the office of the attorney general, no longer objected to the general release of *Titicut Follies.* The series of hearings in response to Wiseman's 1987 motion and the 1989 Meyer decision left Wiseman with far less rhetorical space for his well rehearsed outrage against the Commonwealth and its motives.

In the months after Meyer's 1989 decision, Wiseman's attorney planned to file a motion asking Meyer to reconsider his order.[221] Any appeal Wiseman might make would probably have to rest on his First Amendment claims as an artist and public advocate, and upon the public's right to know. In over twenty years of litigation Wiseman had never constructed a purely art-for-art's-sake argument, but perhaps some variant of that argument would be appropriate and necessary in response to the Meyer decision. In Wiseman's interviews with the press immediately following the decison he seemed to be claiming that blurring would make a substantial and damaging difference in the rhetorical power of *Titicut Follies*. If an appeal were filed and heard on the Meyer decision, that appeal might claim that the right of freedom of expression includes the ability to make an argument on one's own terms. CLUM President Harvey A. Silvergate seemed to anticipate that sort of argument on behalf of Wiseman as artist when he wrote, "Judge Meyer has not really allowed the film to be shown publicly, because to insist that the artist modify the work is not an order allowing the film to be shown, at least not in the form in which the artist completed it."[222]

Hence, the case of *Titicut Follies,* which has made a special contribution to the history of informed consent, once again challenges the definition of informed consent. At the time of the filming, informed consent was typically prior consent, in the sense that at least tacit consent was assumed before filming began. Even when formal consent was obtained immediately or shortly after the filming took place it was granted before the subject had an opportunity to view the completed film and assess its effect on himself. It is for just this reason that scholars have questioned whether prior consent can ever be informed consent. In 1966, the inmates and patients and their guardians at Bridgewater were asked to consent to a film in prospect; in 1989 they were asked to consent to a film with a complicated past, a famous director, and an uncertain future. Apart from the issue of consent, and whatever the views and interests of the immediate parties to the case, the judge's decision will inevitably affect not only their interests but also the interests of the community, and the scope and protection of the First Amendment.

Chapter 5

The Contradiction of
Restricted Exhibition

Despite Wiseman's efforts, as of this writing, the exhibition status of *Titicut Follies* has remained fixed since 1969. Hence, Wiseman, as a filmmaker and a businessman, is confronted with the problematic situation of simultaneously marketing his film, of following the restrictions of the modified decree, and of preparing himself for a possible Supreme Court review or further litigation in the Massachusetts courts. The Commonwealth, on the other hand, is caught in the awkward position of enforcing a ban that can function as a promotional device.

Before its exhibition was legally restricted, *Titicut Follies* was shown at several film festivals and had a brief run in commercial theaters, which is unusual for a documentary film. After the Kalus decision of January 1968, Grove did not book *Titicut Follies* in any commercial theaters. In the May 1968 trial of the respondents, Grove Press, Inc., and Titicut Follies Distributing Company., Inc., the Commonwealth objected to screenings of *Titicut Follies* at the Florence Festivale dei Popoli and at St. Elizabeth's Hospital in Washington, D.C., and charged the New York companies with contempt. Grove was, therefore, aware that the Commonwealth was carefully monitoring distribution of *Titicut Follies*. Judge Kalus found no evidence to support the contempt charge. He refused to accept newspaper articles describing the exhibition of the film as evidence of contempt, since one could not infer admission had been charged based on the articles. The judge also refused to reevaluate the film's merits after it won two prizes at the Italian film festival. Kalus said the prizes "may be very interesting as a commentary on our times and on those who make literary judgments as to artistic value, but I doubt whether it has any relevancy" (Tr. 18:37).

In June 1969, after the Massachusetts Supreme Judicial Court modified the Kalus decree to permit exhibition of the film to selected professional audiences, Grove marketed *Titicut Follies* on the non-theatrical university film society–museum–classroom circuit as a winner of several international awards. Speaking several months after Grove's distribution contract with Wiseman and BFC expired on December 31, 1976, the director of the film division for Grove Press said that Grove had initiated a voluntary policy of limited distribution nationally "to insulate Wiseman, a Massachusetts resident, in the on-going case against the film's exhibition in Massachusetts."[1] During the nearly ten years when Grove held exclusive distribution rights to *Titicut Follies,* the company sold approximately 110–120 prints of the documentary. University libraries, medical schools, law schools, and teaching hospitals were the typical buyers, frequently following a pattern of renting the film several times, then deciding to purchase it, since the rental fee was $100 and the purchase price went from $500 in 1968 to $600–700 in 1976.[2] Although Grove did not file records with the clerk of the Suffolk County Court regarding all screenings—as Wiseman did and does—the film seems to have been generally, if not exclusively, exhibited to the professional groups named in the modified decree during the period when Grove held the distribution rights.

After Films, Inc., bought the distribution rights to most of the titles in the Grove film collection in the mid-seventies, Grove expended little effort in marketing its remaining film holdings, which included *Titicut Follies.* Wiseman has been blunt about his dissatisfaction with Grove in numerous interviews. "You never get accurate reporting, you never get any money and all that sort of stuff." His solution: "Because I've been screwed so badly in distribution, I set up my own distribution company, Zipporah Films."[3]

In a 1974 interview, Wiseman said that "the conditions under which I can show the *Follies* [in Massachusetts] are so restrictive that I have not shown the film rather than comply with the terms of the restraining order."[4] The terms of the SJC restraining order have changed only once since the modified decree of 1969; that change was the result of an appeal filed by Wiseman's attorney the year he founded his own distribution company. On November 5, 1971, Blair Perry argued before the SJC that provisions regarding restricted exhibition were unnecessarily burdensome for the defendants. Within a week, the SJC bench decided that, at the option of the defendants, the provisions could be modified, but only in the following respects:

> (a) notices of future showings of the film (to categories of persons permitted to see it) may be combined in a single advance notice covering the next succeeding thirty days; (b) notices of such showings in Massachusetts need be filed only three days in advance of such showings, respectively, in instances where longer notice is impracticable; and (c) reports of showings, after the event, may be made by filing a written report . . . during the first seven days of each calendar month, covering showings during the next preceding calendar month.[5]

The terms of the restraining order did not change between 1971 and 1977. But first distribution control, then exhibition patterns, did change. Wiseman began to show *Titicut Follies* in Massachusetts.

When Zipporah Films began distributing *Titicut Follies* as of January 1, 1977, the company instituted a comprehensive reporting system for all screenings of the documentary nationwide. Since 1977, prospective exhibitors of *Titicut Follies* have received some close variation of the following instructions:

> By order of the Supreme Judicial Court of Massachusetts, TITICUT FOLLIES may be shown only to legislators, judges, lawyers, sociologists, social workers, doctors, psychiatrists, students in these or related fields, and organizations dealing with the social problems of custodial care and mental infirmity.
>
> TWO statements regarding the screening of TITICUT FOLLIES must be completed in full, signed and returned as specified.
>
> The first statement must be completed and received in Boston along with the rental agreement form at least *12 business days* prior to your scheduled screening date. No prints will be shipped before the statement has been received. Please check the appropriate categories; no additional categories may be added.
>
> The second statement, which confirms your intended screening of the film, will be enclosed in the film case and must be completed and returned *immediately* following your screening. It must arrive in Boston no later than *five days* following the screening.
>
> Prints of TITICUT FOLLIES are available on both a rental and long term lease to anyone who wishes to show the film in compliance with the Final Decree of the Supreme Judicial Court.
>
> Should you have any questions concerning the procedure please do not hesitate to contact us.[6]

The first statement is a declaration of intent to screen *Titicut Follies* to an audience composed only of people who meet the qualifications as defined in the final decree; the second statement is an acknowledgment that the documentary was seen only by persons meeting the court specifications. For Massachusetts screenings only, Wiseman's company requires that the exhibitor demand that each audience member sign an individual statement claiming membership in at least one of the designated categories.[7] The exhibitor is admonished to collect these affidavits before the film begins, deny admittance to anyone who does not sign such a form, and return all signed statements with the print of *Titicut Follies* to the Zipporah office immediately following the screening. In this way, Wiseman and his company meet the personal knowledge stipulation of the decree, since Wiseman is legally responsible for verifying that each person who sees the film is a member of one of the allowed groups.

Zipporah files a statement of intent for each scheduled screening and then either a statement of cancellation or, far more often, a statement that *Titicut Follies* was shown as described. All statements are filed with the clerk of the Suffolk Superior Court in Boston; copies are sent to the attorney general's office. Audience member affidavits are not required by the decree and remain in Wiseman's possession. Although Wiseman himself has signed some of the statements, especially for the foreign screenings in the 1974–77 period and for showings at his studio, most statements bear the signature of "an authorized person claiming through him," that is, a Zipporah staff member. Since 1977, the authorized person has changed—Jennifer Ettling, Iris Berry, Gayle Taylor (then Gayle Taylor-Sutton), Ann Kahn, Karen Konicek, Eleanor Elizabeth Mettent—but the tedious clerical routine has not. Each statement also contains a notice to the clerk of the court that requests that the form be returned to the Zipporah office if it is not accepted for filing.

Those filed statements leave a paper trail marking where, when, and to whom *Titicut Follies* has been exhibited since January of 1977. The trail indicates that a 1968 prediction that "soon *Titicut Follies* will be of interest only to movie buffs, organizers of film festivals, and . . . social historians and anthropologists" underestimated the long-term interest in the film.[8] According to the filed statements, students and working professionals in sociology, law, medicine, and social work most frequently compose the audience for the film, but the actual breadth of the audience is not ascertainable, especially when the film is screened, as it is infrequently, for general audiences.

The first year that Zipporah distributed the film was the most active in rental exhibition in the 1977–87 period, with approximately 160 rental screenings nationwide in 1977; 1978 followed in rental volume, with only a slightly lower number of bookings. Reductions in rental totals may disguise actual increases in screenings, since regular exhibitors will often lease a print after several rentals. Rental activity in Massachusetts has been far greater than in other states.

Before 1977, *Titicut Follies* had been screened in the Commonwealth only to select groups and individuals. After 1977, the groups broadened, but continue to comprise a viewing elite, following the lines drawn by the Supreme Judicial Court of Massachusetts. The SJC stipulation on audience composition institutionalized the exhibition of the film; members of groups, rather than individuals, see *Titicut Follies* in Massachusetts, since the film is booked almost exclusively in institutional viewing situations. An individual involved in arranging one of the first Boston screenings, at the University of Massachusetts-Boston in the spring of 1977, described a "sense of paranoia around the showing," with Zipporah Films anxious to have the *Titicut Follies* print returned to the distributor's office by taxi immediately after the screening.[9] Such nervousness has diminished as Boston screenings in academic environments have become increasingly common, but careful monitoring continues.

The first screening of *Titicut Follies* in Amherst, Massachusetts, was sponsored by the law program at Hampshire College on April 5, 1977. When delivered, a print of *Titicut Follies* includes, among other exhibition directions, the notification that the scheduled screening cannot be advertised in any way. If an exhibitor planned to advertise, the message is somewhat late in arriving. The Hampshire showing was perhaps not advertised, but certainly it was announced publicly, among other places, in the *Five-College Calendar,* a monthly publication available to the Amherst, Hampshire, Mt. Holyoke, Smith, and University of Massachusetts-Amherst communities. The announcement indicated that the screening was free and would be followed by a panel discussion of mental-health and law experts.[10] There was no indication of any audience restrictions. At the screening, audience members were asked to sign individual affidavits before the film began in a manner that resembled a request for signatures on a petition. An individual could easily have neglected to sign an affidavit without being recognized or refused admission.

A flier posted in various locations on the University of Massachu-setts-Amherst campus announced a free showing of *Titicut Follies* on May 6, 1982, at the Hampden Student Center, Southwest Residential College. The flier included a long excerpt from Robert Coles's lauda-tory description of the documentary, labeled the film as "banned in Massachusetts," and cautioned audience members that each would have to sign a statement acknowledging membership in one of the allowed categories in order to see the film. The dormitory showing was cosponsored by the Hampden Board of Governors and the Human Services Program as part of the prison film series, and was attended largely by students enrolled in a one-credit colloquium in criminal justice. Two student moderators, both exconvicts, distrib-uted and collected affidavits from all audience members, but no attempt was made to verify the status of those who sought admission and no one was turned away. One of the student moderators, Jerry Sousa, who had been confined at Bridgewater on two occasions, led a discussion following the film. He was not at Bridgewater when *Titicut Follies* was made, but claimed he spoke for the men pictured in the documentary when he advocated exhibition in the cause of reform. He knew some of the men in the film and discussed their lives with no hesitation. A graduate student in anthropology in 1982, Sousa had recently won a settlement against Walpole, Massachu-setts, prison guards who had brutalized him; he planned to partici-pate in a maltreatment case to be filed against Bridgewater guards.[11]

Others in the prison studies program at the University of Massa-chusetts-Amherst have also been regular users of *Titicut Follies*. In any other state, such regular use would encourage an institution to have its own copy of *Titicut Follies*. For copyright protection, Wise-man retains property rights for the documentary; therefore, an organ-ization or individual actually leases a print, rather than purchases it, although for practical purposes the lease is equivalent to purchase. The Zipporah lease contract, however, stipulates that the film must be exhibited "in its entirety without the addition or deletion of any matter" and that it may be exhibited "only upon premises owned or controlled by the exhibitor." Grove had offered a life-of-print sale and did not attempt to control use of prints. In the late 1970s at Zippo-rah, a lease was for five years or the life of the print, whichever came first. At the end of five years, the print was recalled or the long-term lease was renegotiated. The change in terminology between the Grove and Zipporah offices is more than a semantic technicality; it is indicative of a general difference in attitude toward control of *Titicut Follies* and other Wiseman films. Since 1983, life-of-the-print contracts are available only to institutions unable to lease for the five-year period. Prices are somewhat higher than lease contracts for such arrangements. Renewals of leases for additional five-year periods are available at 50 percent of current lease prices. Replacement prints are available at a 10 percent discount of current lease prices. Zipporah has obviously discovered that Wiseman's documentaries have regular users over decades.

In 1967, Grove sold copies of *Titicut Follies* for $500. In 1977, the price of a leased print from Zipporah was $900; in 1989, $1,200. The rental cost for high schools or charity/civic/church organizations has remained at $100, while the college/corporation/government agency rental fee has increased from $125 to $150. Videotape lease copies of *Titicut Follies* ($900) became available (outside of Massachusetts) for the first time in 1983 but as of April, 1984, only one tape of *Titicut Follies* had been leased.[12] Pirated videotapes have been a problem for Wiseman, as well as for others, for years; this is one of several reasons he demands an immediate return of a print after its rental screening(s).[13] However, what is unique to *Titicut Follies* is that a pirated tape presents problems beyond lost revenue: Wiseman loses control over the exhibition situation and audience composition, for which he is responsible. Screenings of pirated tapes are thus illegal in several senses of the word. Since access to video recorders is increasing, it is not suprising that Zipporah does not offer rentals in video format.

Of course, the most common source for unauthorized videotaping is not from a rental tape, but off-broadcast. *Titicut Follies* and *High School* are the only Wiseman documentaries that have not been aired nationally on NET-PBS, although the Public Broadcasting Laboratory "almost ran [*Titicut Follies*] as its first show." On 25 August 1987, ABC-TV broadcast a special "Nightline" report on *Titicut Follies* and the conditions at Bridgewater State Hospital. Included in the program were clips from what host Ted Koppel called a "bootleg print" of *Titicut Follies*. Wiseman, one of several people interviewed on the show, objected to this use of *Titicut Follies*.[14]

Wiseman is faced with the dilemma of expediting the procedures for reaching the allowed audience for *Titicut Follies* in direct and efficient ways so that his business will operate smoothly and profitably, yet also arguing that the terms of the edict are unduly complicated at best and unconstitutional at worst. Wiseman is thus trying to reach an audience as large as possible and as often as possible in Massachusetts, while simultaneously claiming that the Massachusetts public is being denied its constitutional right to see the Bridgewater documentary. The air has never completely cleared of the early charge of commercialism; Wiseman must continually protect himself from that charge, even though he is operating a business.

For Zipporah Films to remain solvent and retain exclusive distribution control of the Wiseman films, it is necessary to market the documentaries aggressively. Independence has its price. The annual Zipporah brochure is an example of stylish promotion—the graphic design is handsome; the excerpts from critical reviews are impressive; the directions for ordering the films are clear. Additional materials such as reprints and film reviews, brochures, and still photographs are available to exhibitors from the Zipporah office on request. For *Titicut Follies* exhibitors, these materials are considered informational rather than promotional. Among the reprints of *Titicut Follies* reviews that are issued by Zipporah are Robert Coles's lengthy piece from *The New Republic,* Richard Schickel's *Life* review, the *Newsweek* article about the controversy surrounding the film, and a description of the ban written by Harvey Cox and published in *Playboy.* The Zipporah brochure contains no editorial description of the content of *Titicut Follies,* as it does with all other Wiseman films. It suggests *Titicut Follies* as a possible selection for courses in health, medicine, psychology, social work, legal studies, philosophy and, with all other Wiseman titles, in cinema studies and sociology-anthropology. The filmmaker himself is marketed as well: "Mr. Wiseman is available for lectures and workshops. Requests for guest appearances should be made well in advance."[15]

After its New York screenings in the fall of 1967, Grove Press did not book *Titicut Follies* in commercial theaters. There were some public showings with admission charges in states outside of Massachusetts while Grove held the distribution rights to the documentary, but these were usually film society showcases on university campuses. Zipporah brochures announce that all Wiseman films are for nontheatrical use only, yet rates for screenings where there is an admission charge are listed: one hundred and fifty dollars or 50 percent of the gross box office receipts, whichever is greater. What seems to be a contradiction is actually an accommodation for film society and art house exhibition.

Very soon after Wiseman took distributive control of *Titicut Follies,* he made arrangements for a public showing in a commercial Massachusetts theater. After contacting several theater owners, Wiseman scheduled the first public Massachusetts showing of the restricted film at the Pleasant Street Theater in Northampton.[16] The small (135 seat) theater had just opened under new ownership in the college town the previous November, but it already was establishing a reputation for innovative programming of American revival films, contemporary European features, and various types of alternative cinema. Owned by two former professors with extensive film society experience, the Pleasant Street Theater had a sophisticated ambiance, a liberal clientele, and a 16mm projector. Like the rest of western Massachusetts, the provincial art theater and its operations were of no interest to the Boston press and public.

In what co-owner John Morrison described as "leisurely four-walling," Zipporah and Pleasant Street agreed on a rental price of $75 for each of four showings on February 14 and 15, 1977, as long as there were more than forty people in the audience. There were far more than forty people in each audience; several screenings could not accommodate all those who wished to purchase tickets at the special events price of $3, an amount dictated by the Zipporah office. Three Zipporah staff members were present at all showings; they taped the introductory message about the required affidavit signatures each time it was delivered. Affidavits were collected from all audience members at each screening. The exhibition of *Titicut Follies* had been advertised by fliers and in newspapers, which mentioned the special premiere status of the engagement and also the audience restrictions.

The following week, another set of fliers and advertisements announced that *Titicut Follies* was "back by popular demand," a typical promotional phrase, but either a mistaken or a subversive description for a *Titicut Follies* audience.[17] For the February 21–22 engagement, Zipporah charged the Pleasant Street Theater $100 a show; however, the crowds at the theater were not nearly as large as they had been the previous week. No showing had an audience demand that could not be met in the tiny theater; only four of the five showings had more than forty patrons. There were no complaints about the showings registered with the management, nor did any complaints about the screenings or the audience restrictions appear in the local press. The affidavits seemed a silly technicality not worth protesting in a community known for its civil rights protests.

Even after these benign public showings, Zipporah Films did not book *Titicut Follies* as part of Wiseman retrospectives in the Boston-Cambridge area during 1977. Institute of Contemporary Art curator Michael Leja wished to include *Titicut Follies* in the museum retrospective in the fall of 1977, but was told by Wiseman that the filmmaker-distributor was not yet ready to test the court order with a public showing.[18] Similarly, the Bridgewater documentary was excluded from a Wiseman retrospective at the Orson Welles Cinema in Cambridge that same fall.

The Boston public showing test came in May of 1980 when *Titicut Follies* played at a large public theater during "Boston 350," a citywide birthday celebration organized by a deputy mayor of Boston, Katherine Kane. As part of the Boston 350 festivities, the Sack theater chain, the Boston Museum of Fine Arts (MFA), and the city of Boston jointly sponsored screenings of films written, produced, directed, or starring current or former Boston residents. For a thirty-five-cent admission charge, Boston moviegoers could see films of Boston's own and be treated to guest appearances of the local celebrities. The suggestion to include *Titicut Follies,* if Wiseman agreed, came out of a group discussion of the festival organizers from the mayor's office, the Sack theaters, and the MFA.[19] May 12 was designated as "Fred Wiseman Day" and as early as May 7, Boston newspapers announced that *Hospital, High School,* and *Titicut Follies* would be screened as part of the month-long Jubilee 350 Film Festival at the Saxon Theater.[20] Located in the heart of the theater district in downtown Boston, the Saxon originally was a site for stage plays; it operated as a cinema for only several years. On May 8, a Boston film critic, after garbling the documentary's legal history, wrote that the inclusion of *Titicut Follies* in the Jubilee 350 was possible because "it falls under one of the many exceptions that allow the film to be shown for 'educational purposes.' It's the film in the festival that any serious film-goer shouldn't miss."[21] That same day, another Boston paper reported that a spokesman for the attorney general's office said he was unaware of the planned showing of *Titicut Follies* and had no comment. In the same article, Wiseman was quoted as saying, "People will have to decide for themselves whether they're in the categories allowed to see the film. But they will be told if they are not, they are not allowed to see the film."[22] By May 9, the two planned Boston screenings of *Titicut Follies* were described in an Associated Press story as "under terms supposedly allowed by the Court."[23]

Advertisements for the screenings in the Boston papers carried the disclaimer, "Shown under terms of restraining order."[24]

Two weeks before the May 12 play dates, Sack submitted the required statement announcing plans for two screenings of *Titicut Follies* to the clerk of the court and the attorney general's office, but the statement of intent apparently had gone unnoticed until members of the Boston press brought the screenings to the attention of the attorney general's office. On Friday afternoon, May 9, Assistant Attorney General Anthony P. Sager of the Civil Rights Division filed an affidavit in which, among other statements, he recounted a telephone conversation with Alan Friedberg, president of Sack Theaters, earlier that same day that confirmed the scheduled showings of *Titicut Follies* at the Sack's Saxon Theater. Friedberg had told Sager that a notice regarding the viewing restrictions would be placed in the box office and that, before each showing, the theater manager would announce that anyone in the theater who was not a member of one of the listed categories would be asked to "leave the theater so as to satisfy the requirement of the Court."[25] Sager also stated that, based upon information received from Superintendent Gaughan, he believed the inmates who appeared in *Titicut Follies* had been released to the community or transferred to civil facilities.

Assistant Attorney General Robert H. Bolin, Jr., moved for an injunction against the showing of *Titicut Follies* at the Saxon Theater. The Commonwealth's motion for supplemental relief implicitly questioned the general audience's motives for seeing the film and its ability to effect change. "The scheduled showings of 'Titicut Follies' in the Boston Film Festival do not primarily serve the purpose of informing an audience of professional persons with a serious interest in the rehabilitation of mentally ill persons and with the potential capacity to ameliorate the conditions and treatment of mentally ill persons in institutions."[26] That same day, May 9, U.S. District Judge Rya W. Zobel denied the motion for injunctive relief.

Three hours before the afternoon showing of *Titicut Follies* on May 12, the Civil Rights Division of the attorney general's office hand delivered copies of a sternly worded letter to Zipporah Films and the Sack Theaters executive office, suggesting that the Saxon management get full identification from each person attending the showings of *Titicut Follies* at 3:00 and 8:00 P. M. that day. Although the Saxon ignored the suggestion, anyone who did not sign an affidavit was denied entrance. A private police guard was stationed outside the theater for this purpose. A representative from the attorney general's office, attempting to enter the theater without signing an affidavit, was not admitted. A *Boston Globe* reporter interviewed six patrons before the matinee screening, all of whom had signed the document, but none of whom belonged to the professions listed on the form.[27] Six people admittedly comprise a very small sample, but one gets a scent of audience autonomy. According to a spokesperson for Wiseman, "technically, [anyone who signed the affidavit under false pretenses] could also be hauled into court for violating the edict."[28] But no action was taken by the attorney general's office against theater patrons. The court order regarding specialized audiences seemed a paper tiger to the Boston audience. Here, as in other showings of *Titicut Follies,* the force of the court order has been diluted.

In sharp contrast to the press furor regarding the exhibition of the film in the fall of 1967, the Boston press commented little about the public showings of *Titicut Follies* in May of 1980. Two days after the screenings, the film seemed to have been forgotten. There were no printed letters to the editors of Boston newspapers criticizing or praising the screenings.

On May 22, 1977, Assistant Attorney General Sager filed a request for the production of documents concerning the composition of the audience to which *Titicut Follies* was shown: "(a) on May 12, 1980, at 219 Tremont St., Boston, Mass.; (b) on April 10, 1980, at Twentieth Century Fox, Beverly Hills, California; (c) on April 6, 1980, at Facets Multimedia, Chicago, Illinois; (d) on April 14, 1980, at Columbus Branch Library, Tucson, Arizona; (e) on February 4, 1980, at 3657 Springfield Road, Indianapolis, Indiana; (f) on December 16, 1979, at Panorama Studios, Vancouver, B.C."[29] Wiseman was also requested to produce "all documents pertaining (a) to the showing(s) of 'Titicut Follies' from December 27, 1971, to the present at any commercial establishment, public accommodation, or other place to which the public usually may gain admission (such as a movie theater, public library, or public auditorium) or (b) to the nature of the audience at any showing(s) at such places."[30] The attorney general's office had, surprisingly, missed the Pleasant Street Theater screenings in its review of the exhibition statements, but its request for production of documents would have revealed these showings, if followed. It was not. The Commonwealth's motion for a hearing as to this request before the superior court department of the trial court was denied; but the request itself served as a reminder of the continuingly rigid position of the attorney general's office toward the exhibition of *Titicut Follies.*

There were no additional public screenings of *Titicut Follies* in Massachusetts between May 1980 and April 1987. A Wiseman retrospective sponsored by the Institute of Contemporary Art and held at the Coolidge Corner Theater in Cambridge in the fall of 1982 omitted *Titicut Follies* from the series. The guest curator of the retrospective, Ned Rifkin, made a special note of this omission and the court-ordered reasons for it in the series program notes.[31] On May 4, 1987, the John W. McCormack Institute of Public Affairs and the College of Public and Community Services at the University of Massachusetts-Boston cosponsored *"Titicut Follies* Twenty Years Later" at the JFK Library. The free program consisted of the screening of *Titicut Follies* (simultaneously in two auditoria, with the audiences divided into one auditorium for those with invitations and another for the general public, all of whom were required to sign the usual affidavit), light refreshments, and a public forum moderated by Charles Nesson of Harvard Law School. Panelists (all of whom received a framed poster announcing the event) included June S. Binney (supervising attorney at Bridgewater State Hospital), John W. Briggs, Jr. (associate commissioner and general counsel, Department of Correction), George C. Caner, Jr., Judi Chamberlin (chairwoman, National Committee on Patients' Rights), Alan Dershowitz, Blair Perry, Wesley Profit (forensic director, Bridgewater State Hospital), Harvey Silvergate, Howard Simons (former managing editor of the *Washington Post* and curator of the Nieman Foundation, Harvard University), and Frederick Wiseman.[32] During the panel discussion, Wiseman estimated that between 150,000 and 200,000 people had seen *Titicut Follies.*

In March 1988 *Titicut Follies* was shown for the first time at Bridgewater State Hospital. Superintendent Gerard Boyle, himself a former correction officer, approved the showings of the film to the hospital staff. Charles Gaughan remained bitter about *Titicut Follies* until the end of his life and never allowed the film to be shown at the facility while he was superintendent.[33] After serving as superintendent of MCI-Bridgewater for twenty-six years, Gaughan retired in the spring of 1985.[34]

In June 1989, Bridgewater State Hospital hosted the first annual conference on "The Study of Violence: A Clinical and Forensic Perspective." As part of that national, two-day conference for mental health and criminal justice professionals, *Titicut Follies* and the WCVB-TV series "Inside Bridgewater" were screened for conference participants on the night of June 2. On June 3, Frederick Wiseman returned to Bridgewater for the first time in twenty-three years. Wiseman had been invited to join WCVB-TV producer Neil Ungerleider, Department of Correction attorney June S. Binney, and Superintendent Boyle on the last conference panel. Charles Gaughan had been invited to participate in the panel and had indicated his willingness to attend. According to Wesley Profit, the planning committee had an expectation of "this rousing kind of panel discussion" between the producer-directors and the two superintendents. But Gaughan became ill, died on May 25, and was buried the day before the conference.[35] Gaughan was replaced on the panel by Deputy Superintendent Charles Correia, who had been an officer at Bridgewater when *Titicut Follies* was made and had sometimes escorted Wiseman and his crew. The audience of approximately three hundred included some retired nurses who had been at the hospital when Wiseman and Marshall filmed there, and also the parent of a patient. One of the retired nurses announced that, to her surprise, *Titicut Follies* was "not a bad film." Some audience members complained that more of "the good things" done by volunteers had not been included in Wiseman's film; others disapproved of the behavior of the clinical and medical staff pictured in the film. The privacy issue was discussed at length, but when Wesley Profit took a poll, asking if *Titicut Follies* "should have been banned" in 1967, 90 percent of the audience said no. The same strong majority felt that *Titicut Follies* should not "be banned" in 1989.[36]

After Judge Andrew Meyer's September 1989 decision, which required Wiseman to blur the identities of some men pictured in *Titicut Follies* as a condition for the film's general release (a condition that Wiseman immediately and unequivocally refused and planned to appeal), *Titicut Follies* continued to be screened for members of the professional groups allowed to see the film.

In a state bulging with law schools, medical schools, colleges, and universities, people in Massachusetts could probably see *Titicut Follies* more easily than most other documentaries made in 1967. There have been no published complaints in recent years from Massachusetts residents "unqualified" to see the documentary and unwilling to lie about their professional status on affidavits, yet demanding a right to see the Bridgewater documentary. The continuing struggle over exhibition freedom on Wiseman's part seems to be far more an issue of constitutional principle than a matter of actual audience denial.

As long as the conditions of the restraining order remain in effect, there will be a paper stream between the secretaries at Zipporah Films and those at the office of the clerk of the Suffolk Superior Court. At the courthouse, the roles of the Commonwealth as plaintiff, judge, and keeper of the records all merge. In that temple of red tape, the file for *Commonwealth v. Wiseman* is just one more pile of papers, left on the floor and stuck into a corner because it is too cumbersome to be shelved with the other files. In true civil-servant style, the woman assigned to the record keeping does not file equity docket no. 87538 with the equity cases that have been disposed. Those dockets are filed one floor up from her desk and she must enter statements into the no. 87538 docket on a routine basis. Yet, since it is stamped "disposed," the *Titicut Follies* docket is not allowed in the pending files in the area where she works. Dilemma seems too grand a term for what a file clerk is to do with a case that was legally closed in 1971, but remains obviously open to the routine additions that are her responsibility. Entries in the *Titicut Follies* docket exceed 3000.[37] The statements will keep rolling in as long as the court order remains and Wiseman exhibits the film. There is no place for such an anomaly as the closed, yet open, *Titicut Follies* docket in the institutional maze, but the government worker assigned to administering the case clerically has found a way to ignore the rules and make her job more reasonable. In a gesture right out of a Wiseman film, this woman has found a place for the *Commonwealth v. Wiseman* docket: in the middle drawer of her own desk, next to a change of shoes and an umbrella.

Chapter 6

Dilemmas of Documentary Construction and Use

Titicut Follies has much to teach about the dilemmas of documentary construction and use. Dilemmas of negotiation immediately confront a filmmaker who proposes a potentially controversial documentary project: how does one convince people to consent to participate in a film, to sponsor its production, to work on its crew, to support it financially without using guile, misrepresentation, or coercion when risk is not only possible, but probable? The dilemma of consent is partly practical (how to get it), but essentially ethical (how to get it fairly and then not abuse it). Without the participation of social actors, the documentary form known as direct or observational cinema could not exist. Without the informed consent of the subjects, the form lacks ethical integrity; without freedom for the filmmaker, it lacks artistic integrity. The dilemmas of documentary construction are both procedural and artistic. The mix of the two creates its own dilemma: Wiseman could not have made any documentary film about Bridgewater without the active participation of others; he could not have made *Titicut Follies* without independence. Thus, Wiseman relied upon cooperation while filming; he demanded independence while editing. He expected the impossible. In turn, subjects and audiences often expect the impossible from his work. Reviewing the steps of the constructive process and the eventual use of *Titicut Follies* reveals not just its dilemmas, but the dilemmas that shape the documentary enterprise.

To film a Bridgewater documentary, Wiseman had to get permission from others before he could approach the individuals who would be social actors on screen to obtain their consent. Even in this most bureaucratic of settings, the supposed state rule for institutional consent procedures (head of institution–department head–governor's office) was not followed. Governor John Volpe's office was unaware of the project's existence. This violation of protocol made the film susceptible to criticism.

Another chain of consent particular to this case, but quite possibly common in its variance from the orthodoxy of official procedures, was substituted. Lieutenant Governor Elliot Richardson's and Representative Katherine Kane's intercessions changed the permission structure, yet the chain in use retained hierarchical features. Bridgewater was not a closed system, an important consideration when identifying the subject of the film and reactions to it. Wiseman later disclaimed any political motivations in making the documentary, yet he was willing to use the influence of friends who held elective office in order to gain permission to film. It is arguable whether a film about a publicly supported institution can ever be apolitical, whatever its maker's stated or unstated intentions. Thus, both in the narrow sense of partisan politics and in the larger sense of political philosophy, those who had assisted Wiseman were identified with and held accountable for the final product.

The exact, final terms that were being consented *to* by both the state and the filmmaker were vague. It is difficult to imagine a filmmaker with the fierce independence Wiseman later displayed ever consenting to state censorship as an initial and continuing condition of filming. It is also difficult to imagine a state official like Commissioner John Gavin not expecting final state control. It is equally surprising that a sophisticated politician and experienced lawyer like Attorney General Edward Brooke would not anticipate Superintendent Charles Gaughan's position as a man caught in the middle and, therefore, suggest the legal protection of a written contract. Certainly Wiseman, himself an attorney, understood the legal importance of a written contract, but its absence also had advantages for him. Nowhere in writing was there any claim by Wiseman of the rights of the press or the public's right to know; nowhere in writing was there any claim by the state to a right of censorship. In their delay in clearly asserting what were later claimed as rights, both Wiseman and the Commonwealth of Massachusetts positioned themselves for an inevitable confrontation.

The consent pattern had both vertical and horizontal dimensions. Every link in the consent chain was a potential breaking point, but also a point of obligation. Individuals could say no—as the filmmak-ers claimed—but they were expected to say yes. Often the individu-als filmed said nothing. Silence was considered consent. Staff mem-bers had been directed by their superiors to cooperate with the filming. Although privacy and consent are usually discussed as indi-vidual matters, they have social as well as personal dimensions.

Many social activists advocate protection in inverse relationship to power; many documentary film projects work the other way around.[1] John Galliher thinks that some of the controls on research to protect human subjects "limit both research and consequent criticism of offi-cials."[2] He argues against the protection of superordinate subjects when "studying up" and cites Wiseman's "muck-raking" films as suc-cessful attempts at learning about the powerful.[3] Wiseman does not see protection, selective or otherwise, as his obligation or his privi-lege. Just the reverse, he puts the responsibility and—in Wiseman's view of the world, an equally important word—the *choice* of protec-tion or disclosure on his subjects and their guardians.

Since some of the subjects to be photographed were wards of the state in a prison mental hospital, both freedom to consent and mental competence, on which legal competence rests, became highly proble-matic. In court, the Commonwealth cast doubt on the competency of some of the subjects in the film. Wiseman's defense took the position that the filmmakers assumed *all* subjects were competent unless spe-cifically informed otherwise by the superintendent and his staff at the time of shooting.

In all his subsequent documentary films, Wiseman's consent proce-dures have remained stable, with two crucial modifications, both of which provide Wiseman legal protection and were prompted by the litigation surrounding *Titicut Follies*. After initial conversations with administrators, Wiseman summarizes his plans in a letter in which he mentions why he wants to make the film, the filming procedures, the types of events that might be filmed (indicating that these exam-ples are merely suggestive), and the duration of filming and editing. He explicitly states his claim of complete editorial control over the completed film. The persons (or person) in charge of this initial per-mission decision sign(s) Wiseman's letter, thus indicating consent to the filming agreements in this contract of sorts.

On the advice of his lawyers, Wiseman has not obtained written releases since *Titicut Follies*. Before or, more frequently, just after shooting a sequence, Wiseman audiotapes his explanation that he is making a film for public television that will be widely seen by the general public and may be shown theatrically. He explains that he will not use all the film he shoots and offers to answer any questions. If an individual consents, Wiseman asks for a full name, address, and phone number. Thus, he has a contemporaneous record of subject assent.[4] The procedure of consent before, during, or immediately after the act of filming creates a situation of trust in the filmmaker's judgment, rather than a situation of truly informed consent. Subjects who say yes to the film in a camera sometimes say no to the film screened. Ideally, consent is processural, not contractual.[5] But the process of making meaning of filmic images continues into the viewing situation and beyond. It is a never-ending process; neither subjects nor filmmaker can ever fully anticipate audience response.[6] Subjects cannot anticipate their own reactions to the responses of others.[7] Even Calvin Pryluck, an outspoken critic of many direct cinema procedures, admits that "obviously a filmmaker's commitment to a subject cannot be open-ended."[8] But collaborative editing may merely diffuse, rather than solve, the ethical dilemma of informed consent.

There are ways of constructing documentaries that incorporate the consent of crew members, subjects, sponsors, and financial backers into the editing process for reasons that range from democratic idealism to artistic indecision. Fred Wiseman did not work that way with *Titicut Follies,* or with any of his later films. He thoroughly rejects collaborationist cinema when he constructs his personal "reality fictions." If we consider Wiseman's entire career, editorial autonomy may be seen as a central feature of a pattern of independence that has remained consistent.

Titicut Follies set Fred Wiseman on the path to distinction as a documentary filmmaker. Did it help or hurt the inmates at Bridgewater? Charles Gaughan thought *Titicut Follies* had negative effects on plans for the new hospital at Bridgewater (which did open in December 1974). He remembered the film project with bitterness:

> I can only reiterate that, instead of being of help, he [Wiseman] was responsible for our almost complete loss of the whole venture. Many months preceding the bringing out of his film, we had had a media campaign initiated by the Mass. Medical and the Mass. Bar Associations. We also had had the escape of Albert De Salvo and a series of other front page events. These basically enabled us to tell our story and secure the cooperation of the Legislature and the Governor's office. Wiseman's lame and highly peculiar method of breaching the problem was initially considered as a violation of faith in the professional organizations involved. However,

as a result of the series of court hearings and their legal criticism of Mr. Wiseman, the work initiated by others, went forward.[9]

Speaking at the time of the legislative hearing, Dr. William Chasen of the Massachusetts Medical Society also thought "if anything [*Titicut Follies* has] hurt our cause."[10] When the governor's special commission filed a comprehensive Bridgewater reform report on the eve of the New York commercial showing of *Titicut Follies,* Volpe claimed that he did not know about the film until after he had appointed a commission to develop a construction program for Bridgewater.

Looking back on events years later, many people familiar with MCI-Bridgewater, the Departments of Correction and Mental Health, and Commonwealth operations think *Titicut Follies* played a small, but positive, role in improvements at Bridgewater. A Correction Department official has said it is hard to conclude that the film itself is an agent of change, but it did publicize the issue of forgotten people.[11] The legal counsel to the psychiatric staff at McLean Hospital sees *Titicut Follies* as part of a chain of events that led to improved conditions.[12] A psychiatrist with the Mental Health Department speculates that the legal action in right-to-treatment cases had more effect on changes than the documentary.[13] Shortly after the documentary was released, approximately three hundred men were transferred from Bridgewater when the superior court sat on the grounds for months and conducted hearings.[14] In December 1974 the new Bridgewater State Hospital opened. Its completion was expected to coincide with major improvements in treatment, but some critics claimed that the changes at the institution in the mid-seventies and later were more apparent than real.[15] Nevertheless, most agree that vast improvements have been made since Charles Gaughan first became superintendent of MCI-Bridgewater. When Gerard Boyle became superintendent of Bridgewater State Hospital in July 1987, he insisted that all men confined to the hospital be referred to and treated as "patients," even those transferred from maximum security prisons. He transferred and even dismissed correction officers who resisted his emphasis on treatment.[16] In addition to the new hospital facility, changes since the completion of *Titicut Follies* include a reduction in population from approximately eight hundred to around four hundred men, the negotiation of medical personnel contracts with various medical groups, and considerable improvements in the size and training of the professional staff of psychiatrists, clinical psychologists, social workers, and mental health workers.[17]

Wesley Profit, director of forensic services at Bridgewater, describes *Titicut Follies* as a "two-by-four" in getting the attention of the state legislature in the 1960s, but at the same time stresses the continuing struggle to hold that attention in the 1980s and beyond, and to translate it into support for competent and humane psychiatric treatment for the most violent and most disturbed men in the Commonwealth.

Fred Wiseman, who is often asked in interviews and public question-and-answer sessions about improvements effected by the film, gives some variation on this answer: "I no longer have the view that I had in the beginning that there might be some direct relationship between what I was able to show in these films and the achievement of social change. . . . I guess I've gone very far away from the liberal cliches and bromides that I started with, especially the simpleminded social work view of help and intervention."[18] He speaks of change working in oblique, subterranean ways and labels as presumptuous the claims of others that the new hospital at Bridgewater was a direct result of *Titicut Follies*.[19] Nevertheless, in the affidavit accompanying Wiseman's 1987 motion to release the film to general exhibition, a motion filed amidst news reports of recent violent deaths of inmates at Bridgewater, he claimed:

> One of my primary reasons for making the film "Titicut Follies" was to try to bring about improvements in the way in which inmates of M.C.I., Bridgewater, were treated, by showing conditions at M.C.I., Bridgewater, to members of the public. I have been told that as a result of the making of the film, and the public interest which was engendered by the initial public exhibition of the film, conditions at M.C.I., Bridgewater, were improved significantly for a period of time (in that additional staff members were hired, new buildings were built, and some inmates who had been held at the M.C.I. for many years were released from the institution). I have no personal firsthand knowledge that this is true, but of course I am pleased that the film has been credited with bringing about various improvements in conditions at the institution. . . .
>
> . . . I believe that showing of the film "Titicut Follies" to members of the general public at this time would help to arouse public concern about the conditions at M.C.I., Bridgewater, and thus would help to bring about changes in conditions there and lessen the probability of additional deaths of the types described above or other injuries to inmates there.[20]

James F. Gilligan, a psychiatrist who later became treatment director at Bridgewater and then consultant to the new treatment program there thinks *Titicut Follies* changed the moral climate, so that a group of lawyers started a class action suit and the courts then ordered the state to build a new facility and provide better treatment. Gilligan argues that the controversy surrounding *Titicut Follies,* despite the pain it brought the central participants, also was of good use to them. "Ironically, for all the *sturm und drang,* I think the controversy helped Wiseman. I think Wiseman's film helped Bridgewater, and yet neither party could see this [so great were their feelings of betrayal]."[21]

Those feelings of betrayal surface again and again in Wiseman interviews. "The lesson of *Titicut Follies* for me was cowardice, and the biggest coward of all was Elliot Richardson."[22] In Wiseman's office, an old newspaper photo of Richardson being sworn in as ambassador to England by Gerald Ford hangs above the toilet.[23] Richardson does not mention *Titicut Follies* in a book-length political memoir that examines the difficult political choices of his life.[24] Katherine Kane "really [does] not remember much about it, since it was so long ago."[25] It was a long time ago, yet Wiseman and Marshall still do not speak to each other. Marshall is proud of his work on *Titicut Follies* and recalls the experience of working with Wiseman with fondness.[26] Yet he is also critical of Wiseman's work, claiming that, especially in the early films, the sequences are not rich enough, people and situations not followed closely enough, to permit audiences to draw inferences.[27] Eames remembers the filming of *Titicut Follies:* "Working alongside Fred when he is shooting is a singular experience, perhaps like being invited to ride with Santa in his sleigh on Christmas Eve. A lot of hard work is required; the hours kept are odd and long; the trip is likely to take you places you never expected to be, involve encounters you never imagined with people you otherwise wouldn't believe; you may count on plenty of mishaps and screw-ups and moments of high farce. I never had so much fun."[28]

The uses of *Titicut Follies* will continue to grow—a coffee house in Berkeley and a hotel on Martha's Vineyard have been named after the film—but mostly it will be used for the educational purposes originally intended by Wiseman and Gaughan. The reasons for constructing and using documentaries are various; they are tied to complex motives both personal and social and are ultimately unknowable. Projects begin in a mood of cooperation that sometimes diminishes as choices are made and disappointments accumulate. The Bridgewater film project began without easy cooperation, without full disclosure of goals and consequences, among individuals and institutions that held different, even contradictory, values and sensibilities.

Some of the problems *Titicut Follies* faced, and faces, were particular to the film itself, but many were related to the general social and political climate of the times and to tensions at the heart of all realist art. The litigation concerning the documentary has allowed us to overhear a debate among participants about expectations, intentions, procedures, and disappointments that goes on privately in many documentary projects. The litigation has forced the courts to consider a cluster of relationships among filmmakers, subjects, and audiences, and to strike a balance among competing constitutional rights. Those who care about documentary film need to attend to and participate in the debate on these issues.

The history of *Titicut Follies* reveals a substantial gap between the ideal of informed consent and the practice of direct cinema. Would the general good have been better served had *Titicut Follies* not been made? We think not. We believe the general good would be better served if *Titicut Follies* could be shown without restriction. Alone, Wiseman's first film is a work of considerable social and artistic value; as part of his ongoing documentary series, *Titicut Follies* is of even greater worth. The struggle for control of this film tells us much about documentary film and its social context. We are fortunate that Wiseman's experience with *Titicut Follies* did not extinguish his desire or his ability to explore other American institutions. Sometimes comically, but more often sadly, the history of *Titicut Follies* fulfills a central promise of Frederick Wiseman's original Bridgewater film proposal: "To portray that we are all more simply human than otherwise."[29]

Appendix: Chronology of
Titicut Follies
Notes
Bibliography
Index

Chronology of *Titicut Follies*

1 February 1959	Charles Gaughan becomes superintendent of Massachusetts Correctional Institution at Bridgewater.
Spring	Frederick Wiseman, law instructor at Boston University, teaches a summer seminar in legal medicine and takes his class on a tour of MCI-Bridgewater.
10 May 1965	Wiseman visits Gaughan at Bridgewater. Gaughan supports the idea of a documentary film.
18 June	Wiseman screens *The Cool World,* a fiction film he produced in 1964, for Gaughan and James Canavan, public relations director for the Department of Correction.
8 July	Wiseman writes to Gaughan requesting permission to film, enclosing a proposal for the Bridgewater film.
11 August	Gaughan, Wiseman, and Commissioner of Correction John Gavin meet in Gavin's office to discuss Wiseman's proposed film. (Gavin later testified that at this meeting the right of the state to approval of the finished film was discussed as a condition. Wiseman testified that there was no such discussion at the meeting.)
19 August	Wiseman writes to Gavin requesting permission to film, enclosing a five-page description of the project.
27 September	Gavin writes to Wiseman, denying request to film.
September	Representative Katherine Kane of the Massachusetts legislature (D-Beacon Hill), a personal friend of both

	Wiseman and Lieutenant Governor Elliot Richardson, calls Richardson and requests a meeting between Richardson and Wiseman.

6 October

Kane accompanies Wiseman to Richardson's office to introduce the two men. Richardson telephones Gavin requesting a reconsideration of his earlier decision to deny permission for the film.

January 1966

Kane calls Gavin, supporting the Wiseman film project.

28 January

Gavin meets with Wiseman and Gaughan. (Gavin later testified that at this meeting he obtained an oral agreement from Wiseman acknowledging the state's right to final approval of the film. Wiseman denied this allegation.) Gavin tells Wiseman to go ahead, pending advice from state Attorney General Edward Brooke.

21 March

Brooke's office issues an advisory opinion that the film can be made if certain conditions are met.

NET offers advice but no money and suggests that broadcasting the completed film is a possibility.

28 March

Wiseman gets permission from Gaughan to make a documentary at Bridgewater. (Gaughan later testified that he told Wiseman permission was contingent on approval of the finished film by state officials. Wiseman testified that there was no discussion of or agreement to such an arrangement.)

Spring

Wiseman and associate producer David Eames raise money for the film project. John Marshall is recruited as cinematographer. Wiseman, Eames, Marshall, and five of their friends contribute money to the project.

6 April

Gaughan calls a staff meeting at Bridgewater and asks for full cooperation with the film crew. He introduces Wiseman, who screens *The Cool World*. (Gaughan later testified that at this meeting he announced that state officials would have final approval of the film. Wiseman contested this assertion in his testimony.)

22 April	Wiseman and Marshall begin filming at Bridgewater; David Eames assists.
27–29 April and 6 May	The inmate-staff variety show, "The Titicut Follies," is performed before an audience at MCI-Bridgewater. Portions of the show are filmed by Marshall and Timothy Asch, who operates a second camera.
2 May	Dr. Harry Kozol, director of the Treatment Center for the Sexually Dangerous, strongly objects in writing to any filming at the center that does not comply with explicit written conditions. No footage is shot at the center.
April or May	Wiseman drafts a release form naming Bridgewater Film Company (BFC) as released from liability.
29 June	Filming is completed after 29 shooting days.
August	Eames returns to Bridgewater to obtain additional releases.
July	Editing begins. Wiseman and associate editor Alyne Model spend 11 months—until May 1967—editing 80,000 feet of film into an 84-minute feature (32,000 feet).
14 November	Wiseman organizes the Bridgewater Film Company, Inc. The incorporators are David Eames and John and Heather Marshall. Wiseman is neither shareholder nor stockholder.
February 1967	Albert De Salvo—the "Boston Strangler"—and two other inmates escape from Bridgewater. Gaughan describes the security as that of a hen coop.
Spring	At Gaughan's direction, correction officers Edward Pacheco and Joseph Moran visit Wiseman at his Cambridge office. Wiseman shows the men some Bridgewater footage and says the editing is going more slowly than he had expected, then takes them to lunch at a Cambridge restaurant.
April–August	Wiseman submits *Titicut Follies* to thirteen international film festivals.

1 June	Gaughan is among a group of twelve who view the Bridgewater documentary at Wiseman's studio in Cambridge. The screened footage does not include titles or credits.
27 June	Wiseman shows *Titicut Follies* to Richardson, who is now attorney general of Massachusetts, Assistant Attorney General Frederick Greenman, Gaughan, and Richardson's driver.
5 July	Gaughan writes Wiseman that "at some point the Commissioner will have to be drawn in." He sends the letter to Wiseman at 60 Martin Street, Cambridge, the address on Wiseman's 1965 letterhead. (Wiseman had moved from that address and testified that he never received the letter. Gaughan testified that the post office never returned the letter.)
10 July	Wiseman goes to Greenman's office to discuss the memorandum the attorney general's office is preparing about Gaughan's liability regarding *Titicut Follies*.
14 July	Wiseman submits a print of *Titicut Follies* to the New York Film Festival.
18 August	In response to inquiries from the New York Film Festival, Wiseman, in a letter to the festival director, claims that he has "secured releases from those people in the film or from their authorized representatives."
August	Amos Vogel notifies Wiseman that *Titicut Follies* has been accepted in the New York Film Festival.
September	Wiseman negotiates with Grove for exclusive distribution rights to *Titicut Follies*.
5–8 September	(According to Wiseman's trial testimony, Wiseman informs Greenman, around 5 September, by telephone, of the New York Film Festival acceptance. Greenman testified that the conversation took place on 8 September and that Wiseman told him that the film had been screened by a selection committee and praised as one of the best documentaries of the year, but that Wiseman did not inform him that the film was scheduled for public showing at the festival.)

9 September	Arthur Knight's review of *Titicut Follies* appears in the *Saturday Review*.
14 September	Mildred Methven, a former Massachusetts social worker, writes Gavin a letter of complaint about *Titicut Follies,* based on Knight's description of the film. Methven sends copies of the letter to Governor John Volpe, Senator Edward Kennedy, and the Civil Liberties Union of Massachusetts (CLUM).
After 14 September	Gavin calls Gaughan about Methven's letter. Volpe contacts Richardson, who says he is unaware of plans for a public showing of *Titicut Follies.*
16 September	An article appears in the Quincy *Patriot Ledger* quoting Gaughan as asserting that he has informed Wiseman that the film cannot be shown in New York until it is approved by three censors. Dr. Ames Robey, former medical director at Bridgewater, is quoted as saying that he had a written agreement with Wiseman regarding censorship rights.
17 September	An advertisement for the New York Film Festival in the Sunday *New York Times* announces a screening and discussion of *Titicut Follies* for 28 September.
18 September	Wiseman calls Gaughan about the 16 September *Patriot Ledger* article and voices his concern about the assertion of censorship rights (which he later testified he became aware of for the first time in reading the article). Wiseman calls Greenman to suggest a meeting of the key people. Plans are made for a meeting on 20 September at the attorney general's office. Wiseman later postpones the meeting for a day, without informing one of his attorneys, Gerald Berlin, who arrives at the attorney general's office on 20 September.
19 or 20 September	Wiseman engages Harvard law professor Alan Dershowitz and CLUM chairman Gerald Berlin as his legal counsel.
21 September	Wiseman, Berlin, and Dershowitz meet with Richardson, Gavin, Gaughan, and the attorney general's staff at the state house. Richardson expresses concern for the privacy of the inmates and questions the validity of the releases Wiseman has obtained.

Dershowitz argues that oral consent is sufficient and suggests that a guardian be appointed to represent the interests of the inmates and patients. Dershowitz says he sees no reason for Wiseman to hand over the releases, as requested by the attorney general's staff, if they are alleged to be invalid. Wiseman refuses to relinquish the signed releases.

Wiseman, Eames, and Marshall meet at Eames's house; Marshall brings the distribution contract for his 1958 film, *The Hunters.*

Gavin, three deputies, James Canavan, and Marshall see *Titicut Follies* in Newton.

22 September

In New York, Wiseman and Eames, titular president of BFC, negotiate a distribution contract transferring ownership of *Titicut Follies* and leave a print of the film at Grove Press.

Leaving Eames at the Grove office, Wiseman goes to the office of Ephraim London, whom he retains as his counsel. The contract with Grove is prepared in London's office.

Wiseman carries a copy of the distribution contract to Du-Art Film Labs, which holds the negative of *Titicut Follies.*

Excerpts from *Titicut Follies* are broadcast on channel 13.

In Massachusetts, Richardson sends Gavin a hand-delivered letter saying that *Titicut Follies* violates the privacy of the inmates. Gavin then writes Wiseman denying approval to show the film in its present form and sends a copy to Berlin. The letter is sent by registered mail to Wiseman at 60 Martin Street, Cambridge, and is later returned unopened.

Greenman files a bill of complaint signed by Gaughan and Gavin to enjoin Wiseman from showing *Titicut Follies* in Massachusetts.

In a special, and unusual, evening session, Suffolk Superior Court Justice Joseph Ford, without having seen *Titicut Follies,* issues a temporary restraining order on the exhibition of the film. The order is granted without notice to or presence of Wiseman's counsel.

25 September   In New York, Wiseman and Eames meet with Grove executives, who then sign the distribution contract.

In Massachusetts, Greenman files a motion to add Bridgewater Film Company, Inc., as a named defendant.

In New England, the Boston media broadcast news of the court injunction against the exhibition of *Titicut Follies*.

In New Hampshire, John and Heather Marshall resign as officers of the Bridgewater Film Company.

26 September   Counsel for the attorney general of Massachusetts files papers in New York Supreme Court to halt the showing of *Titicut Follies* in New York.

28 September   (According to Wiseman's testimony, Wiseman offers a six week's delay on commercial showing of *Titicut Follies* if the state will allow the New York Film Festival showing, but Richardson, through his attorney, refuses. Wiseman's testimony was contested by Richardson.)

New York Supreme Court Justice Francis Murphy, Jr., denies Massachusetts's request to enjoin the showing of *Titicut Follies* in New York.

First public showing of *Titicut Follies,* at the Lincoln Center Library Theatre, as part of the New York Film Festival; a public discussion with Wiseman and London follows the screening.

Before 2 October   Grove forms the Titicut Follies Film Distributing Company, Inc., to distribute the film.

2 October   New York Supreme Court Justice Saul Street denies a motion to ban the commercial showing of *Titicut Follies*.

3 October   New York commercial opening of *Titicut Follies* at the Cinema Rendezvous.

15 October	*Titicut Follies* begins a three-week run at the Carnegie Hall Cinema in New York.
16 October	The Commonwealth further amends its 22 September bill of complaint to add inmate James Bulcock as a plaintiff. A second injunction, running against Grove Press and Titicut Follies Film Distributing Company, is issued in Suffolk Superior Court.
17 October	Legislative hearings by the State Commission on Mental Health begin. *Titicut Follies* is shown to legislators; others are barred from the screenings.
20 October	A cartoon ridiculing Gerald Berlin appears in the *Boston Herald Traveler*. Berlin withdraws from the Wiseman case.
23 October	Wiseman and others are enjoined in Suffolk Superior Court from disposing of any profits pending trial and barring use of out-takes; the temporary restraining order against exhibition is continued.
1 November	Gaughan files a petition to be appointed legal guardian for Bulcock.
	Cullen v. Grove Press, Inc., a damage suit by Bridgewater guards, is filed in federal court.
2 November	Legislative hearings are thrown into confusion by the discovery that the sessions have been taped and photographed by Timothy Asch.
4 November	*Titicut Follies* concludes a three-week run at the Carnegie Hall Cinema.
Before 10 November	Grove representative Edith Zornow refuses NET's offer to broadcast *Titicut Follies* when they cannot agree on financial terms.
17 November	Trial of *Commonwealth v. Wiseman* begins in Suffolk Superior Court before Judge Harry Kalus, without a jury. At issue: (1) breach of oral contract, (2) invasion of privacy of one of the inmates (James Bulcock), (3) financial gain (the state requests a trust requirement whereby all receipts for the film will be held in trust for inmates). Edward Hanify and George Caner, Jr., appointed as special assistant attorneys

general, act as counsel for the Commonwealth. James St. Clair and Blair Perry represent Wiseman and the Bridgewater Film Co., Inc. There are eighteen days of trial, over four weeks, with 64 exhibits and 2,556 pages of proceedings. The court allows Grove's and Titicut's motion for severance from state to federal court.

20 November   Kalus views *Titicut Follies.*

28 November   Federal judge Francis Ford rules to remand the case of Titicut Follies Film Distributing Company and Grove Press, both of New York, back to Suffolk Superior Court in Massachusetts.

30 November   U.S. district judge Walter Mansfield denies the injunction sought by the Bridgewater guards in *Cullen v. Grove.*

14–15 December   Final oral arguments are heard in *Commonwealth v. Wiseman.*

4 January 1968   Judge Harry Kalus rules on two of the issues in *Commonwealth v. Wiseman.* Kalus rules (1) breach of oral contract and (2) invasion of privacy, in the first decision in Massachusetts to be based on the right to privacy. Kalus describes *Titicut Follies* as a "nightmare of ghoulish obscenities." *Titicut Follies* is permanently banned in Massachusetts.

23 May   *Commonwealth v. Wiseman* continues, now including Grove and the Titicut Follies Film Distributing Company as defendants. At issue is the state's request that a trust fund be established to hold all profits from the film for the benefit of the inmates.

6 August   Kalus enters his final decree in *Commonwealth v. Wiseman.* In settling the remaining issue, Kalus rejects the Commonwealth's request to assign the profits from the film to a trust fund for the inmates.

6 May 1969   The Commonwealth and Wiseman both appeal the lower court decision before the Massachusetts Supreme Judicial Court. The Commonwealth appeals Kalus's decision not to require a trust fund. Wiseman appeals Kalus's rulings on breach of oral contract and invasion of privacy. *Amicus curiae*

briefs are filed by CLUM, the American Sociological Association, and the American Orthopsychiatric Association.

24 June

The Supreme Judicial Court unanimously (5–0) modifies the Kalus decree of 4 January 1968 so that *Titicut Follies* may be shown in Massachusetts to special audiences with a brief explanation that changes and improvements have taken place in the institution since 1966. Preservation of additional footage is allowed. The court refuses to order the $14,451 in profits to be turned over to the state for the benefit of the inmates.

3 November

Thirty-five patients at Bridgewater, through their guardians, file suit against Wiseman and his related corporations for five million dollars.

15 June 1970

U.S. Supreme Court refuses Wiseman's request to review the state court finding on *Titicut Follies*.

7 December

U.S. Supreme Court again denies *certiorari*.

30 June 1971

Titicut Follies Distribution Company and Grove Press file a civil suit in federal court against the attorney general of Massachusetts, Robert Quinn, for restraint of free expression.

10 November

Massachusetts Supreme Judicial Court decides to lessen the procedural burden for Wiseman in exhibiting *Titicut Follies* to professional audiences.

1 March 1972

Suffolk Superior Court Judge Robert Sullivan rules in favor of Wiseman in the five-million-dollar damage suit that had been brought against him by 35 patients.

May 1974

CLUM Board votes unanimously to support court action to remove restrictions from the exhibition of *Titicut Follies*.

1 January 1977

Distribution rights to *Titicut Follies* are transferred from Grove Press to Zipporah Films, Wiseman's company.

14 February

First public showing of *Titicut Follies* in Massachusetts, at Pleasant Street Theater in Northampton.

Spring	A student at the University of Massachusetts-Boston, who appears in *Titicut Follies,* protests the showing of the film on the U-Mass campus, claiming violation of his privacy.
9 May 1980	Attorney general's office moves for an injunction against the public showing of *Titicut Follies* in Boston; the injunction is denied by Rya Zobel, U.S. district judge.
12 May	First public showing in Boston of *Titicut Follies*—two screenings at Saxon Theater as part of the celebration of the 350th anniversary of Boston.
1983	Wiseman's attorney begins preparation for a third petition for *certiorari* to the U. S. Supreme Court.
4 May 1987	*"Titicut Follies* Twenty Years Later" is sponsored by the University of Massachusetts-Boston at the John F. Kennedy Library; a public forum moderated by Harvard law professor Charles Nesson follows screenings of *Titicut Follies.*
23 July	Wiseman files motion in Suffolk Superior Court to permit general exhibition of *Titicut Follies.*
25 August	ABC-TV broadcasts clips from a "bootleg" print of *Titicut Follies* on "Nightline". Ted Koppel interviews Wiseman and others about Bridgewater and the restrictions on *Titicut Follies.*
28 September– 2 October	WCVB-TV, the Boston ABC affiliate, broadcasts scenes from *Titicut Follies* on its evening news program as part of "Inside Bridgewater," a five-part special report on the hospital. The series later wins two national broadcasting awards.
17 December	Suffolk Superior Court Judge Andrew Meyer appoints Mitchell Sikora, Jr., as guardian *ad litem* as part of his deliberation on Wiseman's motion to permit general exhibition of *Titicut Follies.*
January 1988	Massachusetts newspapers run an advertisement from the attorney general's office soliciting information on the whereabouts of men pictured in *Titicut Follies.* Several men are located.

24 and 25 March	*Titicut Follies* is screened for the staff at Bridgewater State Hospital.
Spring and Summer	Sikora travels throughout Massachusetts, interviewing men who are pictured in *Titicut Follies,* to determine each man's competency to make his own decision regarding Wiseman's motion to withdraw restrictions on the showing of the film. For each man judged to be incompetent, Sikora is to advise the court whether any restrictions on the film are recommended. Men considered competent by Sikora are to decide for themselves whether they wish to consent to unrestricted exhibition of the film.
March 1989	Sikora sends his report to Judge Meyer; he recommends that general exhibition of *Titicut Follies* would not cause harm at this time to the incompetent men pictured in the film.
5 April	*Nightline* broadcasts "Horror Story Continues at Bridgewater."
11 April	*Titicut Follies* is shown in the screening room of the Boston public television station, WGBH, to some of the competent men pictured in the film; also present are attorneys involved in the case, the brother of one former patient, Wiseman, and his assistants.
19 May	Meyer sees *Titicut Follies* at Zipporah Films offices in Cambridge.
2 June	*Titicut Follies* is screened as part of a national conference on the treatment of violence, hosted by Bridgewater State Hospital on the hospital grounds.
3 June	Fred Wiseman returns to Bridgewater for the first time in twenty-three years to participate in a panel that discusses *Titicut Follies* with conference participants.
7 June	Meyer conducts a hearing in Suffolk Superior Court, Boston, on Wiseman's motion to remove restrictions on the exhibition of *Titicut Follies.* The Massachusetts attorney general's office does not oppose the motion, but objections to general exhibition are raised by two of the men pictured in the film.

21 June

Titicut Follies is screened in Montreal as part of "A Salute to Documentary," an international celebration of the fiftieth anniversary of the Canadian National Film Board.

22 September

Judge Meyer rules that *Titicut Follies* can be shown to general audiences only if the identities of incompetent, unlocated, and non-consenting competent men are blurred.

29 September

Wiseman announces that he will appeal Meyer's decision.

Chapter 1. Trials of *Titicut Follies*

1. Wiseman has produced, directed, and edited more than twenty documentary films: *Titicut Follies* (1967); *High School* (1968); *Law and Order* (1969); *Hospital* (1970); *Basic Training* (1971); *Essene* (1972); *Juvenile Court* (1973); *Primate* (1974); *Welfare* (1975); *Meat* (1976); *Canal Zone* (1977); *Sinai Field Mission* (1978); *Manoeuvre* (1980); *Model* (1980); *The Store* (1983); *Racetrack* (1985); a four-film series, *Deaf, Blind, Multi-Handicapped,* and *Adjustment and Work* (1988); *Missile* (1988); *Near Death* (1989); *Central Park* (1990); and *Aspen* (1991); and a fiction film, *Seraphita's Diary* (1982).

2. See John Grierson, *Grierson on Documentary*, ed. Forsyth Hardy, rev. ed. (Berkeley: University of California Press, 1966). For other accounts of Grierson's work, see especially Paul Rotha, *Documentary Film*, 3d ed. (New York: Hastings House, 1963); Erik Barnouw, *Documentary: A History of the Non-Fiction Film*, rev. ed. (New York: Oxford University Press, 1983). For Grierson, the "creative treatment of actuality" was not a matter of turning life into art, but of using the art of cinema to address the needs of society. It has long been accepted that Grierson was the first to use the term *documentary* as a description of film, in a review of Robert Flaherty's *Moana*. In the same review, Grierson described *Moana* as a "poetic record," a phrase that addresses some of the same paradoxes as "reality fictions." John Grierson, "Flaherty's Poetic *Moana*," *New York Sun*, 8 February 1926; reprinted in Lewis Jacobs, ed., *The Documentary Tradition*, 2d ed. (New York: Norton, 1979), 25. In a 1988 review of Richard Barsam's *The Vision of Robert Flaherty* (Bloomington: Indiana University Press, 1988), Brian Winston reported that as early as 1914, Edward S. Curtis, whose film on the Kwakiutl of the Pacific Northwest, *In the Land of the Head Hunters*, was in some ways a "direct precursor of Flaherty," used the term *documentary* to describe his own work. Furthermore, reports Winston, Robert Flaherty met Edward S. Curtis in 1915 and "showed Flaherty the way to make his own contribution in *Nanook*" (Brian Winston, "Before Grierson, Before Flaherty: The Documentary Film in 1914," *Sight and Sound* 57, no. 4 (1988): 277–79). Winston seems to attribute part of his own discoveries about the connection between Flaherty and Curtis to Jay Ruby, who seems to have pointed Winston to a crucial entry in the diary of Frances Flaherty. See Jay Ruby, "A Re-Examination of the Early Career of Robert J. Flaherty," *Quarterly Review of Film Studies* 5, no. 4 (1981): 431–57. Wiseman's films bear a strong generic similarity to the form of documentary generally called "direct cinema," a "type of location, non-fiction, close observation cinema in which lightweight cameras

and sound recorders are used to record action as it actually happens with indigenous sound only" (*Glossary of Film Terms* [Philadelphia: University Film Association, 1978], 27). Direct cinema was pioneered in American film by Robert Drew, Richard Leacock, Donn A. Pennebaker, Albert and David Maysles, and, slightly later, Frederick Wiseman, and in Canada by Allan King and several of his associates, including Richard Leiterman and William Brayne (Leiterman and Brayne later working as Wiseman's cinematographers). A parallel development, pioneered by Jean Rouch and Edgar Morin, is the cinema verite documentary, which, as employed by Rouch and Morin, typically involved active interviews and interventions by the filmmakers and the use of nonsynchronous sound. In practice, the terms are often used interchangeably to refer to modern (since about 1960) documentary, beginning with the Drew-Leacock *Primary* (1960) and the Rouch-Morin *Chronique d'un été* (1961). For histories of these developments see, for example, Barnouw, *Documentary;* Stephen Mamber, *Cinema Verite in America: Studies in Uncontrolled Documentary* (Cambridge: MIT Press, 1974); Robert C. Allen and Douglas Gomery, "Case Study: The Beginnings of American Cinema Verite," in *Film History: Theory and Practice* (New York: Knopf, 1985), 215–41. In a letter of application to the Fifth International Film Festival, Wiseman described *Titicut Follies* as "done in the 'cinema verite' style" (26 April 1967, exhibit 44 in *Commonwealth v. Wiseman*). In this book we shall follow the common practice of using *cinema verite* (without italics or accent marks) as the covering term for the two forms and their many variants, *direct cinema* as the somewhat narrower term usually used to refer only to the Anglo-Canadian-American movement. In this usage, common in the documentary movement as well as in writings about it, cinema verite includes direct cinema but direct cinema does not include cinema verite.

3. Capote's use of the phrase "nonfiction novel" was made in reference to his *In Cold Blood* (New York: Random House, 1966). Norman Mailer's history-as-novel is invoked in his *Armies of the Night* (New York: New American Library, 1968); Wiseman used the phrase reality dream in a 1970 interview with John Graham, "There Are No Simple Solutions," reprinted in *Frederick Wiseman,* ed. Thomas R. Atkins (New York: Monarch Press, 1976), 35–36; Wiseman used the term *reality fictions* in a 1974 interview with Thomas Atkins, in Atkins, ed., *Frederick Wiseman,* 82. In a 1970 article, Beatrice Berg wrote that there is no correct term for what Wiseman does, but "perhaps film intellectuals will manufacture a new label" ("I Was Fed Up with Hollywood Fantasies," *New York Times,* 1 February 1970, sec. 2, 26). In 1971, M. Ali Issari reported that Wiseman was calling his films "new documentaries," in an apparent parallel to the "new journalism." M. Ali Issari, *Cinema Verite* (East Lansing: Michigan State University Press, 1971), 125. Wiseman is a highly original film artist, but his flirtation with the term *reality fiction* also underscores another theme that is repeated in almost all of his interviews and lectures: an anxiety not to be thought naive or commonplace.

4. Wiseman, in an unpublished interview with Randall Conrad, circa 1978.

5. For recent, fairly comprehensive overviews of contemporary rhetoric

and its place in communication studies generally, see Carroll C. Arnold and John Waite Bowers, eds., *Handbook of Rhetorical and Communication Theory* (Boston: Allyn and Bacon, 1984); Thomas W. Benson, ed., *Speech Communication in the 20th Century* (Carbondale: Southern Illinois University Press, 1985); Gerard A. Hauser, *Introduction to Rhetorical Theory* (New York: Harper & Row, 1986); for a survey of the extension of the rhetorical tradition to the study of film and other media, see Martin J. Medhurst and Thomas W. Benson, eds., *Rhetorical Dimensions in Media: A Critical Casebook,* rev. printing (Dubuque: Kendall/Hunt, 1986).

6. In an interview with Alan Rosenthal in *The New Documentary in Action: A Casebook in Film Making* (Berkeley: University of California Press, 1971), Wiseman claimed, based on his attorneys' research, that *Titicut Follies* was the first "publication of any sort which has not been judged to be obscene" to be banned from public viewing by an American court (68). Brian Winston has challenged Wiseman's characterization: "Rather it was the first time that an injunction was obtained on the grounds that there was a failure to obtain consent outside of advertising. The case, although therefore important, still does not acknowledge the existence of a right of privacy in any well-defined way. It joins Binns and Vitagraph Inc. among the few precedents which go against the interests of the press and which, almost all, turn on consent issues" (Brian Winston, "The Tradition of the Victim in Griersonian Documentary," in Larry Gross, John Stuart Katz, and Jay Ruby, eds., *Image Ethics: The Moral Rights of Subjects in Photographs, Film, and Television* [New York: Oxford University Press, 1988], 49). More recently, Karen Konicek, director of distribution at Wiseman's company, Zipporah Films, said that *Titicut Follies* was the only film in the United States censored for reasons other than obscenity or national security (Helen M. Wise, "Coursework vs. Career Choices: Two Roads Taken," *The Alumnus* [University of Massachusetts], August–September 1987, 6). Harvey Silvergate, president of the Civil Liberties Union of Massachusetts (CLUM), described the *Titicut Follies* case by saying that "twenty years ago the state judiciary for the first (and still the only) time in modern American history issued an unprecedented order, a prior restraint injunction that suppressed a motion picture neither legally obscene nor a 'clear and present danger' to the national security" ("President's Column: *Titicut Follies* Revisited," in *The Docket* [CLUM] 17, no. 4 (1987): 3). Legal scholars on a *"Titicut Follies:* 20 Years Later" panel held at the University of Massachusetts-Boston, 14 May 1987 repeated the claim about the film's unique legal status ("Film on State Hospital Provocative after 20 Years," *New York Times,* 17 May 1987, 27). Other American films have had unusual restrictions placed on their exhibition. For example, although the Rolling Stones, a rock music group, had commissioned Robert Frank to film their 1972 U.S. tour, they sued to block the release of Frank's documentary, *Cocksucker Blues.* "Litigation on the part of the Rolling Stones has guaranteed the film can be shown only a few times a year and only when Frank is in attendance" (Sean Elder, "Darkness Visible: Robert Frank and the Real Rolling Stones," Berkeley *Express,* 30 October 1987, 6). Marlaine Glickman claims that Frank's film "remains banned (by legal order) to this

day" ("Highway 61 Revisited," *Film Comment* 23, no. 4 [1987]: 33). For a comprehensive review of restrictions on film exhibition see Edward De Grazia and Roger K. Newman, *Banned Films: Movies, Censors, and the First Amendment* (New York: R. R. Bowker, 1982).

7. Bridgewater has been referred to for many years as the "state hospital for the criminally insane" by professionals and lay people. Robert H. Weber, executive director of the Mental Health Legal Advisors Committee, and his legal intern David Twohig have argued that the "phrase 'criminally insane' is an inaccurate and oxymoronic description of Bridgewater's clientele" since "those who are judged insane are, by definition, excused from criminal responsibility." The managing editor of the *Boston Globe* was sufficiently impressed by their argument to issue a directive that the state's most influential newspaper would revise its style book to eliminate the objectionable phrase (Robert L. Kirstead, "Dropping a Stigmatizing Phrase," *Boston Globe*, 2 November 1987, 18).

Chapter 2. Informed Consent

1. "Frederick Wiseman on the Films of Frederick Wiseman," an appearance sponsored by the Student Cultural Events Organization, University of Massachusetts Boston, 6 April, 1977.

2. Wiseman, U-Mass-Boston, 6 April 1977.

3. For an analysis of informed consent, see Ruth R. Faden and Tom L. Beauchamp, in collaboration with Nancy H. P. King, *A History and Theory of Informed Consent* (New York: Oxford University Press, 1986).

4. Mass. Gen. Laws Ann., ch. 127, section 36 (1958).

5. Wiseman, as quoted in Alan Westin, "'You Start Off with a Bromide': Wiseman on Film and Civil Liberties," *Civil Liberties Review* 1, nos. 1 and 2 (1974): 65.

6. Christina Robb, "Focus on Life," *Boston Globe Magazine*, 23 January 1983, 17 and 26; Robb's is the most detailed published account of Fred Wiseman's background and early years. See also Silvia Feldman, "The Wiseman Documentary," *Human Behavior* 5, no. 2 (1976): 64–69 for personal background on Fred Wiseman. Information on Jacob Wiseman's early life and education is available in his Massachusetts bar applications, nos. 9717, 9752, and 9852, filed in the office of the clerk of the Supreme Judicial Court of Massachusetts in Boston. For condensed biographies of Jacob Wiseman see the obituary sections of the *Boston Globe*, 3 July 1971, 27; and the *Boston Herald Traveler*, 3 July 1971, 7. Obituaries for Gertrude Wiseman appeared in the *Boston Globe*, 6 July 1976, 33; and in the *Boston Herald American*, 6 July 1976, 10.

7. Robb, "Focus on Life," 26. Zipporah Batshaw's parents had career interests that resembled those of her in-laws: her father was a judge of the Quebec Superior Court and her mother a practicing physician. (See Batshaw's application, no. 53945, to the Massachusetts bar.) Zipporah Wiseman later became a member of the law faculty at Northeastern University, taught as a visiting professor at Harvard Law School and the University of Texas, and in January 1990 became the Joe A. Worsham Centennial Professor of Law at the University of Texas.

8. In December 1957, in Paris, a mutual friend of Wiseman's and Phil Green's explained Wiseman's absence from the social activities of the group by telling Green that "Freddy had gone to Algeria to do documentaries for French TV." Green was never able to ascertain any more about the alleged project, nor have we. Interview with Professor Philip Green by Carolyn Anderson, Northampton, MA, 26 September 1986.

9. Wiseman, as quoted in Robb, "Focus on Life," 27. In *Commonwealth v. Wiseman,* when asked about his occupation, Wiseman replied, "I am a filmmaker, an attorney, and a consultant on social problems" (trial transcript, volume 13, p. 4; in *Commonwealth v. Wiseman,* Suffolk Superior Court, no. 87538 Equity). All subsequent references to this trial transcript will be by speaker, volume, and page number only (for example, Wiseman, tr. 13:4). References will be placed within the text when the speaker is easily identified therein. Wiseman describes his hope for *The Cool World* in "The Talk of the Town: New Producer," *The New Yorker,* 14 September 1963, 33–35. Wiseman and an associate formed a social-science consulting company in the spring of 1966.

10. Gaughan, tr. 4:12.

11. We use the terms *correction officer, correctional officer,* and *guard* as synonyms throughout this work; we mean to imply no offense when the word *guard* is used as an occupational description. In *Screw: A Guard's View of Bridgewater State Hospital* (Boston: South End Press, 1981), Tom Ryan says that the security staff at Bridgewater wished to be called "correction officers" (21). Daniel Golden confirms the preference: "Traditionally, correctional officers have formed the lowest caste in the law enforcement hierarchy. They're often called 'guards' or 'screws,' two names that many of them dislike" ("Undermanned and Vulnerable," *Boston Globe Magazine,* 30 July 1989, 37).

12. Charles Gaughan, "History of MCI-Bridgewater," p. 3, enclosure in correspondence with Carolyn Anderson, 9 May 1977. See also Russell C. Petrella, Maurice H. Richardson, and June S. Binney, *Final Report: Governor's Special Advisory Panel on Forensic Mental Health* (September 1989), 99–105. A section of the report contains a history of MCI-Bridgewater written by Binney, in her capacity as executive director of the special panel appointed by Governor Michael S. Dukakis to recommend policy regarding mental health and substance abuse services within the criminal justice system in the Commonwealth.

13. Michael Perleman, psychiatrist, made this comment as a participant in a panel discussion after the exhibition of *Titicut Follies* at Hampshire College, Amherst, Massachusetts, 5 April 1977.

14. Robert Perrucci, *Circle of Madness: On Being Insane and Institutionalized in America* (Englewood Cliffs, NJ: Prentice-Hall, 1974), 27.

15. Gaughan, tr. 4:86, 5:82.

16. Wiseman, U-Mass-Boston, 6 April 1977.

17. Exhibit 1, *Commonwealth v. Wiseman.* Subsequent references to exhibits will be noted in the text.

18. The issue of competency later became crucial. Wiseman's defense took the position that he and the state agreed that competency would be

determined at the time of shooting, as a procedural matter. The state took the position that it had a continuing obligation to determine the competency of subjects in the film. Wiseman's letter could support either interpretation.

19. The plaintiffs did not enter the proposal with Wiseman's letter in their original petition against Wiseman. The defense introduced the proposal in Wiseman's reply to the Bill in Equity.

20. Commonwealth of Massachusetts, Suffolk Superior Court for Civil Business, Equity no. 87538. "Findings, Rulings, and Order from Decree," docket entry no. 75, 4 January 968, 3–4.

21. Christopher Lydon, "Richardson Victory Fruit of Shrewd Analysis and Action," *Boston Globe,* 5 November 1964, 11.

22. Jerome M. Mileur and George T. Sulzner, *Campaigning for the Massachusetts Senate: Electioneering Outside the Political Limelight* (Amherst: University of Massachusetts Press, 1974), 4.

23. Brooke, citing 41 Am. Jur. 888.

24. Gavin, "Hearings on the Bridgewater Film before the Special Commission on Mental Health," Boston, 17 October–9 November 1967, 28 (quoted by counsel for the defense, tr. 3:104–5). Subsequent references to the legislative hearings will cite "Hearings" and page number only.

25. Eames, tr. 6:167–68. Interview by Carolyn Anderson with John Marshall, Cambridge, 13 April 1984.

26. For a brief account of the circumstances that led to a remarkable family research project that has continued for over three decades, see Lorna Marshall, *The !Kung of Nyae Nyae* (Cambridge: Harvard University Press, 1976), 1–4.

27. Wiseman, tr. 13:143.

28. According to Pacheco's testimony, he never worked at the hospital before his escort assignment; he was a sanitation officer in the alcoholic section (Tr. 10:27).

29. Marshall interview (1984).

30. Kozol, memorandum, 2 May 1966. Exhibit 14.

31. Wiseman, tr. 13:121; Eames, tr. 6:114.

32. During the *Commonwealth v. Wiseman* trial, the Commonwealth tried to demonstrate that subjects were sometimes unaware of the recording of picture or sound. George Caner, questioning David Eames about the capabilities of a directional mike, asked, "And thus, to the extent that when it is directed at an object it screens out sounds coming from elsewhere, to that extent, it is able to pick up meaningful sounds that your ear might not be able to pick out?" Eames replied, "That is correct" (Tr. 7:55). In a memorandum to the authors, Wiseman said it was inaccurate to assume that "the mike could pick up sounds the ear could not. I think it is difficult not to notice a camera, tape recorder, mike, a bag with film and magazines and 3 strangers" (4 August 1987). In another context, Alan M. Dershowitz has noted that in Massachusetts in the mid-1980s "it is a felony to 'secretly record' conversations. Massachusetts also makes it a crime to disclose surreptitiously recorded conversations" (*Reversal of Fortune: Inside the Von Bulow Case* [New York: Random House, 1986], 266n.).

33. Wiseman, tr. 13:108; Joseph F. Moran, tr. 6:79.

34. George J. Lepine, Jr., tr. 5:125; Wiseman, tr. 13:126; Marshall interview (1984).

35. Wiseman and Marshall have differing current memories about Marshall's independence while shooting. In various published interviews, Wiseman has claimed he directs the shooting on all his films. He noted to us that "Marshall stated in [his] deposition that he did all camera work under my direction" (4 August 1987 memorandum). The Marshall deposition is not included in the public file of *Commonwealth v. Wiseman*. In his trial testimony, Wiseman said, "We might be seven or eight feet apart. Mr. Marshall might be in one place with a camera and I would be in another place with a tape recorder" (Tr. 14:153).

36. Marshall interview (1984). See Lisa Henderson, "Photographing in Public Places" (Master's thesis, University of Pennslvania, 1983). Following Goffman, Henderson provides an analysis of strategies and justifications used by still photographers.

37. Wiseman testified (Tr. 14:139-44) that Vladimir was eager to be filmed. According to Wiseman, "during the trial a letter was received from Vladimir giving his consent" (memorandum to the authors, 4 August 1987).

Chapter 3. Aesthetics of Uncertainty

1. See Anthony J. Lucas, *Common Ground: A Turbulent Decade in the Lives of Three American Families* (New York: Knopf, 1985).

2. Bud Collins, "Marty and Benny Show Tries Out," *Boston Globe,* 24 April 1967, 10. See also "King Begins Anti-War Bloc Here," *Boston Globe,* 24 April 1967, 1, 22.

3. Ronald A. Wysocki, "Bridgewater Lacks Medics," *Boston Globe,* 2 January 1967, 1.

4. Bailey, as quoted in Ray Richard, "Bridgewater: An Emergency Situation," *Boston Globe,* 21 January 1967, 1, 4.

5. Gaughan, as quoted in Wysocki, "Strangler Escapes—Manhunt On," *Boston Globe,* 24 February 1967, 1.

6. Edward G. McGrath, "Public Reaction: Disgust," *Boston Globe,* 24 February 1967, 1.

7. Gaughan, tr. 4:200–201.

8. Moran, tr. 6:86–88, 90–91; Pacheco, tr. 10:31–35.

9. Wiseman, tr. 13:6.

10. Wiseman, as quoted in Westin, "You Start Off with a Bromide," 62.

11. Wiseman, tr. 13:76

12. Marshall interview (1984). Marshall repeated this account of his role in the editing process in an interview with the authors, 27 December 1986, in Peterborough, New Hampshire. During the trial, Wiseman said that sometimes Eames and Marshall gave their views on what had been edited (Tr. 13:140). In a memorandum to the authors, Wiseman said that "Marshall and Eames did not see the film (apart from rushes) until I screened a rough cut for them. Marshall played no part in the editing and does not have co-editor's

credit. I gave Marshall co-director's credit in appreciation for his working without pay and providing equipment free" (memorandum to authors, 4 August 1987).

13. Liz Ellsworth, *Frederick Wiseman: A Guide to References and Resources,* (Boston: G. K. Hall, 1979), 33.

14. Ira Halberstadt, "An Interview with Frederick Wiseman," *Filmmaker's Newsletter* 7, no. 4 (1974): 22.

15. Wiseman, in Randall Conrad, "An Interview with Frederick Wiseman," unpublished transcript, circa 1978, 15.

16. Eames, tr. 7:41, 44; Wiseman, tr. 15:15; John Marshall, Hearings, 821–29; Heather Marshall, Hearings, 868–74.

17. Eames, tr. 7:42. According to Marshall, the company existed primarily to protect Wiseman from potentially overlapping liabilities with *The Cool World* (Marshall interview [1986]).

18. Shirley Clarke, who directed *The Cool World,* produced by Wiseman, was one of three directors of the Film Maker's Distribution Cooperative. As early as 1966, she complained about Wiseman's distribution arrangements for *The Cool World,* charging that he turned out to be much like other purely commercial producers and that she had never seen any of the profits from the film. See "What Is the New Cinema? Two Views—Paris and New York," *Film Culture,* no. 42 (1966): 59.

19. Wiseman, letter to the Fifth Moscow International Film Festival, 26 April 1967. Exhibit 44.

20. Wiseman, description of film sent to Mme. Flavia Paulon, Venice, 26 May 1967. Exhibit 51.

21. Wiseman, tr. 13:172.

22. Gaughan, tr. 4:54; Wiseman, tr. 13:178.

23. Wiseman, as quoted in Thomas R. Atkins, ed., *Frederick Wiseman* (New York: Monarch Press, 1976), 62.

24. Richardson, as quoted in Atkins, *Frederick Wiseman,* 68.

25. Wiseman, as quoted in Atkins, *Frederick Wiseman,* 73.

26. Gaughan, tr. 5:25. Gaughan sent the 5 July 1967 letter to 60 Martin Street, Cambridge, the address on Wiseman's 1965 letterhead (Exhibits 1, 10, and 12). During direct examination of Gaughan, St. Clair objected to Hanify's submission of a copy of Gaughan's letter, on the grounds that Wiseman had not lived at 60 Martin Street in July of 1967. St. Clair claimed his client had never received the 5 July letter from Gaughan and argued that, therefore, it should not be entered as evidence against Wiseman. Gaughan testified that the letter he sent was never returned to him. Kalus accepted a copy of Gaughan's letter of 5 July 1967 as Exhibit 15 (Tr. 4:62–64; 5:21–25).

27. Gaughan, tr. 5:21. In cross-examination of Gaughan, St. Clair asked, "I thought the Commissioner was already 'in'?" Gaughan replied, "This refers to a showing of the film" (Tr. 5:21). When questioned about why this sentence, the last one in Gaughan's letter to Wiseman, was underlined in red in the copy submitted to the court as Exhibit 15, Gaughan said that he had not done it and did not know who did (Tr. 5:21).

28. Wexler, in Ernest Callenbach and Albert Johnson, "The Danger Is

Seduction: An Interview with Haskell Wexler," *Film Quarterly* 21, no. 3 (1968): 7.

29. In his testimony, Wiseman described himself as "one of the authors of a feature film shot in Boston last summer . . . [then titled] *The Crown Caper*" (Tr. 13:9). Wiseman does not list this film in his curriculum vitae. Wiseman recalls, "I met Haskell Wexler for the first time when he was in Boston as Director of Photography for *The Thomas Crown Affair*. I worked solely on the script of the film and had nothing to do with the production" (memorandum to the authors, 4 August 1987).

30. See Leonard Maltin, *Behind the Camera: The Cinematographer's Art* (New York: New American Library, 1971), 57–60; and Dennis Schaefer and Larry Salvato, *Masters of Light: Conversations with Contemporary Cinematographers* (Berkeley: University of California Press, 1984), 247–66. Later, Wexler was the cinematographer for Milos Forman's film of Ken Kesey's novel, *One Flew over the Cuckoo's Nest,* about a mental hospital. Wiseman told us that the producers of *Cuckoo's Nest* rented a print of *Titicut Follies* and screened it repeatedly for the cast and crew before shooting began (Wiseman, in conversation with Thomas W. Benson, Bucknell University, 12 November 1985).

31. Wexler, in Callenbach and Johnson, "The Danger Is Seduction," 7.

32. Rossett deposition in *Commonwealth v. Wiseman,* 10 November 1967, 15–16.

33. *Attorney General v. The Book Named "Tropic of Cancer,"* 1984 N.E.2d 328 (1962); 345 Mass. 11 (1962). Other relevant cases involving Grove Press include *Grove Press, Inc., v. Christenberg,* 276 F. 2d 433 (1960); *Grove Press, Inc., v. Gerstein,* 378 U.S. 577 (1964); *A Book Named "John Cleland's Memoirs of a Woman of Pleasure" v. Attorney General,* 86 S. Ct. 975 (1966).

34. De Grazia and Newman, 123. According to the 1975 Rockefeller Commission Report, Grove was the only American publisher whose activities were monitored.

35. Rossett deposition, 19.

36. Rossett deposition, 20.

37. In *Film as a Subversive Art* (New York: Random House, 1974), Vogel labels *Titicut Follies* "a major work of subversive cinema" (187).

38. Richardson, in Atkins, *Frederick Wiseman,* 68.

39. Richardson, in Atkins, *Frederick Wiseman,* 68.

40. By order of the Supreme Judicial Court of Massachussets, a statement regarding improvements at Bridgewater was added to the film in 1971.

41. Exhibit 1, p. 2.

42. Breitrose, review of *Documentary,* by Erik Barnouw, *Film Quarterly* 28, no. 4 (1975): 38.

43. Bill Nichols, *Ideology and the Image: Social Representation in the Cinema and Other Media* (Bloomington: Indiana University Press, 1981), 209.

44. Rouch, as quoted in G. Roy Levin, *Documentary Explorations: 15 Interviews with Film-Makers* (Garden City: Doubleday, 1971), 141–42.

45. Nichols, *Ideology,* 198.

46. Kalus, "Findings, Rulings, and Order for Decree," 4.

47. Wiseman, U-Mass-Boston, 6 April 1977.

48. Robb, "Focus on Life," 26.

49. Wiseman, in Conrad, "An Interview."

50. Eames, "Watching Wiseman Watch," *New York Times Magazine,* 2 October 1977, 102.

51. Jean-Claude Bringuier, as quoted in Louis Marcorelles, *Living Cinema* (New York: Praeger, 1973), 98. See Mark Roskill and David Carrier, *Truth and Falsehood in Visual Images* (Amherst: University of Massachusetts Press, 1983) for a cogent analysis of visual "truth" by an art historian and a philosopher.

52. Wiseman, as quoted in Atkins, *Frederick Wiseman,* 35–36.

53. Wiseman, as quoted in Halberstadt, "An Interview," 22.

54. Wiseman, as quoted in Deckle McLean, "The Man Who Made *Titicut Follies,"* *Boston Sunday Globe Magazine,* 27 July 1969, 13.

55. Memorandum to authors, 4 August 1987.

56. Marshall interview (1984).

57. Dowd, "Popular Conventions," *Film Quarterly* 22, no. 3 (1969): 29. Dowd's speculation flows from confusion about the suicide discussion early in the film. It is not the body pictured on the television monitor, but the man being led to his cell who is (mistakenly) described as suicidal.

58. Figure 3.1 reproduces Ellsworth's divisions as she presents them in *Frederick Wiseman,* 12–14. Heyer, in "The Documentary Films of Frederick Wiseman: The Evolution of a Style" (Master's thesis, University of Texas, 1975), 28–42, divides *Titicut Follies* into acts and scenes but she does not number the scenes in her text, and so it is sometimes not entirely clear where a scene would break in her interpretation of the film. Heyer uses the terms *scene* and *sequence* somewhat inconsistently, sometimes indicating that a sequence is composed of a group of scenes (in the usage familiar to film critics), but sometimes referring to an *act* as being composed of a number of scenes, which may in turn be divided into sub-units (in a usage borrowed from theatrical terminology). In Figure 3.1, we have created an outline based on Heyer's prose and using her vocabulary, to compare graphically how she and Ellsworth have interpreted the structure of *Titicut Follies.* The vertical arrows in the figure indicate Heyer's descriptions of cross-cutting between scenes two and three in Act I and within scene one in Act II.

59. Marshall interview (1986).

60. Marshall interview (1984).

61. Cf. Robert Phillip Kolker, *A Cinema of Loneliness* (New York: Oxford University Press, 1980), 103. Kolker equates uncertainty with meaninglessness. He makes a distinction between openness and ambiguity and argues that open films engage viewers in constructing plural meanings, while ambiguous films promote passivity.

62. Wiseman, tr. 13:149. The amount of footage that was usable attests to Marshall's skill as a (direct) cinematographer.

63. Wiseman, panel discussion as part of a Wiseman retrospective at the Institute of Contemporary Art, Boston, 30 October 1977.

64. Wiseman, as quoted in Halberstadt, "An Interview," 22.

65. Elizabeth Jennings [Liz Ellsworth], "Frederick Wiseman's Films: A Modern Theory of Documentary" (Master's thesis, University of Wisconsin-Milwaukee, 1975), 199.

66. See Barry Salt, *Film Style and Technology: History and Analysis* (London: Starword, 1983), 345. The *Titicut Follies* averages are based on the figures provided by Ellsworth, *Frederick Wiseman,* 14–32.

67. Marshall interview (1984); Wiseman, tr. 14:117–19.

68. Wiseman, as quoted in Janet Handelman, "An Interview with Frederick Wiseman," *Film Library Quarterly* 3, no. 3 (1970): 7.

69. Wiseman, tr. 14:28, 30; Greenman, tr. 12:13–14, 53, 61; Richardson, tr. 12:118–20.

70. Arthur Knight, "Cinema Verite and Film Truth," *Saturday Review,* 9 September 1967, 44. In his testimony before the legislative hearings, Gavin called the publication *The Saturday Evening Review* (Hearings, 17).

71. Wiseman, tr. 14:29.

72. Wiseman, tr. 14:30, 33.

73. Wiseman, tr. 12:94.

74. Wiseman, memorandum to the authors, 4 August 1987.

75. Greenman, tr. 12:94.

76. Greenman, tr. 12:20, 88, 92–93.

77. Richardson, tr. 12:119.

78. Greenman, tr. 4:76.

79. Richardson, as quoted in a letter by Gavin to Volpe, itself quoted in the *Boston Herald Traveler,* 15 October 1967, 6C.

80. Gavin, tr. 3:57.

Chapter 4. Competing Rights

1. Bill in Equity, docket entry no. 1, 22 September 1967, 5.

2. Equity no. 87538, docket entry no. 2, 25 September 1967. On 16 October 1967, the plaintiffs further amended their bill by adding as a party plaintiff James C. Bulcock, appearing by Gaughan.

3. Memorandum from Wiseman to the authors, 4 August 1987.

4. Wiseman, as quoted in William McGrath, "'Titicut' Winner at Film Festival," *Boston Herald Traveler,* 15 October 1967, 7.

5. Wiseman testimony before the legislative commission, as reported by David B. Wilson, "Producer of 'Titicut' Denies Doublecross," *Boston Globe,* 25 October 1967, 25.

6. As reported by Sara Davidson, "N.Y. Justice Denies Bridgewater Film Ban," *Boston Globe,* 29 September 1967, 9.

7. "N.Y. to Show Film on Bridgewater," *Boston Herald Traveler,* 29 September 1967, 3.

8. Street, as quoted in Peter Lucas, "What Are the Rights of the Insane?" *Boston Herald Traveler,* 16 October 1967, 15.

9. Eames, tr. 7:72–73; Marshall interview (1984). In his testimony, Eames recalled a discussion, probably on 21 September, at which Wiseman told him of a newspaper story reporting a claim by Gaughan that the film was subject to state approval (Tr. 7:73).

10. Eames, tr. 7:147; Marshall interview (1984). According to Wiseman, he had "shown the almost completed film to Mr. and Mrs. Marshall, Mr. and Mrs. Eames, and my wife," sometime before 27 June 1967 (memorandum to authors, 4 August 1987). Eames testified that he saw the finished film in May 1967 (Tr. 7:14).

11. Wiseman, tr. 15:36; Marshall interview (1984).

12. The figures are from Gallen's deposition, 10 November 1967, 5; the quotation is from a memo of 25 September 1967, exhibit 22. Wiseman's advance on *The Cool World* had been six thousand dollars (Wiseman, Hearings, 375).

13. Zornow deposition, 10 November 1967, 12.

14. Exhibit 22.

15. This delicate term is from the "Brief for the Respondents," 23.

16. Eames, tr. 7:76; Wiseman, tr. 15:61.

17. Rossett deposition, 20.

18. Rossett deposition, 20–21.

19. *Burstyn v. Wilson,* 343 U.S. 495 (1952). See De Grazia and Newman, *Banned Films,* 231–33.

20. "Statement by Arthur L. Mayer," in Mary Batten, "An Interview with Ephraim London," *Film Comment* 1, no. 4 (1963): 2, 19.

21. Wiseman, tr. 15:49.

22. Exhibits 24 and 23.

23. Wiseman, tr. 15:40; Eames, tr. 7:110. The Marshalls had a family fortune to protect. John's father, Laurence Kennedy Marshall, founded the Raytheon Company in 1922 and was its president until his retirement in 1950. In a memorandum to the authors, Wiseman wrote, "Marshall was frightened that his own assets would be involved. They never were. He failed to support the film because of his fear. His failure to stand by the film was extremely damaging to the defense" (4 August 1987). Marshall explained his resignation to us differently: "I didn't know what Fred had said to various people. I didn't know the obligations he'd undertaken, with respect to the film or with respect to the state, or the institution at Bridgewater, or Charlie Gaughan. I didn't know what he'd said. And Heather and I were holding the bag on the corporation. We were the majority of this corporation and, in theory, if it was a real corporation, we would have to say 'yea' or 'nay' as to whether the film was to be released or how or what was to become of it and I didn't want to be in that position not knowing all the facts. And I had, besides that, a personal reason—that I didn't know what would happen about some of the people who had been in the film. In these hearings with that guy Robey, they are basically being evaluated to see if they're crazy, or sane enough to stand trial. And I thought, you know, what if it gets around and somebody who's going to be on the jury someday sees them in the film and thinks they're crazy or they make a bad impression on the juror and they go in the slammer when they shouldn't or the lawyers say, well, you know, we'll never get a fair trial in Massachusetts for these people and they just keep putting it off and putting it off—putting their trial off. In Bridgewater, you go there and stay there until you are adjudged competent to stand trial

and it's a way of putting people away forever. It's one of the glaring loopholes, in our country anyway, in which you can get incarcerated and you go to jail, basically to jail, without ever meeting your accusers, without ever going before a court, before God and the people. And I thought, well, hell, if somebody has to spend another three years in Bridgewater because their trial keeps being postponed because of a film, that seems a little extreme. So the real reason was I just didn't know, and that was in my deposition. I think they didn't ask me to come to court because, on the one side, Fred's lawyers would be afraid I'd just tell the truth and, on the other side, because they knew I didn't have any—I thought the film was a good film. I thought it should not be changed or varied or censored" (interview with the authors, Peterborough, New Hampshire, 27 December 1986).

24. Marshall interview (1984).

25. According to Willard Van Dyke, tr. 17:10–17, *Titicut Follies* was screened either 2 or 3 September 1967. The annual seminar, in honor of Robert Flaherty, is devoted exclusively to documentary film.

26. Sara Davidson, "'Titicut Follies' Switches Moods," *Boston Globe*, 29 September 1967, 8.

27. Advertisement, *New York Times*, 3 October 1967, 55.

28. Gallen affidavit in opposition, *Commonwealth v. Lincoln Center*, index no. 15866/67, 3.

29. Gallen affidavit, 4.

30. Information obtained from Zornow deposition, 27; *Commonwealth v. Wiseman* and Vincent McNally, theater manager of Carnegie Hall Cinema, as quoted in Peter Lucas, "Follies Doing Only 'Fair' Business in New York," *Boston Herald Traveler*, 19 October 1967, 3.

31. Thomas C. Gallager, "Furor Sure Over 'Follies,'" *Boston Herald Traveler*, 4 October 1967, 34.

32. Advertisement, *New York Times*, 14 October 1967, 13.

33. "Brief for the Petitioners as Cross-Appellants," 7. These figures are drawn from records of Grove and Titicut produced in the course of discovery. See also tr. 18:8–16.

34. "Never Termed 'Titicut Follies' Film Superb, Says Richardson," *Boston Herald Traveler*, 30 October 1967, 6.

35. Zornow deposition, 22, 26.

36. Wiseman (Tr. 15:62) testified that he neither arranged nor knew of this screening. Eames often traveled to Rhode Island, but the circumstances of the exhibition were not pursued in his examination.

37. Van Dyke, tr. 17:10.

38. Joseph Goldstein, tr. 16:147.

39. Zornow deposition, 24–25.

40. Wiseman interview in Rosenthal, *The New Documentary in Action*, 68.

41. Robert Healy, "Mrs. Hicks Collects the 'Anti' Votes," *Boston Globe*, 27 September 1967, 1.

42. Bud Collins, "Louise, Luis Fan Eight Batters Apiece," *Boston Globe*, 27 September 1967, 23.

43. Kane, letter to the editor, *Boston Herald Traveler*, 3 October 1967, 28.

44. Cornelius J. Noonan, "Gavin, Gaughan Face Questioning on Bridgewater Hospital Film 'Indiscretions,'" *Boston Globe,* 9 October 1967, 13.

45. "Blunder at Bridgewater," *Boston Herald Traveler,* 2 October 1967, 16.

46. Gallager, "Furor Sure Over 'Follies,'" *Boston Herald Traveler,* 4 October 1967, 34.

47. Gallager, "Where Are the Liberals?" *Boston Herald Traveler,* 6 October 1967, 18.

48. Gallager, "More Answers Required," *Boston Herald Traveler,* 12 October 1967, 26.

49. Frank Reilly and John Sullivan, "Hospital Film Maker Hit," *Boston Record American,* 12 October 1967, 2.

50. Peter Lucas, "Follies 'Double Cross' Charged," *Boston Herald Traveler,* 12 October 1967, 1.

51. Wiseman, as quoted in "'Titicut Follies' Producer Blasts Atty. Gen. Richardson," *Boston Herald Traveler,* 13 October 1967, 10.

52. Ray Richard, "Richardson Backed Filming, Gavin Says," *Boston Globe,* 15 October 1967, 1.

53. Gallager, "'Follies' Film Could Cost State Millions," *Boston Herald Traveler,* 17 October 1967, 20.

54. Richard, "Tuesday's 'Titicut Follies' Showing May Cause Legislative Fury," *Boston Globe,* 15 October 1967, 39.

55. Reilly, "Bridgewater Hearing Set," *Boston Record American,* 13 October 1967, 10.

56. John H. Fenton, "Film Stirs Furor in Massachusetts," *New York Times,* 18 October 1967, 40.

57. Richard, "Film Probers Seek Information in N.Y.," *Boston Globe,* 21 October 1967, 4; H. Marshall, Hearings, 872.

58. Ronald A. Wysocki, "Gaughan Says State Tricked by Titicut Showing," *Boston Globe,* 18 October 1967, 3.

59. Reilly and Gordon Hillman, "Sex Criminals Filmed after Doctor's Bar," *Boston Record American,* 27 October 1967, 5.

60. Reilly and Hillman, "Top 'Follies' Figures in Heavy Grilling," *Boston Record American,* 27 October 1967, 5.

61. Bob Creamer, "Wiseman Assails Prober," *Boston Herald Traveler,* 23 October 1967, 3.

62. Lucas, "Wiseman Says Volpe Barred from Preview," *Boston Record American,* 31 October 1967, 3.

63. "Claim Follies Filmed Just to Make $$," *Boston Record American,* 31 October 1967, 3.

64. "Claim Follies Filmed," 3.

65. On four occasions (at a funeral mass for a prisoner and at three rehearsals or performances of the variety show, "The Titicut Follies"), Asch and Marshall both operated cameras. According to documentary filmmaker Ed Pincus, his partner David Neuman took sound one day with the BFC crew. Pincus interview in Levin, *Documentary Explorations,* 367.

66. Richard, "Cameraman Told to Get a Lawyer," *Boston Globe,* 3 November 1967, 10.

67. Richard, "Cameraman," 10.

68. Wiseman, press conference held 14 October 1967.

69. Gallager, *Boston Herald Traveler,* 18 October 1967, 66.

70. Robert F. Muse, counsel for the plaintiffs in *Cullen v. Grove* was one of several who used the expression.

71. Senator Beryl Cohen, as quoted in Richard, "Cameraman Told to Get a Lawyer."

72. Lucas, "'Follies' Aide Filmed Fernald," *Boston Herald Traveler,* 4 November 1967, 1.

73. Richardson, as quoted in "State to Probe Fernald Filming," *Boston Globe,* 5 November 1967, 2.

74. Asch, as quoted in "'Titicut' Cameraman Denies Taking Fernald School Pix," *Boston Herald Traveler,* 8 November 1967, 72.

75. Gavin, tr. 3:28.

76. Wiseman, tr. 14:29–30.

77. Eames, tr. 7:111; Marshall interview (1984).

78. *Boston Herald Traveler,* 15 October 1967, 6

79. *Boston Herald Traveler,* 27 October 1967, 1.

80. Wiseman, as quoted in Richard, "Richardson 'Excluded' Volpe from Seeing Film—Wiseman," *Boston Globe,* 27 October 1967, 16.

81. St. Clair, tr. 3:124.

82. *Boston Record American,* 18 October 1967, 29. Harold Banks quoted Wiseman: "Since I grew up in a household where 'things legal' were discussed with some frequency, neither my family nor myself were particularly surprised when I decided to become a lawyer. It would not be honest if I did not admit that this familial condition probably determined my choice. Coupled with this seemingly negative reason is a strong desire to spend my time at a profession that will require the active use of my mind in solving technical and difficult legal problems, as well as affording some chance to become skillful in understanding—coping with human problems. I, of course, did not overlook the possibility of remunerative reward."

Wiseman's sponsors at the bar were attorney David M. Watchmaker and Superior Court Judge Lewis Goldberg. Both men were long-time friends of attorney Jacob L. Wiseman, the applicant's father, and had known Fred Wiseman, then twenty-four years old, since his birth. Wiseman took the Massachusetts Bar Examination in July 1954 and December 1954. He passed the December 1954 exam. His applications (nos. 54175 and 54439) are filed in the office of the clerk of the Supreme Judicial Court in Boston.

83. Reporters returned to their filed accounts of the 24 April 1967 visit.

84. Harold Banks, *Boston Herald Traveler,* 1 November 1967, 20.

85. Richard, "Confident Film Maker," *Boston Globe,* 26 October 1967, 2.

86. Gallager, "Rep. Kane Was Financial Backer for Earlier Wiseman Documentary," *Boston Herald Traveler,* 22 October 1967, 2. In her collection of essays *Civil Wars* (Boston: Beacon Press, 1981), June Jordan relates how she watched the shooting of *The Cool World* in her old Harlem neighborhood and

"ended up assistant to the producer"; she offers this description of the film project: "Directed by a white woman, Shirley Clarke, and produced by a white man, Frederick Wiseman, the film 'starred' Black kids from the street; it was the only feature film about what it means to be Black in a racist white country from 1954 to 1964 that I can recall" (xix). See 3–16 for Jordan's account of the filming and premiere and for interviews with some of the participants.

87. Richard, "Confident Film Maker," 26 October 1967, 2.

88. "Tempest in a Snakepit," *Newsweek*, 4 December 1967, 109.

89. "Comr. Gavin Guarded after Acid Threat," *Boston Record American*, 21 October 1967, 1.

90. See Anderson, "Documentary Dilemmas: An Analytic History of Frederick Wiseman's *Titicut Follies*" (Ph.D. diss., University of Massachusetts, 1984), 284–91, for a more complete description of newspaper coverage.

91. *Boston Globe*, 30 September 1967, 6.

92. *Boston Globe*, 18 October 1967, 23; 19 October 1967, 17; 20 November 1967, 14.

93. *Boston Globe*, 29 October 1967, 26.

94. Although supportive enough to appear as a witness for the defense in *Commonwealth v. Wiseman*, Boston print and television newsman Louis M. Lyons made no mention of the *Titicut Follies* story in his history of the *Globe* told through an examination of its most important stories (*Newspaper Story: One Hundred Years of* "The Boston Globe" [Cambridge: Harvard University Press, Belknap Press, 1971]).

95. The academic was G. D. Wiebe, "'Follies' Film Neither Lurid Nor Shocking," *Boston Herald Traveler*, 2 November 1967, 21; the analysis was by James Southwood, "The Story behind 'Titicut Follies' Row," *Sunday Herald Traveler*, 8 October 1967, 57.

96. National press attention to *Titicut Follies* from the fall of 1967 through 1969 included: Arthur Knight, "Cinema Verite," 44; "Bay State in Move to Bar Prison Film," *New York Times*, 27 September 1967, 42; "Cinema: Festival Action, Side Show Action, *Titicut Follies*," *Time*, 29 September 1967, 101; "Court Here Refuses to Bar Film at New York Film Festival," *New York Times*, 29 September 1967, 55; "Controversial Film to Have Six Day Run at Cinema Rendezvous," *New York Times*, 30 September 1967, 27; Vincent Canby, "The Screen: *Titicut Follies* Observes Life in a Modern Bedlam," *New York Times*, 4 October 1967, 38; Linda Searbrough, "'Follies' Is Jolting Film about Insane," *New York Daily News*, 4 October 1967, 89; reviews of *Titicut Follies* by "Byro" in *Variety* and Judith Crist on "Today," NBC-TV, reprinted in *FilmFacts* 60 (1967): 314–16; John H. Fenton, "Film Stirs Furor in Massachusetts," *New York Times*, 18 October 1967, 40; review of *Titicut Follies* in *Film Society Review*, October 1967, 17–19; William Wolf, "A Sane Look at an Insane Situation," *Cue*, 21 October 1967; Joseph Morgenstern, "Movies: Bedlam Today," *Newsweek*, 23 October 1967, 100–101; Brendan Gill, "The Current Cinema," *The New Yorker*, 28 October 1967, 166–67; Robert Hatch, "Films," *The Nation*, 30 October 1967, 446; review of *Titicut Follies* in *Films in Review*, November 1967, 580; Andrew Sarris, review of *Titicut Follies* in

The Village Voice, 9 November 1967, 33; *"Titicut Follies," America,* 11 November 1967, 539; Richard Schickel, "The Frightful Follies of Bedlam: *Titicut Follies," Life,* 1 December 1967, 12; "U.S. Court Refuses to Ban *Titicut Follies* to Public," *New York Times,* 1 December 1967, 52; "Tempest in a Snakepit," *Newsweek,* 4 December 1967, 109; Robert Coles, "Stripped Bare at the Follies," *The New Republic,* 20 January 1968, 18, 28–30; separate "Correspondence" from Ronald Kessler, Elliot Richardson, and Robert Coles, *The New Republic,* 10 February 1968, 35–36; Wilfred Sheed, "Films," *Esquire,* March 1968, 52, 55; Deac Rossell, *"Titicut Follies," Christianity and Crisis,"* 18 March 1968, 43–45; Harvey G. Cox, "Massachusetts Movie Ban," in "The Playboy Forum," *Playboy,* March 1968, 45; *"Titicut* Ban Affirmed," in "Forum Newsfront," *Playboy,* April 1968, 62; "Film-Festival Firsts for *Follies,"* in "Forum Newsfront," *Playboy,* June 1968, 54; Paul Bradlow, "Two, But Not of a Kind: A Comparison of Two Controversial Documentaries about Mental Illness, *Warrendale* and *Titicut Follies," Film Comment* 5, no. 3 (1969): 60–61; Dowd, "Popular Conventions," 28–31; *"Titicut Follies* Is Banned to Bay State Public," *New York Times,* 25 June 1969, 41.

97. Docket entry no. 15, 7.

98. Wiseman, "Letters: Focusing again on *Titicut Follies," Civil Liberties Review* 1, no. 3 (1974): 151.

99. Letter to Carolyn Anderson, 11 October 1979.

100. Gallager, "Where Are the Liberals?" *Boston Herald Traveler,* 6 October 1967, 18.

101. Gallager, "Beatniks Aided, Insane Aren't," *Boston Herald Traveler,* 18 October 1967, 66. For the same criticism, more calmly stated, see "Titicut Follies: A Grotesque Invasion," *Boston Herald Traveler,* 20 October 1967, 18.

102. Berlin, as quoted in Harold Banks, "Today's Periscope: Baron Watch Went Deep," *Boston Record American,* 28 October 1967, 19.

103. Wiseman, as quoted in Westin, "You Start Off with a Bromide," 64, 66.

104. See Aryeh Neier (executive director of ACLU), "Letters," *Civil Liberties Review* 2, no. 2 (1975): 151.

105. Berlin's deposition was taken on 9 November 1967. See docket entry no. 36. The deposition transcript is not included in the case file.

106. "'Titicut Follies' Movie Case Presents Complicated Issues," *Civil Liberties in the Bay State,* Winter 1968, 5. All subsequent quotations are from this source. See also "Civil Liberties Union Postpones Stand on 'Follies,'" *Boston Globe,* 29 October 1967, 26, and Bill McGrath, "CLU Explains Its Silence on 'Follies' Film," *Boston Herald Traveler,* 29 October 1967, 20.

107. 356 Mass. 251; 249 N.E.2d 610 (1969).

108. Wiseman, as quoted in Westin, "You Start Off with a Bromide," 66. The *Titicut Follies* controversy goes unmentioned in the *American Civil Liberties Union Annual Reports,* volume 7 (New York: Arno Press and The New York Times, 1970).

109. "Elliot Richardson on *Titicut Follies,"* a letter originally appearing in the *Civil Liberties Review* 1, no. 3 (1974): 150, and reprinted in Atkins, *Frederick Wiseman,* 67.

110. Wiseman, in Atkins, *Frederick Wiseman,* 69.

111. Feingold, *"Titicut Follies* and Competing Rights," *Civil Liberties Review,* 2, no. 2 (1974): 145–51.

112. Telephone interview between Carolyn Anderson and Roberts, 3 June 1977. Attached to Wiseman's personal affidavit on behalf of his 1987 motion to remove the ban from exhibiting *Titicut Follies* to the general public was a letter of support sent to Wiseman from Harvey A. Silvergate, president of the CLUM Board of Directors. See docket entry no. 2512, 20 July 1987. While Wiseman's July 1987 motion was under consideration, CLUM was a plaintiff in court action against the Commonwealth. On 14 September 1987, Suffolk Superior Court Judge James P. Lynch, Jr., ordered changes in procedures used for isolating violent and suicidal patients at Bridgewater State Hospital in response to the CLUM suit, one of a series of Bridgewater maltreatment suits filed by CLUM since the late sixties. See "CLUM Wins Major Victory in Bridgewater State Hospital Suit," *The Docket* 17, no. 4 (1987): 1, 6; and Diane E. Lewis, "'Pain in the Neck' Lawyer Reaps Gains for Bridgewater Patients," *Boston Globe,* 6 December 1987, 37, 42, 43.

113. Richardson, in response to a series of questions asked by Carolyn Anderson during Richardson's U.S. Senate campaign appearance at the University of Massachusetts-Amherst, 27 April 1984.

114. Reitman, "Past, Present, and Future," in *The Pulse of Freedom: American Liberties, 1920–1970s,* ed. Alan Reitman (New York: Norton, 1975), 334.

115. "How CLUM's Legal Program Works," *The Docket,* August 1983, 2.

116. N.Y. Civil Rights Law 50, 51 (McKinney 1948).

117. 276 F. Supp. 727 (S.D.N.Y. 1967).

118. Muse, as quoted in "4 Guards File Suit vs. Movie," *Boston Globe,* 2 November 1967, 9.

119. Crist, *FilmFacts,* 316.

120. Plaintiffs, as quoted in the Mansfield decision, attached as Appendix B to the Wiseman-BFC brief on appeal before the Massachusetts Supreme Judicial Court, in *Massachusetts Reports, Papers, and Briefs,* 356 part 5 (20–24 June 1969): 362–66.

121. 385 U.S. 374 (1967).

122. As paraphrased by Mansfield, 364.

123. Gallager, "'Follies' Film Could Cost State Millions," *Boston Herald Traveler,* 17 October 1967, 29.

124. "Comment: The 'Titicut Follies' Case: Limiting the Public Interest Privilege," *Columbia Law Review* 70, no. 2 (1970): 360, n. 4.

125. Richard W. Daly, "Guards Plan Suit in N.Y. to Block 'Titicut Follies,'" *Boston Herald Traveler,* 31 October 1967, 1.

126. "5 Million Sought in 'Titicut Follies' Case," *Boston Globe,* 4 November 1969, 33.

127. Sullivan, as quoted in Joseph Harvey, "Titicut Follies Survives $5M Suit," *Boston Globe,* 2 March 1972, 10. Subsequent quotations from the Sullivan decision are from this article.

128. Donald M. Gillmor and Jerome A. Barron, *Mass Communication*

Law: Cases and Comment, 4th ed. (St. Paul: West Publishing Company, 1984), 311.

129. Telephone interview between Carolyn Anderson and Ellen Feingold, 23 May 1977. Attorney Feingold was the instructor of the class mentioned.

130. Ford's order is docket entry no. 21, filed 23 October 1967. A pretrial conference was held on 17 November 1967; the trial began 20 November 1967.

131. Nathan Cobb, "James St. Clair," *Boston Globe,* 13 February 1983, A17–18. Much less well known is the fact that St. Clair was also approached to serve as chief litigator for the prosecution of the Nixon case.

132. St. Clair, tr. 1:23. See docket entry no. 55, "Petition for Removal," Civil Action no. 67–846–F.

133. Holmes, from *The Common Law* (1881), cited in Arthur R. Miller, *The Assault on Privacy: Computers, Data Banks, and Dossiers* (Ann Arbor: University of Michigan Press, 1971), 210.

134. Kalus's obituary headline ("Judge Harry Kalus, 76—He Barred Showing of 'Titicut Follies' in Mass," *Boston Globe,* 8 October 1980, 49) speaks to the importance of this case in his judicial career. The *Boston Herald American* obituary (8 October 1980, C10) does not mention the case.

135. Interview between Carolyn Anderson and Francis X. Orfanello, executive secretary to administrative judges, Suffolk Superior Court, 17 February 1984.

136. Perry made the objection (noted) to a question asked of G. A. Wiebe, tr. 16:133; Kalus, tr. 16:192.

137. Charles Taylor, *"Titicut Follies," Sight and Sound* 57, no. 2 (1988): 101.

138. Hanify, tr. 2:22.

139. See docket entry no. 14. The Marshall deposition was scheduled for 2 November 1967. See Marshall's testimony before the legislative hearing, also 2 November 1967, 800–840, 852–67.

140. The length is described in William F. Doherty, "Wiseman Tells His Side in 'Titicut Follies' Dispute," *Boston Herald Traveler,* 6 December 1967, 2.

141. Tartakoff, tr. 8:92.

142. The count is by a correction officer, George J. Lepine, Jr., who saw the film in New York City and dictated a description into a tape recorder as he viewed *Titicut Follies* (Tr. 5:96–117).

143. See Ellsworth, *Frederick Wiseman,* shots 53–57, pp. 20–21.

144. Docket entry no. 35; the deposition was scheduled for 16 November 1967. The absence of a deposition in the case file does not prove that none was taken, only that its contents were not used as part of the trial record. It seems fair to assume that Bulcock would not have been permitted to leave Bridgewater for his deposition.

145. See David M. O'Brien, *The Public's Right to Know* (New York: Praeger, 1981), for an elaboration of this thesis.

146. The affidavit was filed in U.S. District Court, New York (Civil Action no. 4246). See Wiseman, tr. 15:113–15.

147. Kalus, tr. 15:158–59. See Barbara Sweeney, "The Use of Social Science Research in Supreme Court Opinions Related to Obscenity" (Ph.D. diss., University of Massachusetts, 1981).

148. Kalus [paraphrased], tr. 17:52–54.

149. Don R. Pember, *Mass Media Law,* 3d ed. (Dubuque: William C. Brown, 1984), 10.

150. Kalus, "Findings, Rulings, and Order for Decree," 4–5.

151. Findings, 13.

152. Findings, 5–6

153. Findings, 14.

154. Docket entry no. 106.

155. "Brief for the Petitioners as Cross-Appellants," 17, *Commonwealth v. Wiseman,* 356 Mass. 251; 249 N.E.2d 610 (1969). All subsequent references to the appeal are to this source.

156. "Brief for the Respondents," 101–3.

157. "Brief for the Petitioners as Appellees," i–ii.

158. "Brief *Amicus Curiae* of the American Sociological Association, Inc.," 1–11.

159. "Brief for *Amicus Curiae* of the American Orthopsychiatric Association," 21–22.

160. "Brief *Amicus Curiae* of the Civil Liberties Union of Massachusetts," 1–23.

161. 249 N.E.2d at 615; 356 Mass. at 258.

162. 249 N.E.2d at 619; 356 Mass. at 264.

163. 249 N.E.2d at 619; 356 Mass. at 263. In complying with the court order, Wiseman added the statement that "changes and improvements have taken place at the institution since 1966" but he preceded this statement with an explanation that he had been required to add it, thus mocking the credibility of the alleged improvements.

164. David L. Bennett and Philip Small, "Case Comments," *Suffolk Law Review* 4, no. 1 (1969): 204.

165. "Recent Cases," *Harvard Law Review* 83, no. 7 (1970): 1730–31, n. 42.

166. "Comment: The 'Titicut Follies' Case: Limiting the Public Interest Privilege," 359, 371.

167. "Producers Sue to Show Film," *Boston Globe,* 1 July 1971, 25. The headline is an error, in that it was not Wiseman who sued. Wiseman did not initiate the court action and he said he was unaware of its existence (telephone conversation with Carolyn Anderson, 9 May 1977).

168. According to Judge Murray's clerk, the case (Civil Action no. 71–1341–M) was dismissed 31 March 1972.

169. See docket entries no. 1183, 1184.

170. Wiseman, in telephone conversation with Carolyn Anderson, 14 November 1983.

171. 385 U.S. 374 (1967).

172. 398 U.S. 960 (1970); 400 U.S. 954 (1970).

173. 398 U.S. at 961–63.

174. In a memorandum to the authors, Wiseman recalled the circumstances of Douglas's absence from the vote: "Douglas recused himself because Gerald Ford had instigated hearings in Congress in an attempt to impeach Douglas. Douglas was being very careful and was cautious even about such a remote connection as publishing a chapter of a book in the *Evergreen Review*" (4 August 1987). But Douglas was not, as Wiseman's comment may seem to suggest, making an exception for the *Titicut Follies* case. In two letters to Ramsey Clark, both written early in the year in which William O. Douglas recused himself in the *Wiseman v. Massachusetts* case, the justice described the circumstances of his withdrawal from consideration in a number of other conflict of interest cases involving publication. On 28 April 1970, Douglas wrote "My publications have at times raised conflicts of interest. I have written extensively for *Look,* mostly on foreign travels and experiences. As a result, I have always recused myself in a Cowles Magazine case. See *Polizzi v. Cowles Magazine Inc.* 344 U. S. 853, 345 U. S. 663 [1952]. . . . I also withdrew from consideration of a motion in No. 905—*Grove Press Inc. v. Maryland State Board,* because I was told that Grove Press owned the Evergreen Magazine to which Random House sold, without my knowledge, excerpts from my book *Points of Rebellion.*" (From *The Douglas Letters: Selections from the Private Papers of Justice William O. Douglas,* ed. Melvin I. Urofsky [Bethesda, MD: Adler & Adler, 1987], 396-97. See also Douglas's letter to Clark of 7 May 1970, 402-403. Clark was attorney general from 1967 to 1969 and, as a member of Paul, Weiss, Rifkind, Wharton & Garrison, handled "some of the strategy in WOD's defense against impeachment" (394, note 1).

175. "Public ban stays on 'Titicut' film," *Boston Globe,* 7 December 1970, 3.

176. "Brief for the Respondent Wiseman in Support of Motion to Amend Final Decree After Rescript," docket entry no. 2511, 23 July 1987. In December 1987, Wiseman told Charles Taylor, "I think there's some hope, although how much I don't know, that the film will be sprung some time over the next few months. . . . The attitude toward me might have changed somewhat. I have made a lot of other films in the interim and I'm not seen as a pornographic Cambridge lawyer. The Follies have been legitimised by time." Charles Taylor, "*Titicut Follies,*" 98, 103).

177. "Response of Commonwealth of Massachusetts to Motion to Amend Final Decree After Rescript," docket entry no. 2522A, 12 August 1987, 1.

178. "Order," Judge Andrew G. Meyer, Docket entry no. 2604, 17 December 1987, 2. According to the 1967 testimony of correction officer George Lepine, Jr. (Tr. 5:96–117), 62 inmates or patients were identifiable in the film. At the 7 June 1989 hearing, Deputy Attorney General Stephen A. Jonas announced that in their search the state had located four men "who were not among the initial 62, but who were, nonetheless, depicted in the film."

179. *Boston Herald,* 4 January 1988, 38; *Boston Globe,* 4 January 1988, 4; *Daily Hampshire Gazette,* 4 January 1988, 28.

180. Telephone interview between Carolyn Anderson and Stephen A. Jonas, 4 April 1988. Information on the procedures of the attorney general's office in response to Wiseman's motion and quotations from Jonas are based on this interview and another conducted on 18 May 1989.

181. "Order," docket entry no. 2604, 5.

182. Mitchell J. Sikora, Jr., telephone interview with Carolyn Anderson. All quotations from Sikora and information about his duties and procedures are from telephone conversations (15 and 20 July 1988 and 17 May 1989); a personal interview (3 October 1989); and written correspondence (2 January 1990).

183. Sikora himself had never seen the entire film before his appointment as guardian *ad litem*. He saw the documentary at Zipporah Films before he began his interviews.

184. Mitchell J. Sikora, Jr., "Report of the Guardian Ad Litem," Equity no. 87538, 3 March 1989, 53–54.

185. M. K. played a central role—and perhaps a more important role than did Fred Wiseman—in reforms at MCI-Bridgewater in the 1970s and 1980s. In 1972 M. K., then confined to the Treatment Center for the Sexually Dangerous at MCI-Bridgewater, sued state officials, claiming that his placement in seclusion was unconstitutional. In 1974 the parties negotiated a consent decree and then a supplemental consent decree, but the case was not closed until 1981, when M. K. and the state settled their fee dispute. In a consent decree, the defendant agrees to change the behavior challenged by the plaintiff without admitting wrongdoing. Although M. K. was released from the center in 1975, officials there considered themselves bound by the *King* decrees and did not challenge them until 1989, in response to two right-to-treatment suits filed by patients at the center. U. S. District Judge D. J. Mazzone dismissed those two complaints, but considered *King* "an appropriate vehicle within which to pursue a resolution of the conflicts and ambiguity which continue to plague the sequestration process at the Treatment Center." At the end of a 171-page order that included a review of litigation involving the center, Mazzone wrote, "the *King* case remains open, the consent decrees remain in full force, and *King* will be the vehicle in which all future orders will issue." *Pearson v. Fair,* C.A. No. 81–3219–Mass. 8/28/89; *Bruder v. Johnston,* C.A. No. 86–1092–Mass. 8/28/89 at 169. See also *King v. Greenblatt,* C.A. No. 72–788–W, slip op. (D. Mass. 10/29/74 & 2/17/77), *aff'd* 560 F.2d 1024 (1st Cir. 1977), *cert. denied,* 438 U.S. 916 (1978). *King,* 489 F. Supp. 105 (D. Mass. 1980). Another successful and influential right-to-treatment case—and one based on conditions at the hospital—filed during the era in which *Titicut Follies* was made was *Nason v. the Superintendent of Bridgewater State Hospital,* 351 Mass. 94 (1966); 353 Mass. 604 (1968).

186. *New York Times v. U. S.,* 403 U. S. 713 (1971), 91 S. CT. 2140. In response to Meyer's inquiry whether any of the six cases Perry had cited were relevant to the issue of privacy, Perry described two cases based on allegations of invasion of privacy: *Time, Inc. vs. Hill,* 385 U. S. 374 (1967) and *Cox Broadcasting Corp. v. Cohn,* 420 U. S. 469 (1975). In both cases, which involved media claims of public interest, the Court was sympathetic to the First Amendment defense and decided in favor of the press. All quotations from the hearing of 7 June 1989 are from a transcript based on an audio tape of the hearing recorded by Carolyn Anderson.

187. In *Commonwealth v. Wiseman,* a correction guard testified that 62

inmates or patients were identifiable in *Titicut Follies.* Of those 62, eleven or twelve had signed written releases. Wiseman testified that he had the oral consent of everyone pictured in the film. Wiseman also testified that M. K. was fully aware that his interview by Dr. Ross was being photographed for use in a film and that M. K. gave his oral and written consent to such use (Tr. 14:146–51).

188. An Associated Press story quoted Perry as commenting after the hearing: "The fact that the commonwealth doesn't oppose the motion helps my case but I don't know what the judge will do." "State May Lift Ban on 'Titicut Follies.'" *Daily Hampshire Gazette,* 8 June 1989, 31.

189. In *Titicut Follies* a woman says, "You know that fellow's master of ceremonies. [The man's full name.] You think he's relaxed. You think he's been doing it for years and he's a paranoid. They can't reach him."

190. Michael J. Sullivan, "Brief in Opposition of Motion to Amend Final Decree after Rescript," Equity no. 87538, 29 June 1989, 3.

191. Sullivan, "Brief," 4.

192. In the hearing on 3 September 1987 Meyer asked if any rights were being claimed by the staff. Stephen Jonas replied that he had received a phone call from a guard, one of the plaintiffs in a former case before a New York court (*Cullen v. Grove* [1967]), who was still concerned about the exhibition of *Titicut Follies.* Perry said that the man was bound by the New York decision and did not have rights in the present action.

193. A Boston news story quoted Vladimir, by full name, as saying, "To me, [Bridgewater] was like a concentration camp. I'm glad they're showing the film; I want to expose the state. . . . " Gary Witherspoon, "'Titicut' Director to Fight Restriction on Film's Release," *Boston Herald,* 30 September 1989, 8.

194. 249 N.E.2d 610 (1969) at 618–19.

195. In what may have been an oversight, Meyer made no mention of the previously required "explanation" in his own decision on the film, thus leaving the requirement intact. The explanation was still appended to at least two prints of the film shown after Meyer's decision.

196. "Statement of the Case and Order," docket entry no. 2992, 22 September 1989, 2. Subsequent quotations and paraphrases of Meyer's decision are from this source.

197. Meyer note: *Cullen v. Grove Press, Inc.,* 276 F. Supp. 727, 730 (1967).

198. Meyer note: *Commonwealth v. Wiseman,* 356 Mass. at 261.

199. Meyer note: In the recent case of *Commonwealth v. John McCabe,* Middlesex Superior Court C.A. 84–1750, I noted that, "Dr. Albert Jargela, a clinical psychologist on the Bridgewater staff, estimated 30 to 40 percent of the inmates choose not to participate in treatment programs." This means that approximately 111 of the total 227 inmate/patients want no treatment and receive no treatment.

200. Meyer note: *Kelley v. Post Publishing Co.,* 327 Mass. 275, 276–77, 98 N.E. 2d 286, 287 (1951).

201. Meyer note: *Commonwealth v. Wiseman,* 356 Mass. 251 (1969).

202. Meyer note: In his July 20, 1987, affidavit, Frederick Wiseman said:

"I believe that showing of the film *Titicut Follies* to members of the general public at this time would help arouse public concern about conditions at M.C.I. Bridgewater, and thus would help to bring about changes in conditions there. . . . "

203. Perry specialized in antitrust and high-technology cases. In 1977 he successfully represented another independent filmmaker from Massachusetts, Liane Brandon, in a landmark case against a large distributor. See Charles Schreger, "Court Fades Out Pix-Title Ripoffs," *Variety*, 26 October 1977, 1. Steven Naifeh and Gregory White Smith, in *The Best Lawyers in America: 1987* (New York: Woodward/White, 1987), listed Blair L. Perry as one of thirty-five attorneys outstanding in the area of business litigation in the state of Massachusetts (126). All lawyers mentioned in the "entertainment and intellectual property law" section resided in California or New York. Naifeh and Smith consulted six thousand attorneys in preparing the 1987 edition. Perry was also listed in the business litigation section of the 1989–90 edition of Naifeh and Smith.

204. Massachusetts bar application, no. 55130, filed in the office of the Supreme Judicial Court in Boston.

205. See Walter V. Robinson, "4 Men Named by King to Fill Judgeships," *Boston Globe*, 28 June 1979, 24.

206. Gary Witherspoon, "'Titicut' Director to Fight Restriction on Film's Release," *Boston Herald*, 30 September 1989, 8.

207. These recollections about the hearings are based on notes and audio tapes made by Carolyn Anderson. In a 2 January 1990 letter to Anderson, Mitchell Sikora wrote, "I have a dim and uncertain memory that [at a preliminary, informal meeting of counsel with Meyer in open court on 3 March 1989] the judge may have asked whether such blurring technology, now common in television video tape presentations of sensitive matters, could furnish some help in the present situation. My memory is that Mr. Perry was not receptive to the idea and that neither the judge nor counsel pursued it at all."

208. During the period when Frederick Wiseman's motion was before him, Meyer heard another case case in the Suffolk Superior Court, which also involved the clash of First Amendment and privacy rights, and concerned the flow of information about treatment at Bridgewater State Hospital. The *Boston Globe* and one of its reporters had sought an order to compel the state chief medical examiner to release the autopsy reports of three men who had died at the hospital under questionable circumstances in the spring of 1987. *Globe* reporter Diane E. Lewis had requested the reports in connection with a series she was writing on conditions at Bridgewater. The *Globe* sought disclosure of the autopsy reports, under a Massachusetts statute providing for the inspection of public records. Counsel for the newspaper, Joanne D'Alcomo, argued, much as Wiseman had argued for over twenty years, that the public has a right to know how its institutions are being run. The *Globe* claimed that autopsy reports reveal essential information about the treatment, or lack of it, given to persons entrusted to the state's care and that such a disclosure would not constitute an invasion of privacy since the subject of an autopsy has died and privacy rights end with death. In September

of 1987, Meyer ruled on behalf of the newspaper. The chief medical examiner disclosed the autopsy reports, but stated that he would not be guided by the court's interpretation in the future. A month later, in response to a motion by the *Globe,* Meyer broadened his earlier decision and ruled that autopsy reports written by state and county medical examiners are not "medical files and information," which are exempt from the definition of public records under the statute. In December of 1987 Assistant Attorney General John Corbett filed an appeal. Corbett told a *Globe* reporter, "I don't think privacy ends with death. And I think there is room in the statute's exemption to recognize the rights of relatives of people who may have been incarcerated or may be victims of crimes." D'Alcomo said, "This case may well decide the question of whether, under Massachusetts law, privacy rights terminate at death. That has not as yet been addressed by an appellate court in this state." (Corbett and D'Alcomo, as quoted by Ed Quill, "Shannon Appealing Ruling that Opens Autopsy Records," *Boston Globe,* 25 December 1987, 81.) The case was argued before the SJC on 6 December 1988 and decided 14 February 1989. The SJC unanimously agreed that Meyer had erred in allowing the motion of the *Globe* to amend and broaden his earlier judgment. The SJC ruled that autopsy reports are "medical files or information," which are clearly exempt from the definition of public records, which the statute says must be disclosed. The SJC rejected the argument that the autopsy reports fell within the statutory classification of "any other materials or data relating to a specifically named individual, the disclosure of which may constitute an unwarranted invasion of privacy." The court said that the exemption for medical files or information was absolute, and cited the strong public policy in Massachusetts favoring the confidentiality of medical records. The court refused to consider whether the disclosure of the autopsy reports would constitute a clearly unwarranted invasion of privacy, a consideration that would have been relevant had the reports fallen within the exception relating to "other materials or data." In this way, the SJC avoided directly addressing either the privacy or the First Amendment implications of their decision. *(Globe Newspaper Co. v. Chief Medical Examiner,* 404 Mass. 132, 533 N.E.2d 1356 (1989). Also see Ed Quill, "Judge Rules that Autopsy Reports Can't Be Withheld," *Boston Globe,* 24 October 1987, 19; and Doris Sue Wong, "SJC Rules Autopsies Not Public Data," *Boston Globe,* 15 February 1989, 25.) Meyer cited the SJC *Globe* appeal—in which his own strong First Amendment decision had been overturned just months before—when he constructed his rationale regarding privacy rights in his decision on the Wiseman motion. (We thank Barbara Sweeney for her advice on the analysis of the SJC decision on the *Globe* case).

209. In direct examination, Wiseman contradicted Richardson. Wiseman testified that it was Greenman who mentioned nudity at the June 27 screening and that Richardson "answered him by saying he didn't think the nudity was a problem and that would solely be a concern for any television network or other person or other institution that distributed the film" (Tr. 14:12).

210. "Brief *Amicus Curiae* of the Civil Liberties Union of Massachusetts," *Commonwealth v. Wiseman,* 356 Mass. 251; 249 N.Ed.2d 610 (1969), 20.

211. "Recent Cases," *Harvard Law Review* 83, no. 7 (1970): 1731.

212. "Comment: The *Titicut Follies* Case: Limiting the Public Interest Privilege," *Columbia Law Review* 70, no. 2 (1970):370–71.

213. ABC News *Nightline* Show no. 1631, broadcast 25 August 1987. All quotations from this broadcast are from the transcript provided by ABC.

214. In a hearing on the motion two days after the *Nightline* broadcast, Meyer questioned Perry about the program. The judge had heard of the broadcast, or read about it in the Boston papers, but he had not seen it himself. Meyer wondered if individuals pictured in the clips shown from the film had been identifiable. Perry assured him—an assurance that we think is inaccurate—that individuals had not been identifiable, because of the poor quality of the print. Perry did not mention that the two patients featured in the broadcast clips (which included the most visually shocking images in the film) were both deceased in 1987.

215. Information on the history and techniques of blurring was obtained in a series of interviews conducted by the authors in the fall of 1989 with a number of people professionally associated with educational audio-visual services, commercial special effects labs, psychological services, and independent filmmaking. Interviewees included John Stacey, Jeff Kaplan, a member of the technical staff at EFX Unlimited, Richard Halgin, Mary Jo Sparrow, and P. J. O'Connell. For a discussion of journalistic guidelines in the use of blurring identities in news stories, see John L. Hulteng, *The Messenger's Motives: Ethical Problems of the New Media*, 2d ed. (Englewood Cliffs: Prentice Hall, 1985), especially chapter 9, "Saying It with Pictures," 142–69. Hulteng recalls a survey conducted by the *Columbia Journalism Review* that asked experienced journalists to decide on the publication of a set of actual shots of tragedy, violence, or grief. The responses demonstrated a great diversity of views on what images are appropriate to publish (158–59). An example of the procedure of using actors in place of patients is William H. Reid, *The DSM-III-R Training Program Videotaped Clinical Vignettes* (New York: Brunner/Mazel, Inc., 1989). Some audio-visual centers that show actual clients in counseling situations impose voluntary restrictions on exhibition that are very similar to those imposed on *Titicut Follies* by the SJC in 1971. At Penn State University's audio-visual services center, for example, *The Hillcrest Family,* a series of family counseling films released in 1968, is available for showing only to "advanced college classes, psychiatric and medical societies. A written statement is required stating the intended use."

216. "Petitioners' Demand to Grove and Titicut for Admission of Facts," 23-25.

217. To our knowledge, this transcript has never been published, but published discussions of the film probably have used it as a source by which to identify individuals in the film and some discussions of the film use those full names. Since the Bridgewater Film Company claims a (1967) copyright on the transcript, whether Wiseman has a legal right to publish it is an interesting question and one that has gone heretofore unasked, as far as we know. The guardian *ad litem* did not receive a copy of the transcript.

218. MacLeish and Dershowitz are both quoted in Irene Sage, "Court Eases 22-year Ban on *Titicut Follies,*" *Boston Globe,* 29 September 1989, 22.

219. Wiseman, as quoted by Gary Witherspoon, *"Titicut* Director to Fight Restriction on Film's Release," *Boston Herald,* 30 September 1989, 8.

220. Wiseman, as quoted in "Judge Proposes Compromise on Banned Film," *New York Times,* 30 September, 1989, 24.

221. In telephone conversations with Carolyn Anderson on 3 January and 10 May 1990, Perry confirmed his plans to request a reconsideration by Judge Meyer, but as of 10 May 1990 the request had not yet been submitted. According to Perry, there was no time limit restricting when that motion might be filed. The failure of a motion to reconsider might lead to a series of appeals to higher courts. In a letter of 2 January 1990 to Carolyn Anderson, Mitchell Sikora said he believed "that the case will now proceed to the Supreme Judicial Court for an appellate decision and, conceivably, beyond to the United States Supreme Court if any restriction remains upon the showing of the film."

222. Silvergate, letter to Carolyn Anderson, 11 December 1989. In Silvergate's view, the Meyer decision leaves *Titicut Follies* in the unique position it was in before the decision: as the only American film subject to prior restraint on grounds other than obscenity or national security.

Chapter 5. Restricted Exhibition

1. Kent Carroll, telephone interview with Carolyn Anderson, 12 April 1977.

2. Carroll interview.

3. Wiseman in Levin, *Documentary Explorations,* 327.

4. Wiseman in Westin, "You Start Off with a Bromide," 67.

5. 275 N.E.2d at 148.

6. These instructions are printed in the fall 1988/89 promotional brochure from Zipporah Films, 15. Since 1977, directions have varied only slightly, the greatest substantive change being the receipt of the statement of intent from ten to twelve days. Before 1983, rental instructions for *Titicut Follies* were mailed separately and were not included in the Zipporah brochure itself. All subsequent references to Zipporah prices and policies use these annual brochures as their source of information, unless otherwise indicated.

7. The affidavit that is to be signed by each member of the audience reads: "By order of the Supreme Judicial Court of Massachusetts, *Titicut Follies* may be shown only to judges, legislators, doctors, lawyers, sociologists, social workers, psychiatrists, students in these or related fields and organizations dealing with the social problems of custodial care and mental infirmity. Your signature below certifies that you are within the categories of people allowed to watch *Titicut Follies* as stated in the Final Decree of the Suffolk Superior Court, Eq. No. 87538, and repeated above." The viewer is then requested to sign and print his or her name.

8. Bradlow, "Two, But Not of a Kind," 60.

9. Telephone interview between Carolyn Anderson and Kevin Crain, director of the center for media development, University of Massachusetts-Boston, 13 April 1977.

10. *Five College Calendar,* 15, no. 8 (29 March–16 April 1977).

11. Interview between Carolyn Anderson and Jerry Sousa, 6 May 1982. See also Alice Dembner, "Prison Reform Ex-Con's Goal," *Daily Hampshire Gazette* (Northampton, MA) 24 January 1983, 1, 7.

12. Information provided by Zipporah director of distribution, Karen Konicek, 5 April 1984. A fall 1990/91 Zipporah brochure advertised videotapes of most Wiseman films for sale at $350, but *Titicut Follies* was no longer available on tape.

13. Telephone interview between Carolyn Anderson and Iris Berry, secretary at Zipporah Films, 26 April 1977.

14. Wiseman, in Rosenthal, *The New Documentary in Action,* 68. *High School* was broadcast on WNET-TV. In the "Nightline" broadcast, Koppel and Wiseman were joined in a "live" discussion with Thomas Gutheil, from Harvard Medical School; Philip Johnston, Massachusetts Human Services Secretary; and Roderick MacLeish, a patients' rights attorney. Also included in the broadcast were taped interviews with Elliot Richardson; Frank Gulla, a former Bridgewater patient; Blair Perry; George Caner; psychiatrist Edward Mason; and Stephen Jonas (ABC News, "Nightline" show no. 1631). See Diane E. Lewis, "'Nightline' Airs Segments from 'Titicut Follies,'" *Boston Globe,* 27 August 1987, 66. Scenes from *Titicut Follies* were rebroadcast (28 September–2 October 1987) during a five-part series, "Inside Bridgewater," produced by WCVB-TV, the Boston ABC affiliate. According to reporter Ron Allen, the local station obtained "unlimited access" to Bridgewater while filming its report. Wesley Profit recalled that producer-director Neil Ungerleider worked out a "very elaborate procedure so that nobody who appears in the film is not competent to give away their right to privacy." Patient advocates were present to advise patients before they signed the Channel 5 waivers. Ungerleider also made arrangements to inform the hospital staff as to when the reports would be broadcast so that clinicians would be available to patients at those times. Ungerleider agreed that Channel 5 would not broadcast any of the series on the 11:00 o'clock news, since some Bridgewater inmates had television sets in their rooms and would not have access to clinical staff at that time of night. (Wesley Profit, interviewed by Carolyn Anderson, Boston, 7 June 1989.) The "Inside Bridgewater" series won a George Foster Peabody Award for excellence in broadcasting and the Robert F. Kennedy Award for outstanding coverage of problems of the disabled. Footage from the WCVB series was combined with clips from *Titicut Follies* on a "World News Tonight" (ABC-TV) report on Bridgewater on 12 October 1987. Ted Koppel returned to the story of inadequate treatment and lack of media access on 5 April 1989 when "Nightline" broadcast a report entitled "Horror Story Continues at Bridgewater" with Roderick MacLeish and Edward Murphy, Massachusetts Mental Health Commissioner, as guests. An unidentified clip from *Titicut Follies* was the first shot in a montage of images from Bridgewater that began the program.

15. Brochure for Zipporah Films, fall 1988/89, 14. Wiseman's minimum lecture fee was $1,700, plus expenses.

16. Information regarding these showings was obtained in interviews by

Carolyn Anderson with John Morrison, co-owner of the Pleasant Street Theater, on 1 March and 9 May 1977.

17. In a memorandum to the authors, Wiseman wrote, "Neither I nor Zipporah Films had any connection with the flyer or the advertisements other than to insist that restrictions on the audience be made absolutely clear" (4 August 1987).

18. Telephone interview between Carolyn Anderson and Michael Leja, 4 October 1977.

19. Interviews between Carolyn Anderson and Deac Rossell, May 1980 and July 1982. Rossell, Film Coordinator, Boston Museum of Fine Arts, and co-organizer of the Boston 350 screenings, provided an account of the actions of the attorney general's office.

20. Fran Weil, "Jack Lemmon Kicks Off Jubilee 350 Film Festival," *Boston Herald American,* 7 May 1980, B5.

21. Michael Blowen, "What Do Jack Lemmon, the Brink's Job, and Thirty Five Cents Have in Common?" *Boston Globe* "Calendar," 8 May 1980, 12.

22. Fran Weil, "'Titicut Follies' Showing Set in Hub, Despite Ban," *Boston Herald American,* 8 May 1980, A3.

23. "Movie Banned in 1967 Will Be Shown," *Daily Hampshire Gazette,* 9 May 1980, 4.

24. *Boston Herald American,* 11 May 1980, D11.

25. Docket entry no. 1184, 2.

26. Docket entry no. 1183.

27. Michael Blowen, "Some Told Lies to See 'Titicut,'" *Boston Globe,* 13 May 1980, 17.

28. Unidentified spokesperson from Zipporah Films, as quoted in Blowen, "Some Told Lies," 17.

29. "Commonwealth's Request for Production of Documents," docket entry no. 1193, 2.

30. Docket entry no. 1193, 2–3.

31. Ned Rifkin, "Drama of the Real: The Films of Frederick Wiseman," program notes at Wiseman retrospective sponsored by the Institute of Contemporary Art, Boston, 13–28 October 1982.

32. Several panelists, including state senator Patricia McGovern and Wiseman's former attorney, James St. Clair, who were listed in publicity for the program, were not present. At the 7 June 1989 hearing on Wiseman's motion to open *Titicut Follies* to general audiences, Wiseman's attorney, Blair Perry, recalled that the panelists had expressed a feeling that the film ought to be shown and claimed that "as a result of that, we decided to file a motion to modify the existing decree, so that it could be shown not only to professional audiences, but to the public." The majority of panelists did support public exhibition of the film, but some did not, including George Caner, who had been counsel for the state in *Commonwealth v. Wiseman.* See Diane E. Lewis, "End to 'Titicut Follies' Ban Is Backed," *Boston Globe,* 26 May 1987, 17, 24. Not long after the screening at the JFK Library, three psychiatrists from the Massachusetts Mental Health Center at Harvard Medical School wrote a letter to the editor of the *Boston Globe* opposing general exhibition.

See "Maintain Limit on Showings of 'Titicut Follies,'" 6 July 1987, 16.

33. In an interview with Carolyn Anderson (7 June 1989, Boston), Wesley Profit, director of forensic services and deputy medical director of Bridgewater State Hospital, recalled how nurses at Bridgewater had told him about staff requests over the years to see *Titicut Follies* and about Gaughan's insistence that the film would never be shown at Bridgewater while he was in charge of the institution. In an interview with Barbara Howard for a public radio report on *Titicut Follies,* Gaughan repeated some of his complaints about the documentary, emphasizing his objections to the nudity in the film and speculating that "this thing is for homosexuals" ("Around New England" 29 June 1987).

34. Gaughan was replaced by Joseph Ponte, who was fired four months later by Commissioner of Correction Michael V. Fair. In October 1985, John Noonan succeeded Ponte as superintendent of MCI-Bridgewater (see Kenneth J. Cooper, "Correction Chief Fires Bridgewater Head," *Boston Globe,* 23 October 1985, 21, 24). In 1987, administration of the state correctional institution at Bridgewater was divided so that Bridgewater State Hospital would have its own superintendent. Gerard Boyle was appointed superintendent of the hospital in July 1987 (see Diane E. Lewis, "Hospital Staff Is Blamed in Death," *Boston Globe,* 7 July 1987, 1, 18).

35. See William G. Sullivan, "Charles Gaughan, Bridgewater Supt., Tried to Improve Life of the Inmates," *Quincy Patriot Ledger,* 26 May 1989, 34; and "Gaughan," *Boston Globe,* 29 May 1989, 43. The panel would have had a sort of symmetry, as Gaughan had supported the filming of *Titicut Follies* and Boyle had given his support to the filming of the WCVB-TV documentary.

36. Profit agreed with the majority that disapproved of the original and continuing restrictions (interview with Carolyn Anderson, 7 June 1989). In a telephone conversation with Carolyn Anderson on 29 December 1989, June Binney recalled her amazement at "the extraordinary passion on the part of the staff that *[Titicut Follies]* inspires after all these years." She remembered retired nurses "screaming into the microphone" at Wiseman during the question and answer session. Binney said that Wiseman, having previously agreed to speak at the Saturday morning panel, then gave the impression of making excuses to avoid it during the days and even hours before it began. He insisted on audio taping the panel, and refused an invitation to tour the new hospital.

37. The file, last checked 31 August 1990, listed docket entry no. 3176, dated 30 August 1990, as its most recently entered item. The number 3176 referred to the total number of entries in the case file. Beginning with entry no. 139, dated 17 July 1974, the entries were all exhibition statements, until entry no. 2511, filed 23 July 1987. (Entry no. 2511 was a motion by Wiseman to amend the "Final Decree after Rescript".) Other motions, affidavits, and orders pertaining to Wiseman's motion of July 1987 were also entered from 1987 to 1989. Usually, there were two entries for each showing of *Titicut Follies.* The first was a statement from Zipporah Films indicating date, place, and audience for a scheduled screening. The second statement indicated that a showing took place or, less often, that it was canceled.

Chapter 6. Construction and Use

1. See Levin, *Documentary Explorations* and Alan Rosenthal, *The Documentary Conscience: A Casebook in Film Making* (Berkeley: University of California Press, 1980).

2. Galliher, "The Life and Death of Liberal Criminology," *Contemporary Crises* 2, no. 3 (1978): 251.

3. Galliher, "Social Scientists' Ethical Responsibilities to Superordinates: Looking Up Meekly," *Social Problems* 27, no. 3 (1980): 298–308.

4. Wiseman, as cited in Westin, "You Start Off with a Bromide," 64; Levin, *Documentary Explorations,* 319–20; Atkins, *Frederick Wiseman,* 43–44; and telephone conversation with Carolyn Anderson, 14 November 1983. According to cinematographer John Davey, consent was obtained from the parents of handicapped children in the *Deaf* and *Blind* series (interview with the authors, London, 14 October 1986). In at least one project, Wiseman used a person associated with the host institution being filmed, and presumably carrying the halo of prestige and authority of the institution and the medical profession, to negotiate consent. He discussed this procedure at a question and answer session following the premiere of *Near Death* at the New York Film Festival on 7 October 1989. Wiseman said that while shooting the film in an intensive care unit at Beth Israel Hospital in Boston, "one of the people who was working with me was a fourth-year medical student whose job it was to talk to the families and get their consents."

5. Murray L. Wax, "Paradoxes of 'Consent' to the Practices of Fieldwork" *Social Problems* 27, no. 3 (1980): 282.

6. Karl Heider, *Ethnographic Film* (Austin: University of Texas Press, 1976), 120–21.

7. See Charles Horton Cooley, "The Looking-Glass Self," in *Symbolic Interaction: A Reader in Social Psychology,* ed. Jerome Manis and Bernard Meltzer, 3d ed. (Boston: Allyn and Bacon, 1978), 169–70.

8. Pryluck, "Ultimately We Are All Outsiders: The Ethics of Documentary Filming," *Journal of the University Film Association* 28, no. 1 (1976): 28. In personal correspondence with the authors, Pryluck maintains that direct cinema owes its subjects either "direct" collaboration or, if the subject is helpless, "utter protection" (29 September 1989).

9. Gaughan, personal correspondence with Carolyn Anderson, 9 May 1977.

10. Chasen, as quoted in Peter Lucas, "Film Harms Inmates, Says Doctor," *Boston Herald Traveler,* 24 October 1967, 1.

11. Telephone interviews between Carolyn Anderson and Dave Haley, assistant director, Department of Correction, 4 May and 9 May 1977.

12. Telephone interview between Carolyn Anderson and Ken Colpan, counsel to the psychiatric staff, Institute of Law and Psychiatry, McLean Hospital, 17 May 1977.

13. Telephone interview between Carolyn Anderson and Michael Perleman, Director of Mental Health for Western Massachusetts, 1971–74, 7 May 1977.

14. Information on changes obtained from Charles Gaughan, "Bridgewater State Hospital," 29 April 1977, enclosure in correspondence with Carolyn Anderson.

15. For a highly critical account of Bridgewater, see Tom Ryan, with Bob Casey, *Screw: A Guard's View of Bridgewater State Hospital* (Boston: South End Press, 1981). Ryan was first a volunteer at the hospital, then worked as a guard for eighteen months in 1974–75. He argues that even after the reforms of the late 1960s and early 1970s, brutality by guards was common and treatment by the professional staff inadequate. Ryan remembers correction officers as antagonistic to "do-gooders" and to organized attempts at prison reform, such as the efforts of the New England Prisoners Association (NEPA). He cites a 16 July 1974 memorandum signed by Superintendent Gaughan and posted on hospital bulletin boards as evidence that the superintendent shared this distrust of reformers (73–74).

16. This characterization of Boyle's superintendency is based on interviews by the authors with unit director and forensic psychologist Dr. Thomas Kurcharski and director of forensic services and deputy medical director Dr. Wesley Profit, during a tour of Bridgewater State Hospital on 26 June 1989. According to Kurcharski, the men confined at Bridgewater continue to make distinctions between inmates and patients; they use the terms "cons" and "bugs." In *Screw,* Ryan claims that the clinical staff was often unaware of actual conditions at the hospital. He describes tours for visitors as "snow jobs" (121–26).

17. Bridgewater State Hospital has had contracts with McLean Hospital and Goldberg Medical Associates. Population figures are somewhat misleading, since many men—from 1,200 to 1,300 yearly—are sent to Bridgewater for psychiatric evaluations. For the first time, the hospital was scheduled to have a full complement of psychiatrists (twenty-six) as of July 1989. Population and staff figures were cited by Wesley Profit.

18. Wiseman, as quoted in Atkins, *Frederick Wiseman,* 56.

19. Wiseman, panel discussion at the Institute of Contemporary Art Retrospective, Boston, 3 October 1977.

20. "Affidavit of Frederick Wiseman," docket entry no. 2512, 20 July 1987, 6. In other contexts, Wiseman continues to describe his early notions about the film's role in social change as naive. In December 1987, he told a North Adams State College audience that "there is no direct correlation between any work and social change" (David Tyler, "Bridgewater Filmmaker Defends His Freedom of Expression," *The Transcript,* 2 December 1987, 3).

21. Gilligan, as quoted in Robb, "Focus on Life," 30–31.

22. Wiseman, as quoted in Robb, "Focus on Life," 30.

23. Robb, "Focus on Life," 31.

24. Richardson, *The Creative Balance: Government, Politics, and the Individual in America's Third Century* (New York: Holt, Rinehart & Winston, 1976).

25. Kane, telephone conversation with Carolyn Anderson, 16 June 1982.

26. Marshall interview (1984).

27. John Marshall and Emilie De Brigard, "Idea and Event in Urban

Film," in *Principles of Visual Anthropology,* ed. Paul Hockings (The Hague: Mouton, 1975), 138.

28. Eames, "Watching Wiseman Watch," 102.

29. Exhibit 3, 3.

Bibliography

Newspaper articles cited in the endnotes are not included in the bibliography, with the exception of some feature articles from Sunday magazine sections.

Allen, Robert C., and Douglas Gomery. *Film History: Theory and Practice.* New York: Knopf, 1985.
American Civil Liberties Union Annual Reports. Vol. 7. New York: Arno Press, 1970.
Anderson, Carolyn. "The Conundrum of Competing Rights in *Titicut Follies.*" *Journal of the University Film Association* 33, no. 1 (1981): 15–22.
———. "Documentary Dilemmas: An Analytic History of Frederick Wiseman's *Titicut Follies.*" Ph.D. diss., University of Massachusetts, 1984.
———. "The *Titicut Follies* Audience and the Double Bind of Court-Restricted Exhibition." In *Current Research in Film: Audiences, Economics, and Law,* ed. Bruce A. Austin, vol. 3: 189–214. Norwood, NJ: Ablex, 1987.
Anderson, Carolyn, and Thomas W. Benson. "Direct Cinema and the Myth of Informed Consent: The Case of *Titicut Follies.*" In *Image Ethics: The Moral Rights of Subjects in Photography, Film, and Television,* ed. Larry Gross, John Katz, and Jay Ruby, 58–90. New York: Oxford University Press, 1988.
Armstrong, Dan. "Wiseman's Realm of Transgression: *Titicut Follies,* the Symbolic Father, and the Spectacle of Confinement." *Cinema Journal* 29, no. 1 (1989): 20–35.
Arnold, Carroll C., and John Waite Bowers, eds. *Handbook of Rhetorical and Communication Theory.* Boston: Allyn and Bacon, 1984.
Atkins, Thomas R., ed. *Frederick Wiseman.* New York: Monarch Press, 1976.
Barnouw, Erik. *Documentary: A History of the Non-Fiction Film.* Rev. ed. New York: Oxford University Press, 1983.
———. *The Sponsor: Notes on a Modern Potentate.* New York: Oxford University Press, 1978.
Barsam, Richard Meran. *Nonfiction Film: A Critical History.* New York: Dutton, 1973.
———. *The Vision of Robert Flaherty.* Bloomington: Indiana University Press, 1988.
———, ed. *Nonfiction Film: Theory and Criticism.* New York: Dutton, 1976.
Batten, Mary. "An Interview with Ephraim London. *Film Comment* 1, no. 4 (1963): 2–19.
Bennett, David L., and Philip Small. "Case Comments." *Suffolk Law Review* 4, no. 1 (1969): 197–206.

Benson, Thomas W. "Implicit Communication Theory in Campaign Coverage." In *Television Coverage of the 1980 Presidential Campaign,* ed. William C. Adams, 103–16. Norwood, NJ: Ablex, 1983.

———. *"Joe:* An Essay in the Rhetorical Criticism of Film." *Journal of Popular Culture* 8 (1974): 608–18.

———. "The Rhetorical Structure of Frederick Wiseman's *High School."* *Communication Monographs* 47 (1980): 233–61.

———. "The Rhetorical Structure of Frederick Wiseman's *Primate."* *Quarterly Journal of Speech* 71 (1985): 204–17.

———, ed. *American Rhetoric: Context and Criticism.* Carbondale: Southern Illinois University Press, 1989.

———, ed. *Speech Communication in the 20th Century.* Carbondale: Southern Illinois University Press, 1985.

Benson, Thomas W., and Carolyn Anderson. "Good Films from Bad Rules: The Ethics of Naming in Frederick Wiseman's *Welfare."* In *Visual Explorations of the World: Selected Papers from the International Conference on Visual Communiction,* ed. Jay Ruby and Martin Taureg, 2–27. Aachen, West Germany: Radar Verlag (Edition Herodot), 1987.

———. *Reality Fictions: The Films of Frederick Wiseman.* Carbondale, IL: Southern Illinois University Press, 1989.

———. "The Rhetorical Structure of Frederick Wiseman's *Model." Journal of Film and Video* 36, no. 4 (1984): 30–40.

———. "The Ultimate Technology: Frederick Wiseman's *Missile."* In *Communication and the Culture of Technology,* ed. Martin J. Medhurst, Alberto Gonzalez, and Tarla Rai Peterson, 257–83. Pullman: Washington State University Press, 1990.

Benson, Thomas W., and Richard Barton. "Television as Politics: The British View." *Quarterly Journal of Speech* 65 (1979): 439–57.

Berg, Beatrice. "'I Was Fed Up with Hollywood Fantasies.'" *New York Times,* 1 February 1970, sec. 2, 25.

Blue, James. "Direct Cinema." *Film Comment* 4, nos. 2 and 3 (1967): 80–81.

Bluem, A. William. *Documentary in American Television: Form, Function, Method.* New York: Hastings House, 1965.

Blumenberg, Richard. "Documentary Films and the Problem of 'Truth.'" *Journal of the University Film Association* 29 (Fall 1977): 19–22.

Bradlow, Paul. "Two, But Not of a Kind: A Comparison of Two Controversial Documentaries about Mental Illness, *Warrendale* and *Titicut Follies." Film Comment* 5, no. 3 (1969): 60–61.

Breitrose, Henry. Review of *Documentary,* by Erik Barnouw. *Film Quarterly* 28, no. 4 (Summer 1975): 38.

Bull, Peter L. "Catalyst versus Observer Documentary: Jean-Pierre Gorin's *Poto & Cabengo* and Frederick Wiseman's *High School."* M.F.A. thesis, University of California, San Diego, 1980.

Burke, Kenneth. *A Rhetoric of Motives.* 1950. Reprint. Berkeley: University of California Press, 1973.

Burstyn v. Wilson. 343 U.S. 495 (1952).

Calder-Marshall, Arthur. *The Innocent Eye: The Life of Robert J. Flaherty.* New York: Harcourt, Brace, & World, 1966.

Callenbach, Ernest, and Albert Johnson. "The Danger Is Seduction: An Interview with Haskell Wexler." *Film Quarterly* 21, no. 3 (1968): 3–14.

Campbell, Russell. *Cinema Strikes Back: Radical Filmmaking in the United States, 1930–1942.* Ann Arbor: UMI Research Press, 1982.

Capote, Truman. *In Cold Blood.* New York: Random House, 1966.

Carroll, Raymond L. "Television Documentary." In *TV Genres,* ed. Brian G. Rose, 237–56. Westport, CT: Greenwood Press, 1985.

Cholodenko, Robert A. "The Films of Frederick Wiseman." Ph.D. diss., Harvard University, 1987.

Coles, Robert. "Stripped Bare at the Follies." *The New Republic,* 20 January 1968, 18, 28–30.

"Comment: The 'Titicut Follies' Case: Limiting the Public Interest Privilege," *Columbia Law Review* 70, no. 2 (1970): 359–71.

Commonwealth v. Wiseman. 356 Mass. 251, 249 N.E.2d 610 (1969); cert. denied, 398 U.S. 960 (1970); rehearing denied, 400 U.S. 954 (1970).

Conrad, Randall. "An Interview with Frederick Wiseman." Unpublished transcript, Boston, circa 1978.

Cooley, Charles Horton. "The Looking-Glass Self." In *Symbolic Interaction: A Reader in Social Psychology.* Ed. Jerome G. Manis and Bernard M. Meltzer. 3d ed. Boston: Allyn & Bacon, 1978.

Corner, John, ed. *Documentary and the Mass Media.* London: Edward Arnold, 1986.

Cox, Harvey G. "Massachusetts Movie Ban." *Playboy,* March 1968, 45.

Cullen v. Grove Press, Inc. 276 F.Supp. 727 (S.D.N.Y. 1967).

Curry, Timothy Jon. "Frederick Wiseman: Sociological Filmmaker?" *Contemporary Sociology* 14, no. 1 (1985): 35–39.

Davidson, David. "Direct Cinema and Modernism: The Long Journey to *Grey Gardens.*" *Journal of the University Film Association* 36, no. 1 (1981): 3–13.

De Grazia, Edward. *Censorship Landmarks.* New York: R. R. Bowker, 1969.

De Grazia, Edward, and Roger K. Newman. *Banned Films: Movies, Censors, and the First Amendment.* New York: Bowker, 1982.

Dershowitz, Alan M. *Reversal of Fortune: Inside the Von Bulow Case.* New York: Random House, 1986.

Desilet, E. Michael. "Fred Wiseman: *Titicut* Revisited." *Film Library Quarterly* 4, no. 2 (1971): 29–33.

Dowd, Mary Ellen. "Popular Conventions." *Film Quarterly* 22, no. 3 (1969): 28–31.

Eames, David. "Watching Wiseman Watch." *New York Times Magazine,* 2 October 1977, 96–102, 104, 108.

Eaton, Mick. *Anthropology-Reality-Cinema: The Films of Jean Rouch.* London: British Film Institute, 1979.

Elder, Sean. "Darkness Visible: Robert Frank and the Real Rolling Stones." *Berkeley Express,* 30 October 1987, 6.

Ellis, Jack C. *The Documentary Idea: A Critical History of English-Language Documentary Film and Video.* Englewood Cliffs, NJ: Prentice-Hall, 1989.

Ellsworth, Liz. [Elizabeth Jennings.] *Frederick Wiseman: A Guide to References and Resources.* Boston: G. K. Hall, 1979.

Faden, Ruth R., and Tom L. Beauchamp, in collaboration with Nancy H. P. King. *A History and Theory of Informed Consent.* New York: Oxford University Press, 1986.

Feingold, Ellen. "*Titicut Follies* and Competing Rights." *Civil Liberties Review* 2, no. 2 (1974): 145–51.

Feldman, Silvia. "The Wiseman Documentary." *Human Behavior* 5, no. 2 (1976): 64–69.

"Film-Festival Firsts for *Follies.*" *Playboy,* June 1968, 54.

Friedenberg, Edgar Z. "Ship of Fools: The Films of Frederick Wiseman." *New York Review of Books,* 21 October 1971, 19–22.

Galliher, John. "The Life and Death of Liberal Criminology." *Contemporary Crises* 2, no. 3 (1978): 245–63.

————. "Social Scientists' Ethical Responsibilities to Superordinates: Looking Up Meekly." *Social Problems* 27, no. 3 (1980): 298–308.

Gertz, Elmer, and Felice F. Lewis, eds. *Henry Miller: Years of Trial and Triumph.* Carbondale: Southern Illinois University Press, 1978.

Gilbert, Craig. "Reflections on 'An American Family.'" *Studies in Visual Communication* 8, no. 1 (1982): 24–54.

Gill, Brendan. "The Current Cinema." *The New Yorker,* 28 October 1967, 166–67.

Gillmor, Donald M., and Jerome A. Barron. *Mass Communication Law: Cases and Comment.* 4th ed. St. Paul: West Publishing Company, 1984.

Glicksman, Marlaine. "Highway 61 Revisited." *Film Comment* 23, no. 4 (1987), 32–39.

Glossary of Film Terms. Philadelphia: University Film Association, 1978.

Goffman, Erving. *Asylums.* Garden City, NY: Doubleday, 1961.

Golden, Daniel. "Undermanned and Vulnerable." *Boston Globe Magazine* 30 July 1989, 20–22, 36–42, 49–50.

Graham, John. "Frederick Wiseman on Viewing Film." *The Film Journal* 1, no. 1 (1971): 43–47.

Gross, Larry, John Katz, and Jay Ruby, eds. *Image Ethics: The Moral Rights of Subjects in Photography, Film and Television.* New York: Oxford University Press, 1988.

Halberstadt, Ira. "An Interview with Frederick Wiseman." *Filmmaker's Newsletter* 7, no. 4 (1974): 19–25.

Hammond, Charles Montgomery, Jr. *The Image Decade: Television Documentary: 1965–1975.* New York: Hastings House, 1981.

Handelman, Janet. "An Interview with Frederick Wiseman." *Film Library Quarterly* 3, no. 3 (1970): 5–9.

Hardy, Forsyth, ed. *Grierson on Documentary.* Berkeley: University of California Press, 1966.

Hatch, Robert. "Films." *The Nation,* 30 October 1967, 446.

Hauser, Gerard A. *Introduction to Rhetorical Theory.* New York: Harper & Row, 1986.

"Hearings on the Bridgewater Film before the Special Commission on Mental Health." Massachusetts General Court, Boston, 17 October–7 November 1967.

Hecht, Chandra. [Chandra Mukerji]. "Total Institutions on Celluloid." *Society* 9, no. 6 (1972): 44–48.

Heider, Karl. *Ethnographic Film.* Austin: University of Texas Press, 1976.

Henderson, Lisa. "Photographing in Public Places." Master's thesis, University of Pennsylvania, 1983.

Heyer, Susan J. "The Documentary Films of Frederick Wiseman: The Evolution of a Style." Master's thesis, University of Texas, 1975.

Hockings, Paul, ed. *Principles of Visual Anthropology.* The Hague: Mouton, 1975.

Issari, M. Ali. *Cinema Verite.* East Lansing: Michigan State University Press, 1971.

Issari, M. Ali, and Doris A. Paul. *What Is Cinema Verite?* Methuchen, NJ: Scarecrow Press, 1979.

Jacobs, Lewis, ed. *The Documentary Tradition.* 2d ed. New York: Norton, 1979.

Jennings, Elizabeth. [Liz Ellsworth.] "Frederick Wiseman's Films: A Modern Theory of Documentary." Master's thesis, University of Wisconsin-Milwaukee, 1975.

Jordan, June. *Civil Wars.* Boston: Beacon Press, 1981.

Kalin, Bob. "Frederick Wiseman: From *Titicut Follies* to *Model.*" *Film News,* Fall 1981, 6–12.

Knight, Arthur. "Cinema Verite and Film Truth." *Saturday Review,* 9 September 1967, 44.

Kolker, Robert Phillip. *A Cinema of Loneliness.* New York: Oxford University Press, 1980.

Kracauer, Siegfried. *Theory of Film: The Redemption of Physical Reality.* New York: Oxford University Press, 1960.

Levin, G. Roy. *Documentary Explorations: 15 Interviews with Film-Makers.* Garden City, NY: Doubleday, 1971.

Levin, Murray B., and George Blackwood. *The Compleat Politician: Political Strategy in Massachusetts.* Indianapolis: Bobbs-Merrill, 1962.

Litt, Edgar. *The Political Culture of Massachusetts.* Cambridge: MIT Press, 1965.

Lomperis, Timothy J. *"Reading the Wind": The Literature of the Vietnam War.* Durham, NC: Duke University Press, 1987.

Lovell, Alan, and Jim Hillier. *Studies in Documentary.* New York: Viking Press, 1972.

Lucas, Anthony J. *Common Ground: A Turbulent Decade in the Lives of Three American Families.* New York: Knopf, 1985.

Lyons, Louis M. *Newspaper Story: One Hundred Years of "The Boston Globe."* Cambridge: Harvard University Press, Belknap Press, 1971.

McLean, Deckle. "The Man Who Made *Titicut Follies.*" *Boston Sunday Globe Magazine,* 27 July 1969, 11–15.

McWilliams, Donald E. "Frederick Wiseman." *Film Quarterly* 24, no. 1 (1970): 17–26.

Mailer, Norman. *The Armies of the Night.* New York: New American Library, 1968.

Maltin, Leonard. *Behind the Camera: The Cinematographer's Art.* New York: New American Library, 1971.

Mamber, Stephen. *Cinema Verite in America: Studies in Uncontrolled Documentary.* Cambridge: MIT Press, 1974.

———. "The New Documentaries of Frederick Wiseman." *Cinema* 6, no. 1 (1970): 33–40.

Marcorelles, Louis. *Living Cinema: New Directions in Contemporary Filmmaking.* Translated by Isabel Quigly. New York: Praeger, 1973.

Marshall, John. "Man the Hunter." *Natural History* 67 (1958): 6–7.

Marshall, John, and Emilie de Brigard. "Idea and Event in Urban Film." In *Principles of Visual Anthropology,* ed. Paul Hockings, 133–45. The Hague: Mouton, 1975.

Marshall, John, and Claire Ritchie. *Where Are the Ju/wasi of Nyae Nyae? Changes in a Bushman Society, 1958–1981.* Rondebosch, South Africa: Centre for African Studies, University of Cape Town, 1984.

Marshall, Lorna. *The !Kung of Nyae Nyae.* Cambridge: Harvard University Press, 1976.

Massachusetts Reports, Papers, and Briefs. 356 part 5 (20–24 June 1969): 362–66.

Medhurst, Martin J., and Thomas W. Benson, eds. *Rhetorical Dimensions in Media: A Critical Casebook.* Rev. printing. Dubuque: Kendall/Hunt, 1986.

Mileur, Jerome M., and George T. Sulzner. *Campaigning for the Massachusetts Senate: Electioneering Outside the Political Limelight.* Amherst: University of Massachusetts Press, 1974.

Miller, Arthur R. *The Assault on Privacy: Computers, Data Banks, and Dossiers.* Ann Arbor: University of Michigan Press, 1971.

Morgenstern, Joseph. "Movies: Bedlam Today." *Newsweek,* 23 October 1967, 100–101.

Naifeh, Steven and Gregory White Smith. *The Best Lawyers in America: 1989–90.* New York: Woodward/White, 1989.

Neier, Aryeh. "Letters." *Civil Liberties Review* 2, no. 2 (1975): 151.

Nichols, Bill. "Fred Wiseman's Documentaries: Theory and Structure." *Film Quarterly* 31, no. 3 (1978): 15–28.

———. *Ideology and the Image: Social Representation in the Cinema and Other Media.* Bloomington: Indiana University Press, 1981.

———. "The Voice of Documentary." *Film Quarterly* 36, no. 3 (1983): 17–30.

Nicholson, Philip, and Elizabeth Nicholson. "Meet Lawyer-Filmmaker Frederick Wiseman." *American Bar Association Journal* 61, no. 3 (1975): 328–32.

O'Brien, David M. *The Public's Right to Know.* New York: Praeger, 1981.

O'Connell, P. J. "Robert Drew and the Development of Cinema-Verite in America: An Innovation in Television Journalism." Ph.D. Diss., The Pennsylvania State University, 1988.

Pember, Don R. *Mass Media Law.* 3d ed. Dubuque: William C. Brown, 1984.

Perrucci, Robert. *Circle of Madness: On Being Insane and Institutionalized in America.* Englewood Cliffs, NJ: Prentice-Hall, 1974.

Press, Aric, with Daniel Shapiro and Tom Schmitz. "'Titicut Follies': An Asylum with a Past." *Newsweek,* 20 July 1987, 57.

Pryluck, Calvin. "'Seeking to Take the Longest Journey': A Conversation with Albert Maysles." *Journal of the University Film Association* 28, no. 2 (1976): 9–16.

———. "Ultimately We Are All Outsiders: The Ethics of Documentary Filming." *Journal of the University Film Association* 28, no. 1 (1976): 21–29.

"Recent Cases." *Harvard Law Review* 83, no. 7 (1970): 1722–31.

Reitman, Alan, ed. *The Pulse of Freedom: American Liberties, 1920–1970s.* New York: Norton, 1975.

Renov, Michael. "Re-thinking Documentary: Toward a Taxonomy of Mediation." *Wide Angle* 8, nos. 3 and 4 (1986): 71–77.

Review of *Titicut Follies. Films in Review,* November 1967, 580.

Review of *Titicut Follies. Film Society Review,* October 1967, 17–19.

Richardson, Elliot L. *The Creative Balance: Government, Politics and the Individual in America's Third Century.* New York: Holt, Rinehart, & Winston, 1976.

———. "Letters: Focusing Again on *Titicut Follies.*" *Civil Liberties Review* 1, no. 3 (1974): 150.

Ricoeur, Paul. *History and Truth.* Translated by Charles A. Kelbley. Evanston, IL: Northwestern University Press, 1965.

Robb, Christina. "The Battered American." *Boston Globe Magazine,* 12 August 1979, 8–10, 20, 24.

———. "Focus on Life." *Boston Globe Magazine,* 23 January 1983, 15–18, 25–34.

Rosenthal, Alan. *The Documentary Conscience: A Casebook in Film Making.* Berkeley: University of California Press, 1980.

———. *The New Documentary in Action: A Casebook in Film Making.* Berkeley: University of California Press, 1971.

———, ed. *New Challenges to Documentary.* Berkeley: University of California Press, 1988.

Roskill, Mark, and David Carrier. *Truth and Falsehood in Visual Images.* Amherst: University of Massachusetts Press, 1983.

Rossell, Deac. "*Titicut Follies.*" *Christianity and Crisis,* 18 March 1968, 43–45.

Rotha, Paul. *Documentary Diary: An Informal History of the British Documentary Film, 1928–1939.* London: Secker & Warburg, 1973.

———. *Documentary Film.* 3d ed. New York: Hastings House, 1963.

Ruby, Jay. "The Image Mirrored: Reflexivity and the Documentary Film." *Journal of the University Film Association* 29, no. 4 (1977): 3–11.

——. "A Re-Examination of the Early Career of Robert J. Flaherty." *Quarterly Review of Film Studies* 5, no. 4 (1981): 431–57.

——, ed. *A Crack in the Mirror: Reflexive Perspectives in Anthropology.* Philadelphia: University of Pennsylvania Press, 1982.

——, ed. *Robert Flaherty: A Biography.* Philadelphia: University of Pennsylvania Press, 1983.

Ryan, Tom, with Bob Casey. *Screw: A Guard's View of Bridgewater.* Boston: South End Press, 1982.

Salt, Barry. *Film Style and Technology: History and Analysis.* London: Starword, 1983.

Sarris, Andrew. Review of *Titicut Follies. The Village Voice,* 9 November 1967, 33.

Schaefer, Dennis, and Larry Salvato. *Masters of Light: Conversations with Contemporary Cinematographers.* Berkeley: University of California Press, 1984.

Schickel, Richard. "The Frightful Follies of Bedlam: *Titicut Follies." Life,* 1 December 1967, 12.

Sheed, Wilfred. "Films." *Esquire,* March 1968, 52, 55.

Silvergate, Harvey. "President's Column: *Titicut Follies* Revisited." *The Docket* [Civil Liberties Union of Massachusetts] 17, no. 4 (1987): 3.

Snyder, Robert L. *Pare Lorentz and the Documentary Film.* Norman: University of Oklahoma Press, 1973.

Sobchack, Vivian. *"No Lies:* Direct Cinema as Rape." *Journal of the University Film Association* 29, no. 4 (1977): 13–18.

Sontag, Susan. *On Photography.* New York: Farrar, Straus & Giroux, 1978.

Stevenson, Jack. "Interview with Frederick Wiseman." *Pandemonium* 3 (1989): 145-52.

Stott, William. *Documentary Expression and Thirties America.* New York: Oxford University Press, 1973.

Sullivan, Patrick J. "'What's All the Cryin' About?' The Films of Frederick Wiseman." *Massachusetts Review* 13, no. 3 (1972): 452–69.

Sussex, Elizabeth, ed. *The Rise and Fall of British Documentary: The Story of the Film Movement Founded by John Grierson.* Berkeley: University of California Press, 1975.

Sweeney, Barbara. "The Use of Social Science Research in Supreme Court Opinions Related to Obscenity." Ph.D. diss., University of Massachusetts, 1981.

Szasz, Thomas S. *The Myth of Mental Illness: Foundations of a Theory of Personal Conduct.* Rev. ed. New York: Harper & Row, 1974.

"The Talk of the Town: New Producer." *The New Yorker,* 14 September 1963, 33–35.

Taylor, Arthur R. "An Analysis of the Narrative Content and Cinematic Elements of Frederick Wiseman's Film *Hospital."* Ed.D. diss., Indiana University, 1977.

Taylor, Charles. *"Titicut Follies." Sight and Sound* 57, no. 2 (1988): 98–103.

"Tempest in a Snakepit." *Newsweek,* 4 December 1967, 109.

Thomas, Elizabeth Marshall. *The Harmless People*. London: Secker & Warburg, 1969.
"Titicut Ban Affirmed." *Playboy,* April 1968, 62.
"Titicut Follies."America, 11 November 1967, 539.
Tuch, Ronald. "Frederick Wiseman's Cinema of Alienation." *Film Library Quarterly* 11, no. 3 (1978): 9–15, 49.
Urofsky, Melvin I., ed. *The Douglas Letters: Selections from the Private Papers of William O. Douglas.* Bethesda, MD: Adler & Adler, 1987.
Vaughan, Dai. *Television Documentary Usage.* London: British Film Institute, 1976.
Vogel, Amos. *Film as a Subversive Art.* New York: Random House, 1974.
Waugh, Thomas, ed. *"Show Us Life": Toward a History and Aesthetics of the Committed Documentary.* Metuchen, NJ: Scarecrow Press, 1984.
Wax, Murray L. "Paradoxes of 'Consent' to the Practice of Fieldwork." *Social Problems* 27, no. 3 (1980): 272–83.
Westin, Alan. "'You Start Off with a Bromide': Wiseman on Film and Civil Liberties." *Civil Liberties Review* 1, nos. 1 and 2 (1974): 52–67.
"What Is the New Cinema? Two Views—Paris and New York." *Film Culture,* no. 42 (1966): 56–61.
White, Hayden. *Tropics of Discourse: Essays in Cultural Criticism.* Baltimore: Johns Hopkins University Press, 1978.
Williams, Raymond. *Problems in Materialism and Culture.* London: NLB, 1980.
Wilson, George M. *Narration in Light: Studies in Cinematic Point of View.* Baltimore: Johns Hopkins University Press, 1986.
Winick, Charles, ed. *Deviance and Mass Media.* Beverly Hills, CA: Sage, 1978.
Winston, Brian. "Before Grierson, Before Flaherty: The Documentary Film in 1914." *Sight and Sound* 57, no. 4 (1988): 277–79.
Wise, Helen M. "Coursework vs. Career Choices: Two Roads Taken." *The Alumnus* [University of Massachusetts], August-September 1987, 6.
Wiseman, Frederick. "A Filmmaker's Choices." *The Christian Science Monitor,* 25 April 1984, 30.
———. "Lawyer-Client Interviews: Some Lessons from Psychiatry." *Boston University Law Review* 39, no. 2 (1959): 181–87.
———. "Letters: Focusing Again on *Titicut Follies." Civil Liberties Review* 1, no. 3 (1974): 151.
———. "Psychiatry and Law: Use and Abuse of Psychiatry in a Murder Case." *American Journal of Psychiatry* 118, no. 4 (1961): 289–99.
———. "Reminiscences of a Film Maker: Fred Wiseman on *Law and Order."* *The Police Chief,* September 1969, 32–35.
———. "Time to Unlock the 'Titicut Follies.'" *Boston Sunday Globe,* 7 June 1987, A 2.
"Wiseman on *Juvenile Court." Journal of the University Film Association* 25, no. 3 (1973): 48–49, 58.
Wolf, William. "A Sane Look at an Insane Institution." *Cue,* 21 October 1967.

Youdelman, Jeffrey. "Narration, Invention and History." *Cineaste* 12, no. 2 (1982): 8–15.

Zimmermann, Patricia R. "Public Television, Independent Documentary Producers and Public Policy." *Journal of the University Film and Video Association* 34, no. 3 (1982): 9–23.

Index

219

Carolyn Anderson is Associate Professor of Communication at the University of Massachusetts at Amherst, where she teaches film and television history, criticism, and theory. She has contributed chapters to *Film and the Arts in Symbiosis, American Film Genres,* and *Current Research in Film,* and has written articles appearing in *Post Script* and *Journal of the University Film Association.* Her coauthored work on language use on television has been published in *Journal of Communication, Phylon,* and *Journal of Multilingual and Multicultural Development.* She is the coauthor of *Reality Fictions: The Films of Frederick Wiseman,* published by Southern Illinois University Press in 1989.

Thomas W. Benson is the Edwin Erle Sparks Professor of Rhetoric at The Pennsylvania State University. He has served as editor of *Communication Quarterly* and the *Quarterly Journal of Speech,* and is the recipient of the ECA Scholar and Meritorious Service awards of the Eastern Communication Association and the Robert A. Kibler Award of the Speech Communication Association. He is the author or coauthor of *Readings in Classical Rhetoric, Readings in Medieval Rhetoric, Nonverbal Communication, Rhetorical Dimensions in Media, Speech Communication in the 20th Century, American Rhetoric: Context and Criticism,* and essays on rhetoric, politics, film, and communication. He is the coauthor of *Reality Fictions: The Films of Frederick Wiseman,* published by Southern Illinois University Press in 1989.